OF WORDS AND THE WORLD

OF WORDS AND THE WORLD

REFERENTIAL ANXIETY IN
CONTEMPORARY FRENCH FICTION

DAVID R. ELLISON

PRINCETON UNIVERSITY PRESS

PRINCETON, NEW JERSEY

Library of Congress Cataloging-in-Publication Data

Ellison, David R.
Of words and the world : referential anxiety in
contemporary French fiction / David R. Ellison.
p.   cm.
Includes bibliographical references and index.
ISBN 0-691-06964-6
1. French fiction—20th century—History and criticism—
Theory, etc.   2. Experimental fiction—France—History and
criticism.   3. Reference (Philosophy) in literature.
4. Mimesis (in literature)   I. Title.

PQ671.E55   1993   843′91409—dc20   92-25049

This book has been composed in Adobe Berkeley

Princeton University Press books are printed
on acid-free paper and meet the guidelines for
permanence and durability of the Committee on
Production Guidelines for Book Longevity
of the Council on Library Resources

Printed in the United States of America

10   9   8   7   6   5   4   3   2   1

For Ellen

WEIL DIE STELLE NICHT SCHWINDET

By "theory" I mean the displacement in literary studies from a focus on the meaning of texts to a focus on the way meaning is conveyed. Put another way, theory is the use of language to talk about language. Put yet another way, theory is a focus on referentiality as a problem rather than as something that reliably and unambiguously relates a reader to the "real world" of history, of society, and of people acting within society on the stage of history.

 —J. Hillis Miller, "The Triumph of Theory"

CONTENTS

ACKNOWLEDGMENTS

I N A BOOK devoted to the varied manifestations of the referential function in contemporary experimental fiction, it is especially appropriate and important to acknowledge one's debts to the "world outside." Although literary scholarship is based on private research and the interpretive efforts of the individual, it will be clear to the readers of the present study that I owe much to current literary and cultural theory—notably, to the painstaking work of my colleagues in twentieth-century studies. At the same time, what is less visible but no less crucial is the very real debt I owe to the students at Mount Holyoke College who have taken my courses on the modern and postmodern novel. It is thanks to them that *Referential Anxiety* took shape.

Some of the material contained in this book originally appeared in scholarly periodicals. I would like to thank the editors of these journals for allowing me to reprint, in modified form, the following: "Camus and the Rhetoric of Dizziness: *La Chute*," *Contemporary Literature* 24, no. 3 (Fall 1983): 322–48; "Reappearing Man in Robbe-Grillet's *Topologie d'une cité fantôme*," *Stanford French Review* 3, no. 1 (Spring 1979): 97–110; "Narrative Leveling and Performative Pathos in Claude Simon's *Les Géorgiques*," *French Forum* 12, no. 3 (September 1987): 303–21; and "Beckett's *Compagnie*: Voice, Meta-Discourse, Reference," in *Theories of Narrative and French Literature*, 51–59. French Literature Series, vol. 17. Columbia: University of South Carolina, 1990.

For the encouragement, advice, and invigorating conversations with colleagues and friends during the various stages of my research and writing, I wish to thank especially: Gerald Prince, Peter Brooks, Charles Porter, Richard Macksey, Carol Murphy, Margaret Gray, Claude Pichois, Robert Norton, and William Paulson. I would like to express my gratitude, as well, to Madame Françoise Bermann for her kind bibliographic assistance at the Bibliothèque Nationale. And I am happy to make public my thanks to Mount Holyoke College for its support of my efforts in the form of a sabbatical leave during the 1986–1987 academic year. This period of freedom from administrative duties and teaching obligations made it possible for me to begin steady work on my project.

NOTE ON TEXTS AND TRANSLATIONS

MY PURPOSE in this book is to provide close readings of selected works of contemporary experimental fiction written, for the most part, in French. Because I have read these works in the original language, I refer to the pagination of the original French editions throughout my analysis. At the same time, in the hope that my study might render some of these works more accessible to an English-speaking readership, I have translated all quoted material into English, while indicating, within brackets, French words or phrases on which I have decided to concentrate my attention (I have also supplied bibliographical information on available translations in Works Cited).

The only exception to this scheme occurs in Chapter 6, when I undertake an analysis of some of Samuel Beckett's works. In this case, I quote the English and French versions of each text as written and emended by the author. In the play *Fin de partie* (*Endgame*), certain transformations of the text from its original French writing to its English translation are crucial to my argument and would have gone unnoticed had I not included quoted material in both languages.

OF WORDS AND THE WORLD

INTRODUCTION

> Le théorique est nécessaire (par exemple les théories du langage), nécessaire et inutile. La raison travaille pour s'user elle-même, en s'organisant en systèmes, à la recherche d'un savoir positif où elle se pose et se repose et en même temps se porte à une extrémité qui forme arrêt et clôture. Nous devons passer par ce savoir et l'oublier. . . . Le combat théorique, fût-ce contre une forme de violence, est toujours la violence d'une incompréhension; ne nous laissons pas arrêter par le trait partial, simplificateur, réducteur, de la compréhension même. Cette partialité est le propre du théorique: "à coups de marteau," disait Nietzsche.
> —Maurice Blanchot, *L'Ecriture du désastre*

> [Theoretical activity is necessary (for example, theories of language), necessary and useless. Reason works toward exhausting itself, organizing itself into systems, searching for a positive form of knowledge where it can alight and refresh itself and at the same time move onward toward an extremity that establishes stasis and closure. We should pass through this knowledge and forget it. . . . Theoretical combat, even directed against a form of violence, is always itself the violence of incomprehension; let us not be sidetracked by the partial, simplifying, reductive quality of comprehension as such. This partiality is the distinguishing trait of all theory: "the banging of the hammer," said Nietzsche.]

THEORY AND REFERENTIAL ANXIETY

TO SAY THAT we live in an age of theory is perhaps an understatement. Even a schematic examination of the evolution of literary and cultural criticism during the past thirty years suffices to indicate ever-expanding levels of methodological self-consciousness and of terminological density now achieved in studies aimed at the elucidation of texts. It is not uncommon for a humanities professor to overhear colleagues admitting to each other, sotto voce, that the rereading of a "classic in criticism" written before the advent of the new methods and new vocabularies constitutes a veritable hidden pleasure. Yet many of the same colleagues, this shameful admission made, revert to a more serious tone and declare that, after all, this kind of classic is no longer possible. Our pleasure in its reading is suffused with the regressive forces of nostalgia and guilt. The epistemic field has shifted, perhaps irreversibly, and we are drawn toward increasingly specialized modes of linguistic definition and conceptualization.

All too often, the reception of these advanced modes of discourse takes on the superficial appearance of a splitting of the academy into camps, with "conservative" scholars holding fast to an ideal of clear, jargon-free language, while "progressive" interpreters spin wide webs of technical barbarisms. The danger in both cases is that of intellectual reductionism—in the former case because the conservatives have decided to remain impermeable to sea changes in the way the words of poetic language relate to the world, and in the latter case because it is tempting to confuse terminological innovation and precision with genuine insight into the nature and mode of being of texts.

I have included as a liminary quotation for the present introduction a seemingly curious paragraph by Maurice Blanchot that addresses the issue of theory in a direct, one might say percussive, way (I will examine this statement in context in Chapter 5). Blanchot, whose nonfictional prose writings are among the most important modern theoretical meditations available in their nonsystematic, aphoristic intensity, makes the deliberately provocative assertion in *L'Ecriture du désastre* (*The Writing of the Disaster*) that theory is both "necessary and useless" (*inutile*): necessary in that human *ratio* tends ineluctably toward "using itself up" in organizational schemes and systems; useless because theorizing in this rational sense always implies violence, partiality, reduction, a distinctly unsubtle "banging of the hammer" that bypasses the hidden recesses or silences of the text(s) under examination. Important in Blanchot's assessment is its *both-and* form of argumentation: we must *both* pass through theory (it is impossible not to theorize about literary texts) *and*, in some sense, pass beyond it, refuse it, slip through its imprisoning analytical grid. We do not have the luxury to ignore or avoid the rigors of theoretical cognition (in order to study narrative today, for example, the *savoir positif* of narratology is, to borrow from Jacques Derrida, *incontournable*, not to be merely dismissed, eluded, or "outflanked"). But to remain shut within theory in its classificatory mode, Blanchot suggests, is to remain on the far side of what occurs within texts. Although he does not say in this particular context what such occurrences might be, we shall see in Chapter 5 that it is the weaving *and* unweaving of theoretical positions within textual praxis that creates the complexity, the obscurity, but also the ultimate readability (interpretability) of literary texts.

Before discussing further the precise ways in which literary theory and textual practice overlap in the several chapters of this book, the ways in which theory reveals itself as both necessary and useless in its cognitive rigor, I would like to examine what might be called the origins of the far-ranging *extension* of theory—the sources, within our contemporaneity, of a heightened, increasingly pervasive, self-reflexive theoretical discourse. In the course of this examination, I shall be citing important theoretical statements made by some of our most influential contemporary critics. As will become apparent, these statements often take on a declarative, unambiguous, definitional tone that contrasts with Blanchot's cautious both-and rhetoric of theoretical agnosticism. The cause for such a straight tone or "zero-degree" rhetoric lies both in the nature of theoretical language as such and in the presence of a certain anxiety that inhabits the critic when he or she establishes the primacy of language (either of poetic language or of the language of commentary) over the world to which it refers. The turn from the world and toward the word creates the space for theory, engenders theoretical definitions and classifications; this turn is the founding action that interests me here and in the pages to come.

In his 1986 Presidential Address to the Modern Language Association, J. Hillis Miller describes literary theory as three essential activities or moments: (1) "the displacement in literary studies from a focus on the meaning of texts to a focus on the way meaning is conveyed"; (2) "the use of language to talk about language"; and (3) "a focus on referentiality as a problem rather than as something that reliably and unambiguously relates a reader to the 'real world.' " If we combine these statements into a whole, we find that the difference between literary study as practiced today and its more traditional appearance in past criticism lies essentially in a *turn inward*: the critic no longer tries to extract a meaning or meanings from texts, but attempts to codify the production of meaning as such, and this meaning is a specular reflection of language on and by itself rather than the seductive but problematic pointing of linguistic signs to a world beyond.

If this scheme sounds familiar, it is because Professor Miller's neat formulation captures the categories and results of several important recent contributions to the theory of literature. In his theory of poetry entitled *The Anxiety of Influence* (1973), Harold Bloom stipulates that the study of literature should increasingly focus not on individual texts and their purported singular meanings, but rather on the intertextual dialectic whereby one "strong poet" influences another. One of the intriguing points in Bloom's conception is its historical dimension. As we progress through the chronology of literary history, not only has more and more been said (so that the space to be carved out by the "ephebe" in relation to his strong predecessor seems increasingly narrow), but the newer poet, in creating his language, must turn inward, must adopt a self-involved tone, and he thereby loses the directness of the relation between word and world that had been that of his master:

> To attain a self yet more inward than the precursor's, the ephebe becomes necessarily more solipsistic. To evade the precursor's imagined glance, the ephebe seeks to confine it in scope, which perversely enlarges the glance, so that it rarely can be evaded. As the small child believes his parents can see him around corners, so the ephebe feels a magical glance attending his every movement. The desired glance is friendly or loving, but the feared glance disapproves, or renders the ephebe unworthy of the

highest love, alienates him from the realms of poetry. Moving through landscapes that are mute, or of things that speak to him less often or urgently than they did to the precursor, the ephebe knows also the cost of an increasing inwardness, a greater separation from everything extensive. The loss is of reciprocity with the world, as compared to the precursor's sense of being a man to whom all things spoke. (105–6)

The anxiety of influence, an agonistic state of dialogue that pits one poet against another and makes of intertextuality an active dueling rather than a passive receiving of tradition, is also what I shall call an *anxiety of reference* or *referential anxiety*. The "loss of reciprocity with the world" that Bloom sees as a continual historical movement is a fact of contemporary literary history worthy of close study. What Bloom saw happening in the movement from Milton to Keats to Whitman to Stevens seems to have occurred, in a shorter temporal expanse, in the realm of the novel, from Balzac to Flaubert to Proust to Beckett. While I have no quarrel with the general tenets of Bloom's theory (especially its strengthened view of intertextual relations), the majority of the exemplary texts he chooses for analysis come from the classical, romantic, and modern periods and do not extend to the problematic period of our contemporaneity called *postmodernism* in architecture and the arts and *poststructuralism* in the discourse of critical theory. If there is indeed a movement inward from Balzac to Beckett that bears some analogical resemblance to the passage from Milton to Stevens, what happens as the careers of Stevens and Beckett move toward closure? What remains for the writers who must wrestle with these angels? Might there be a point at which the turn away from the referent reverses itself, where minimalism and textual self-referentiality reach their limits? And if so, can there be something like a *return to the referent* as exterior reality, a new embracing of the world in its extensiveness that is not a pale and naïve reflection of past tradition but a textual praxis reinvigorated by the arduous passage through inwardness as such? These are questions that lie at the center of the chapters that follow.

FICTION AND REFERENCE

In discussing the question of referentiality *in* literature, we run into an immediate and embarrassing problem: Is it not true that imaginative literature, conceived of as *fiction*, is precisely that privileged form of communication that understands itself as separate from the sphere of the real, as self-referential? Does not the difference between a newspaper account of the political and social events of 1848 in Paris and Flaubert's *L'Education sentimentale* lie in the fact that the newspaper refers to events in reality, whereas Flaubert's fiction creates its own self-sufficient topography of significance? In their *Dictionnaire encyclopédique des sciences du langage* (1972) (*Encyclopedic Dictionary of the Sci-*

ences of Language), Oswald Ducrot and Tzvetan Todorov, in defining *le discours de fiction,* declare that

> certain linguistic statements refer to particular extralinguistic circumstances: one says in such cases that they denote a referent. This property, important as it is, is not constitutive of human language: certain statements possess this attribute, while others do not. But there is also a type of discourse called *fictional,* in which the question of reference is posed in a radically different manner: here it is indicated explicitly that the proffered phrases describe a fiction and not a real referent. Of this type of discourse, literature is the most studied. (333)

In this programmatic definition of the notion of reference, Ducrot and Todorov distinguish between the linguistic and the extralinguistic, the act of verbal or written utterance in itself and the pointing effect of the utterance as it designates a realm beyond language. According to the authors of the *Dictionnaire,* it would seem that certain, *but not all,* statements denote a referent, and that literary language as such (the language of connotation) exists within the self-sufficient realm of fiction. In the critical discourse of the 1960s and 1970s it was not uncommon for the referent to be understood primarily, if not exclusively, as the *real referent*—that is, the object in the world beyond the confines of the text. In such a view, it was possible to speak of denotational, "referential language" on the one hand, and of a connotative, "nonreferential" literary language on the other. According to this scheme, literature differentiates itself from all other forms of human communication by being essentially an inward-turning phenomenon, an artifact that does not rely or depend upon referential pointing in the same way that ordinary discourse does. Such appears to be the underlying assumption of one of Paul de Man's most eloquent statements on the nature of literary language:

> For the statement about language, that sign and meaning can never coincide, is what is precisely taken for granted in the kind of language we call literary. Literature, unlike everyday language, begins on the far side of this knowledge; it is the only form of language free from the fallacy of unmediated expression. All of us know this, although we know it in the misleading way of a wishful assertion of the opposite. Yet the truth emerges in the foreknowledge we possess of the true nature of literature when we refer to it as *fiction.* All literatures, including the literature of Greece, have always designated themselves as existing in the mode of fiction; in the *Iliad,* when we first encounter Helen, it is as the emblem of the narrator weaving the actual war into the tapestry of a fictional object. Her beauty prefigures the beauty of all fictional narratives as entities that point to their own fictional nature. The self-reflecting mirror-effect by means of which a work of fiction asserts, by its very existence, its separation from empirical reality, its divergence, as sign, from a meaning that depends for its existence on the constitutive activity of this sign, characterizes the work of literature in its essence. It is always against the explicit assertion of the writer that

readers degrade the fiction by confusing it with a reality from which it has forever taken leave. (*Blindness and Insight*, 17)

In interpreting Helen as figure of the narrator (as weaver of *texts*), and in suggesting that the "actual war" is somehow subsumed in the act of narrating per se, de Man privileges the telling of the story over the elements told *in* the story—elements that, presumably, have been "always already" transformed into fictional phenomena. According to this conception, it is only logical that fictional discourse, in its very separation from the real referent, should emerge as a "self-reflecting mirror-effect." As de Man states polemically in the concluding remarks of his essay, this scheme also presupposes that literature, in knowing its own essential fictional nature, is, from the start, "demystified": "When modern critics think they are demystifying literature, they are in fact being demystified by it" (18). In this view, literature simultaneously produces referential effects *and* undoes, dismantles, deconstructs these effects in revealing them *as* fictitious from the start. The referential sphere has not been eliminated, but it has been contained or enveloped within the self-knowing literary text: the referential outside has been devoured and digested by the fictional inside.[1]

The equivalence established by the authors of the *Dictionnaire* and Paul de Man between the referent and the extralinguistic outside of or beyond (*audelà*) the text has been challenged in recent years by a growing number of scholars whose purpose has been to redefine the concept of referentiality in literature. With the concurrent waning of the technical experimentation of the *nouveau roman* (new novel) in the domain of creative writing and of formalist methodologies in the area of literary theory, the attention of critics has begun to focus on the specificity of literary reference, and, in this process, the exclusive presupposition of the "reality" of the referent has come under scrutiny. In her important study of postmodern experimental French fiction, Dina Sherzer affirms: "Representation in any work of art . . . is a construction that has a reference in that it represents something for the reader/observer; however it may have no referent in that it does not necessarily reproduce anything actual in the real world" (*Representation in Contemporary French Fiction*, 1–2). Similarly, in her theoretical article on novelistic reference contained in the volume *On Referring in Literature* (1987), Linda Hutcheon maintains:

> In the literary text, one could argue that there are no such things as real referents for the reader at least: all are fictive—"table," "forehead," "unicorn," "honesty," "ubiquity"—because their context would be an imagined world. Readers accept this as a given when they accept the fact that what they are reading is a fiction, that is, an imagined construct. (4).

For both Sherzer and Hutcheon, there is always reference in literary texts (to speak of a nonreferential text would make no sense to these critics: all utterances possess some kind of reference, whether real or imaginary), and it is the reader who *actualizes* the referential function of the text by reading it. Because the literary work is essentially a construction, and therefore separate from reality, it is subject to its own laws of reference rather than to the constraints of the world toward which it may or may not point.

In his remarkable speculative study entitled *Fictional Worlds* (1986), Thomas Pavel reminds us that "reference to fictional characters and objects is not a logically strange activity, but rather . . . relates to a common way of making reference" (32). When an author refers to a character, emotion, or imagined landscape in a literary work, he or she is establishing the parameters of a specifically fictional realm. This realm is new and strange to the reader, but the act of reference whereby the imagined world is created is analogous to common, real-world reference. This means that the critic, rather than gauging fiction against nonfictional constructions, should be encouraged to create "an internal approach whose purpose is to propose models representing the user's understanding of fiction" (43). The implicit pact or contract between writer and reader is of paramount importance to our understanding of literary reference as such, and this particular mode of reference need not be considered secondary or derivative vis-à-vis the mode of existence of the extraliterary referent.

What Sherzer, Hutcheon, and Pavel propose in their different languages is a way of approaching the referential function(s) of the literary text *without reference to the real referent*, so to speak. The lucid and interesting results of their interpretations rest, in no small degree, on the clear delineation of literary fiction as a separate, analyzable field. The fact that the text is freed from the constraints of the real referent, the fact that fiction *is* a world of its own, allows the reader or critic to map the self-created topography of the text and view it with the clearsightedness of a theoretical perspective.

From the specific standpoint of critical theory, therefore, the distinction between a "real" and an "imaginary" referent promises to be useful and productive, as both Pavel's book and several of the distinguished essays in *On Referring in Literature* demonstrate unequivocally.[2] At the same time, however, an exclusive concentration on the question of reference *within* fiction (a study of the laws of the imaginary referent) would limit the scope of the literary work to the aesthetic realm (the space of forms, structures, narrative laws, and poetic figures) and would abstract that work from the ethical domain to which it points, or seems to point. I am suggesting here (and shall develop this theme at length in the analyses that follow) that some of the most impressive experimental texts of the past thirty years are built on the *tension* between imaginary and real referents. Several of these texts construct a self-sufficient, highly coherent fictional world whose referential laws seem embedded within the fiction itself, yet *at the same time* refer the reader beyond the borders of the text, to a complex and problematic "outside"—an ethical space that the aesthetic space designates, not transparently (in the simple mimetic mode) but with some mystery, some opacity. This difficult link between the verbal texture of the work (the word) and the world is at the center of the present study.

In choosing to analyze experimental writings of authors whose views on literature are in many cases theoretically sophisticated and avant-garde in their formulation, I enter a mine field of critical controversy. If I have decided to write a book on the subject of referential anxiety in the recent French novel, it is because I have the firm conviction that the most talented representatives of this kind of writing have written works worthy of close scrutiny, intellectually and artistically challenging and achieved forms. This is a personal conviction that is not shared by all readers, especially those who feel that both contemporary novelistic and theoretical discourses are contaminated by an excessive (involuted) attention to form, by an insufficient concentration on the moral message of the work of art. Before returning to a further elaboration of my own thesis on the opaque or difficult link between words and the world, I would like to turn to a critic whose passionate, conservative defense of the moral values of literature occurs within an explicit attack on the contemporary theory and praxis that I shall be studying throughout this book.

CREATION, CRITICISM, AND THE MORAL IMPERATIVE

In his cogent and percussive essay "Real Presences," George Steiner provides us with a *défense et illustration* of the act of reading in its full moral force. In part a polemical piece against the "excesses" of deconstruction, as practiced by Jacques Derrida and his epigones, "Real Presences" proceeds in three distinct stages: First, it locates the "crisis . . . in the concept and understanding of language" (69) in the poetic theory and practice of the symbolist poets Mallarmé and Rimbaud. Second, it demonstrates that the current crisis in philology (textual interpretation in the broadest sense) stems from the radical doubt shared by many critics in the possibility of a "cumulative advance towards textual understanding" (78)—i.e., the act of interpretation has been reduced to the endless proliferation of highly personal readings, none of which builds upon the insights of previous readings. And third, it proposes, as a counterstatement to the theory and practice of deconstruction, a conception of reading formulated in the terms of an ethical imperative: "If we wish to . . . meet the challenge of autistic textuality or, more accurately, 'anti-textuality' on grounds as radical as its own, we must bring to bear on the act of meaning, on the understanding of meaning, the full force of moral intuition" (83).

From this *ethical inference* follow, in the form of logical consequence, three crucial points, which Steiner makes with strong declarative bravado: first, "the poem comes before the commentary" (83); second, "the equalities of weight

and force which deconstruction assigns to the primary [creative] and secondary [critical] texts, are spurious. They represent that reversal in the natural
order of values and interest which characterize an Alexandrine or Byzantine
period in the history of arts and of thought" (84); and third, we [all of us
readers] must read "as if the text (the piece of music, the work of art) *incarnates*
(the notion is grounded in the sacramental) a *real presence of significant being*"
(86). Steiner concludes by stating that criticism has borrowed heavily, in its
vocabulary and in its methods, from "the bank or treasure-house of theology"
(88) and that it is time to recognize explicitly this debt. In historical terms,
whereas art through the ages has spoken of the presence or absence of God, it
may be that modernism and its aftermath constitute the first period in which
God is no longer experienced as a "competitor, a predecessor, an antagonist in
the long night" (90). What remains, once God (and once the question of
meaning in its sacramental sense) has disappeared, is the reflection of literature upon itself, which Steiner describes in these terms:

> There may well be in atonal or aleatory music, in non-representational art, in certain
> modes of surrealist, automatic or concrete writing, a sort of shadow-boxing. The
> adversary is now the form itself. Shadow-boxing can be technically dazzling and
> formative. But like so much of modern art it remains solipsistic. The sovereign chal-
> lenger is gone. And much of the audience. (Ibid.)

Whereas the self-reflecting mirror-effect of fiction understanding (demystifying) itself was a positive element in de Man's theoretical conception, here it
is viewed as narcissism, a glorification of form for form's sake that characterizes those Alexandrine or Byzantine periods of art in which the creative impetus has disappeared in favor of a verbose, pompous, and heavy-handed emphasis on the theoretical. Clearly, "Real Presences" reverses the constitutive
polarities of de Man as it establishes (interpretively and subjectively, to be
sure) a historical context for what Steiner calls our current "language turn"
(70). It may be no coincidence that some of the best interpretive efforts of de
Man, Derrida, and other so-called deconstructionist critics center on the poetry and poetic theory of Mallarmé, in whose work Steiner finds the very root
of our contemporary solipsism. In the following lines, Steiner paraphrases the
aesthetic tenets of the symbolist poet:

> It is from Mallarmé that stems the programmatic attempt to dissociate poetic
> language from external reference, to fix the otherwise undefinable, unrecapturable
> texture and odour of the rose in the word "rose" and not in some fiction of external
> correspondence and validation. Poetic discourse, which is, in fact, discourse made
> essential and maximally *meaning-ful*, constitutes an internally coherent, infinitely
> connotative and innovative, structure or set. It is richer than that of largely indeter-
> minate and illusory sensory experience. Its logic and dynamics are internalized:
> words refer to other words; the "naming of the world"—that Adamic conceit which

is the primal myth and metaphor of all western theories of language—is not a descriptive or analytic mapping of the world "out there," but a literal construction, animation, unfolding of conceptual possibilities. (Poetic) speech is creation. (71)

Central to the entirety of Steiner's polemic and to the unfolding of his argument is the question of the real referent. For Steiner, it is safe to say that words refer *both* to other words *and* to the world; the "Adamic conceit" may be only that, but it has shaped the map of traditional conceptions of language and has informed much of classical literary creation.

The temptation for the reader of this introduction, who is, I assume, not only an interpreter of texts but also a person with tastes and preferences, might well be to take sides in the debate I have arranged with obliging pedagogical clarity. The admirer of Mallarméan poetry and of the specular convolutions of the nouveau roman could find Steiner's argument oppressively old-fashioned and retrograde, while the reader who has struggled in vain to piece together the evanescent "subconversations" of Nathalie Sarraute and the disjointed narrative layers of Claude Simon's prose could find in Steiner's moral imperative a comforting return to common sense. My point is that the either/or alternative set forth in Steiner's opposition to the deconstructionists and other poststructuralist critics is, in fact, *too neat*: it masks, in its theoretical "violence" (Blanchot), the complexity of the referential turn as it occurs, repeatedly and variously, in the challenging texts I shall attempt to interpret. On the one hand, the heritage of Mallarmé and of the symbolist emphasis on words relating to words *rather than* transparently mirroring the world is certainly present in many of the texts I shall be examining; on the other hand, however—and it is here that one must take Steiner seriously even if one finds (as I do) his position suspect in its nostalgic tone and theological emphasis— the question of the moral imperative *in* the literary text is not a dead letter in several of the works I shall be reading, even those works that include strong self-reflexive moments. The way in which texts reintroduce, via a turn toward the real referent, what one might call the ethical dimension of literature (even literature *as* fiction) will inform large sections of my book, especially in Chapters 3 through 6.

Before turning to a preliminary description of the purpose and procedures of the present interpretive study, however, I should like to consider briefly some of the salient characteristics of the short but complicated period of literary history on which I shall be concentrating. Notably, I should like to place in the foreground the question of the transition from modernism to what, for lack of a better word, I am calling *postmodern* writing[3]—those experimental texts spanning the years 1956 to 1984 that stand at the center of my analysis. Although it is quite difficult to be the historian of such recent events, it seems necessary to acknowledge a definite historical dimension to the sometimes disconcerting twists and turns of contemporary literature in its aesthetic transformations.

The Age of Suspicion

In his attack on the deconstructionists, George Steiner singles out one often explicitly stated tenet of poststructuralist literary criticism that he finds particularly dangerous: namely, the assumption that the *intention* of the author in writing a work is both invisible and irrelevant to the reader's understanding or interpretation of that work. Following is Steiner's paraphrase of this contemporary credo:

> The notion that we can grasp an author's intentionality, that we should attend to what he would tell us of his own purpose in or understanding of his text, is utterly naive. What does he know of the meanings hidden by or projected from the interplay of semantic potentialities which he has momentarily circumscribed and formalized? Why should we trust in his own self-delusions, in the suppressions of the psychic impulses, which most likely have impelled him to produce a "textuality" in the first place? The adage had it: "do not trust the teller but the tale." Deconstruction asks: why trust either? Confidence is not the relevant hermeneutic note. (79–80)

If we read against the irony of this formulation, we must assume that for Steiner the intentionality of the author *does* matter, and that true naïveté consists in a surrender to the anarchy of "textuality" as unlimited, uncontrollable semantic proliferation. We can assume, as well, that trust in the author *is* the "relevant hermeneutic note" for Steiner and that the current infatuation with poststructuralist linguistic games is a momentary Alexandrine deviation from this fundamental trust. What Steiner does not do in his polemical presentation is historicize this question of trust or confidence: Is an unquestioning belief in the author's intentions an immemorial characteristic of the reading process, or can we locate a moment, a turn away from such a belief—and if so, when does this swerving take place?

In her influential and now classical collection of essays entitled *L'Ere du soupçon: Essais sur le roman* (1956) (*The Age of Suspicion. Essays on the Novel*), Nathalie Sarraute locates precisely this turn from confidence and toward suspicion in the modernist novel—in an aesthetic form that antedates deconstructionism by more than fifty years. Specifically, Sarraute finds in the more and more pervasive use of an anonymous first-person narrator/protagonist "who is everything and yet nothing," combined with secondary characters "deprived of their own existence," the origin of our era *as* "age of suspicion" (58–59). Indeed, it is the lack of recognizable qualities or characteristics in both narrator and fictional characters—i.e., our inability as readers to identify with their singular, disembodied destinies—that sows the seeds of an ever-expanding crisis in the relation between author and reader. Thus, whereas Steiner found the source of what he considers to be our current confusion of values in Mallarmé's poetics, Sarraute uncovers the prehistory of postmodern textual praxis in the Proustian narrator-hero and the constellation of shadowy figures with which Proust peoples his strange, ego-centered universe. The fundamental difference between Steiner and Sarraute, of course, is that the former decries our poststructuralist and postmodernist radical extensions of Mallarméan textual theory, whereas Sarraute sees the movement through and beyond Proust, Joyce, and Kafka as the only legitimate *challenge* for contemporary literature. The crisis in confidence that seems a dead end for Steiner is the *point de départ* for Sarraute.

According to the sophisticated standards of today, Sarraute's concise and suggestive essays might seem out-of-date in their nontechnical generality. In most current criticism, *L'Ere du soupçon* is recognized as an important seminal work but is relegated to background or footnote status. In retrieving these essays here, I intend to underline their continued relevance to postmodern fictional writing and to contemporary critical debate, notably as concerns what one could call the *collaboration* between reader and author in the constitution of the interpreted text. The reader's suspicion about the author's intentions leads not to an impasse but to a new relation that Sarraute describes in metaphorical terms reminiscent of her fictional vocabulary:

> Thus [as a result of his suspicion] the reader finds himself suddenly on the inside, at the very position of the author, at a depth where nothing subsists of those reference-points [*points de repère*] thanks to which he [the reader] constructs characters. The reader plunges and maintains himself until the end in a substance as anonymous as blood, in a nameless and shapeless magma. If he manages to find direction, it is thanks to the landmarks the author has placed for his own purposes of orientation. No reminders of his familiar world, no conventional concern about cohesion or verisimilitude, can deviate his attention or curb his effort. (74)

Readers of Sarraute's fictions will recognize in this passage a description of the novelist's own technique, which consists of descending beneath the level of daily conversational discourse to the less recognizable stratum of the *sous-conversation*, that "nameless and shapeless magma" which underlies and informs each speaker's attempts to communicate emotion and desire. Sarraute's experimentation with the metaphorical language of fiction depends upon a conception of reading that is itself constructed on one essential metaphor: that of the (lost) landmark, of directionless orientation. We are not far from the infinite peregrinations of the land surveyor in Kafka's novel *The Castle*. And because the reader finds himself in a landscape without points de repère (a central notion to which I shall return in Chapters 3 and 6), there can be "no reminders of his familiar world"—that is, no pointing from the inside recesses of fiction to the referential outside that would result in a clear correspondence between these two domains. Here Sarraute adumbrates a question that I shall consider at some length in Chapters 5 and 6: namely, the possibility of fiction as *relationless* phenomenon, as creation or construction of a universe that stands in no relation to our human world, at a point of apparent zero-degree reference to reality.

Sarraute's description of the reader's "plunge" into the disorientation of the text should not be confused with a statement of despair or anguish. On the contrary, it is this new reading situation that the essayist holds responsible for any possible *progress* in contemporary literary production and reception. Indeed, it would be no exaggeration to say that Sarraute replaces our now irretrievably lost confidence in the author and the believability of his characters with confidence in the forward movement of literary innovation, which is itself completely dependent on the reader's increasingly active involvement in the constitution of the text's meanings. In the concluding paragraph of the essay "L'Ere du soupçon," Sarraute writes:

> Suspicion, which is now destroying the fictional character and the entire outmoded apparatus that once assured his power, is one of those morbid reactions by which an organism defends itself and finds a new equilibrium. Suspicion forces the novelist to acquit himself of what is, according to Mr. Toynbee (reminding us of Flaubert's lesson), "his most profound obligation: the discovery of the new," and stops him from committing "the most heinous of crimes: the repeating of his predecessors' discoveries." (77)

This ideology of the new, of progress conceived as a positive, continual movement forward in the destruction of old forms and the invention of structures and techniques adequate to the expression of today's reality, this ideology that surfaces also in Alain Robbe-Grillet's *Pour un nouveau roman* (1963) (*For a New Novel*), is perhaps the most traditional of Sarraute's propositions, the most vulnerable to demystification as remnant of nineteenth-century cultural mythology. Certainly Sarraute, in representing literary history as a procession of aesthetic renewal, does not face the question of ethics, of critical valuation, in Steiner's sense. The main polemical thrust of *L'Ere du soupçon* consists in its reversal of the polar opposition between realism and formalism: Sarraute argues, against the defenders of classical tradition, that the true realist is the creator of new forms, whereas the formalist is that writer who remains within outdated conventions (143–55)—but this argument does not address the matter of valuation or value as such. Is all renewal of form to be considered progress, or is some innovation truly narcissistic, experimental in a mechanical and unimaginative sense? To be more specific, do Sarraute's own investigations into the meanderings of sous-conversation constitute an advance over Proust, or does the Proustian novel dwarf its successor's experiments in scope and invention?

I do not propose to answer these difficult, perhaps intractable, questions here; I am suggesting that while Sarraute succeeded (convincingly, I think) in locating the crisis of contemporary literary production and reception in the new reading contract presupposed by modernist textual practice, she leaves in abeyance a problem of major importance to my study: namely, what happens when the readers of modernism—the postmodernist novelists and the poststructuralist critics—enter the language laboratory together; what forms of discourse do they produce; and can we as *their readers* remain immune to, stay on the far side of, the questions of value and ethics as they emerge from an analysis of the referential function of literary language? Because her essays appeared in 1956, at the very beginning of the explosion of the nouveau roman, Sarraute cannot be asked (unless as a prophet) to respond to these queries. Therefore I turn now to a more recent critical assessment of experimental fiction for a view of the transformations of the new novel as it develops beyond the formal manifestations and aesthetic ideology of modernism.

THE TEXT AS MIRROR

The phenomenon of the nouveau roman as it developed in France from the late 1950s until at least the late 1970s has been the subject of much journalistic wrangling and spirited academic debate. On the one hand, a large portion of the reading public turned away from the purportedly obscure fictions of Alain Robbe-Grillet, Claude Simon, Nathalie Sarraute, Marguerite Duras, and Michel Butor; on the other hand, professors specializing in twentieth-century literature on both sides of the Atlantic seized upon the nouveau roman as a welcome pretext for aesthetic and political position-taking on issues of criticism and theory. This meant that the flourishing of disconcertingly new novelistic forms caused the already appreciable rift between the general and specialized literary publics to grow larger; yet at the same time, in an interesting shift whose sociopolitical consequences deserve study, two groups of practicing writers that had often been opposed to each other—namely, creators of fictions and critics or theoreticians—came together, joining forces in what can only be called the common cause of experimental writing. Novelists and critics had much to be gained from each other: the critics, in introducing and elucidating the new novels for those readers still willing to furnish the interpretive effort of which Sarraute speaks in *L'Ere du soupçon*, earned the respect of the novelists, while the novelists, most of whom were willing participants in numerous, well-publicized colloquia with the critics, seemed eager to substantiate the theoretical claims of the latter, to confirm the critics' methodological generalizations.[4]

The one professor and critic who identified the common thread uniting the motley productions of these experimental writers was Lucien Dällenbach, whose *Le Récit spéculaire: Essai sur la mise en abyme* (1977) (*The Mirror in the Text*) provides the best overview of the period stretching from 1956 until about 1973. Dällenbach shows that the several authors usually categorized as "new novelists," whose styles are otherwise quite divergent, all make use of one essential technical device inherited from the theory and practice of André Gide—the self-reflecting mirror-effect (de Man) called, in the language of heraldry, *mise en abyme*.[5] In heraldry, we have mise en abyme when one shield contains within itself its own reflection or duplication; in its metaphorical extension to the arts and to literature, this technique serves to place within the macrostructure of the work viewed as a totality a microstructure or structures that "mirror" its effects. Dällenbach convincingly demonstrates that, from the beginning (within Gide's own literary production as well as later, with the early texts of the new novelists), the appeal to mirror imagery as such gradually supplants the actual use of the term *mise en abyme*—which is invoked with increasing rarity and with a notable lack of precision (*Le Récit spéculaire*, 45–51).

Important for our purposes is one of Dällenbach's central theses—that the transformation of the new novel from its first, creatively experimental stage (1954–1958) to its second, more highly theoretical manifestation (1969–1973) can best be understood as a transformation within the practice of textual specularity. Most crucially, the dominance of the macrolevel over the microlevel—of container (*contenant*) over contained (*contenu*) (i.e., of the play *Hamlet* over the smaller "play within a play")—that had characterized the first stage of the nouveau roman tends to disappear in the second, more theoretical stage of its development, where all levels of representation are viewed as equivalent, where the traditional hierarchies and categories of mimesis are abolished in favor of what Dällenbach calls "a dislocated, hyper-reflexive, aleatory, or multipolar text" (200).

It is at this point of "hyper-reflexivity," in which experimental fictions seem to exist exclusively for the purpose of illustrating theoretical propositions, that Dällenbach foresees (in 1977) not only an inevitable disappearance of the mise en abyme as utilized technique but also a probable return to those questions that had been bracketed during the flourishing of the new novel. At the conclusion of his study, Dällenbach writes of the reaction against the continued emphasis on specularity that was becoming visible in the mid-seventies and which promised to extend further in the years to come:

> If the truth be told, this reaction was perfectly predictable: first, because reflexivity is in itself a position that is difficult to maintain and its very proponents have recently made surprising leaps toward exteriority (toward Revolution, or Bliss [i.e., the *jouissance* of Roland Barthes]); second, because it is within the logic of the scansions of History that every excessive tendency (here a literature of the signifier) brings on [calls forth, *appelle*) the opposite tendency (a literature of the signified, of the referent, of instinct or drive [*la Pulsion*]). (211)

Lucien Dällenbach's study of literary specularity (self-reflexivity, self-referentiality) bears the mark of its time as strongly as Nathalie Sarraute's analysis of the age of suspicion. Whereas Sarraute in 1956 was looking back to the literature of modernism for the point of departure toward a new and invigorated fiction, and whereas she could be content at that time with general and nontechnical remarks in her argument, by 1977 the subtle theoretical distinctions and structural diagrams employed by Dällenbach had become necessary for an adequate description of the explosive technical innovations that had made of the nouveau roman a laboratory setting for fictional experimentation. Sarraute and Dällenbach succeeded in characterizing the essential shifts of the periods in which they wrote (Sarraute's new reading contract; Dällenbach's useful equation of the new novel as a whole with self-reflexivity as such), but each also looked beyond to the immediate future—in Sarraute's case to the matter of narrative voice, in Dällenbach's to the problem of what I shall call a *return to the referent* as "outside" reality.

As I proceed now to a preliminary discussion of the contents and purpose of my book, I should like to keep in mind both Sarraute's conception of "active reading" and Dällenbach's analysis of textual self-reflexivity, but I think it necessary to return to the matter of contemporary literary history for a moment, and especially to the thorny related issues of dates, of chronological distinctions, and of the evolution of forms, so that the presentation of my own theses and critical concerns might gain in clarity.

CONTEMPORARY LITERARY HISTORY AND THE STUDY OF INDIVIDUAL TEXTS

In the six essays that constitute the present study, my purpose will be to focus on the problem of referential anxiety as it arises in the narrative texts of Albert Camus, Alain Robbe-Grillet, Claude Simon, Marguerite Duras, Nathalie Sarraute, Maurice Blanchot, and Samuel Beckett. In each essay I shall examine the precise ways in which these writers come to terms with the referential function of language in the elaboration of their experimental fictions. From essay to essay, therefore, stretches a narrative line of my own construction that serves to establish a thematic unity to my critical enterprise. At the same time, however, I have not wished to sacrifice the close examination of particular texts to the overly didactic presentation of a message. For this reason, within each chapter I have attempted to remain in the nearest proximity to the texts under scrutiny, while I have also included, in the introductions that frame Parts 1 and 2, theoretical pauses (in music, these would be called *intermezzi*) during which I establish an overview of the chapters to come, a conceptual bordering-effect that I hope will be a useful guide through the essays. In sum: although I am attentive to the matter of intertextual relations throughout my study, I do not believe that an analysis of the links between and among texts can replace the concrete interpretation of works in their individuality.[6]

I shall concentrate on fictional works that were composed, *grosso modo*, between the mid-1950s and the mid-1980s—a thirty year period remarkable for its innovations and for its diversity of aesthetic form and theoretical intent. I shall begin with a novel written in 1956, the year of publication of Sarraute's

L'Ere du soupçon, the year preceding the publication of Robbe-Grillet's *La Ja-lousie* (*Jealousy*), Simon's *Le Vent* (*The Wind*), and Butor's *La Modification* (*A Change of Heart*). Rather than choose a nouveau roman, however, I have de-cided to analyze Camus's ironical novel *La Chute* (*The Fall*), a work that seems, on the surface, closer to the concerns of existential humanism than to the inventiveness of the new novel. My thesis is that this appearance is deceiving and that *La Chute* stages the "fall" into literary self-reflexiveness or self-referen-tiality with a rigor that is not to be exceeded by any of the *nouveaux romans* of that same era. From this moment of the simultaneous continuation of human-ism in its Sartrian or Camusian guise and the beginning of the new novel I make a jump of twenty years to 1976, the time of the culmination of mise en abyme techniques and of the imprint of literary theory on novelistic practice: In Chapter 2 I analyze Robbe-Grillet's *Topologie d'une cité fantôme* (*Topology of a Phantom City*), a work that elaborates the theories of *topology* and *generativity*. Here, however, I find underneath the topological and generational theoretical stratum an insistent reference to the questioning or interpretive activities of "man" (the human being) that resembles certain key tenets of Heideggerian philosophy and that brings to the text a distinct humanistic resonance. Thus the juxtaposition of Chapters 1 and 2 yields the following paradox: in *La Chute* Camus begins with an existential drama that ultimately explodes into a vertiginous self-referential *abyme*; in *Topologie* Robbe-Grillet begins with a theoretical model of textual self-reflexivity that yields to referential reality when man is reinserted into the text as decipherer of signs, as decryptor of his world.

In these first two chapters, the close reading of individual texts will compli-cate the chronology established by Dällenbach (a chronology whose heuristic value I do not debate or deny), in that the jump from a certain 1956 to a certain 1976 yields not a linear movement whereby literary self-referentiality accentuates itself in a continual manner toward the end point of hyper-reflex-ivity, but rather a more jagged, uncanny design in which the referential and the abyme of the self-reflexive alternate with each other *within each work*.

In Chapters 3 and 4 I move beyond 1980 into the period that Dällenbach correctly prophesied as swerving away from the liberation of the signifier to the anchoring of the signified and to a reestablishing of a concern with the referential, with desire, with pulsion in its Freudian and Lacanian guises.[7] In Chapter 3 I discuss Claude Simon's *Les Géorgiques* (1981) (*The Georgics*), a novel that stages both the breakdown of narrative layering or "leveling" and also what I call *performative pathos*—that is, the hyper-referential move whereby the fictional narrator attempts to "name the world" (taking Steiner's Adamic conceit to its logical end point). And in Chapter 4 I compare three postmodern autobiographies, all published between 1983 and 1984—Robbe-Grillet's *Le Miroir qui revient* (*Ghosts in the Mirror*), Duras's *L'Amant* (*The Lover*),

and Sarraute's *Enfance* (*Childhood*)—as they contrast with Barthes's idiosyncratic self-portrait, *Roland Barthes par Roland Barthes* (*Roland Barthes by Roland
Barthes*). In this chapter my intent is to make clear the problems encountered
by erstwhile *nouveaux romanciers* when they return, explicitly, to the referential sphere, when they face the difficulty of creating a style appropriate to the
depiction of the self in the world.

Whereas Chapters 1 through 4 stage a certain (problematized) chronological evolution from 1956 to 1984 via a series of works written by different
authors, in Chapters 5 and 6 I examine two writers whose long careers encompass this same thirty year span and *within* whose varied literary production I
choose to analyze texts from the fifties in juxtaposition with texts from the
seventies and eighties. In Chapter 5 I discuss Blanchot's theory and complex
praxis of narrative, notably the question of a possible "pure fiction" as it collides with referential constraints. And in Chapter 6 I devote my attention to
the late Samuel Beckett, both as fabricator of postmodern, apparently relationless fiction and as dramatist interested in the narrative possibilities of dialogue
and in the establishing, via the storytelling impulse, of a communicational
community. In focusing on Blanchot and Beckett in some detail, I attempt to
dispel the notion that the supposed obscurity of their fictions is tantamount to
a retreat from the world and its exigencies. In the end, as I discuss Beckett's
antithetical use of the primal word *recueillement* (a term to be understood both
as the solipsistic attitude of meditation and as the act of taking in one's fellow
human, of integrating him or her into a community) in the play *Fin de partie*
(*Endgame*) I return not only to the appeal (*appel*) within the word to the world
but also to the issue of ethical value or valuation that resides within literary
language.

The crux of the interrelated questions with which I deal may be the
problematic interdependence of theory and praxis. From the tone and style of
this introduction, it must seem evident that I find the matter of literary theory
unavoidable, *incontournable*, in the particular context of contemporary literature. I do not think readers can gain access to the texts I have chosen to
analyze without a grounding in theory, and it may be legitimate to ask
whether this fact is itself a sign of the decadence of our postmodern Western
culture, of the Byzantine or Alexandrine era in which we find ourselves. At the
same time, my interpretive efforts are directed at demonstrating that the
practice of writing often undermines the theoretical constructs on which that
writing seems to be based, especially those constructs that center on self-
reflexivity or self-referentiality. It is precisely when a work of fiction asserts
most categorically (most "theoretically," with the loudest "banging of the hammer") that it is a self-sufficient sign which has "forever taken leave" (de Man)
of the referential sphere that the resonance of the referential returns to haunt
the text. In conclusion, I would say that there are two essential forms of
naïveté available to the reader of literature: (1) that which confuses the

fictional text with reality to the point of abolishing all distinctions between the two domains, and (2) that which confuses the fictional narrative with the abolition of the referential *as* question, *as* problem for interpretation. When we encounter Helen in the *Iliad*, she is weaving a text, but the text is *of* war: this envelopment of the said by the saying does not cancel the said, but illuminates it in a light whose brilliance will always exceed our theoretical attempts to capture its enigmatic force.

PART ONE

METAMORPHOSES OF THE REFERENTIAL

FUNCTION, 1956–1984

Chapter One

VERTIGINOUS STORYTELLING: CAMUS'S *LA CHUTE*, 1956

We lived with or against his thought, such as his books revealed it to us—
La Chute [*The Fall*] especially, the most beautiful perhaps and the
least well understood of his works—but always through it [i.e.,
his thought]. His literary enterprise was a singular adventure
of our culture, a movement whose phases and end
point we tried to guess and to imagine.
He represented in this century, and against History, the current inheritor
of that long line of moralists whose works constitute perhaps that which
is most original in French letters. His obstinate humanism, narrow
and pure, austere and sensual, had to wage a questionable battle
against the massive and grotesque events of our time. But, on the
other hand, by the obstinacy of his refusals, he reaffirmed, at the
very heart of our epoch, the existence of the moral fact.
—Sartre, "*Albert Camus*"

Since the end of the war, French literature has been dominated by a
succession of quickly alternating intellectual fashions that have kept
alive the illusion of a fecund and productive modernity. First came the
vogue of Sartre, Camus, and the humanistic existentialism that followed
immediately in the wake of the war, soon to be succeeded by the
experimentalism of the new theater, bypassed in turn by the advent
of the *nouveau roman* and its epigones. These movements are, to a
large extent, superficial and ephemeral; the traces they will leave on
the history of French literature are bound to be slighter than it
appears within the necessarily limited perspective of our own
contemporaneity. . . . When we are able to observe the period
with more detachment, the main proponents of contemporary
French literature may well turn out to be figures that now seem
shadowy in comparison with the celebrities of the hour. And
none is more likely to achieve future prominence than the
little-publicized and difficult writer, Maurice Blanchot.
—de Man, *Blindness and Insight*

I S *LA CHUTE* READABLE? Can its resistance to analytical probing be overcome? Is it possible to arrive at a consensus on the main vectors of its significant multiplicity? To those familiar with criticism on Camus, such questions might sound both naïve and overstated, after all, it can be countered that although *La Chute* is an enigmatic *récit* (narration), the most allusive, textually complex, and personally (autobiographically) revealing of Camus's late works,[1] thirty-five years of commentary have uncovered many of its secrets and progressively illuminated its dark recesses. To say that a text is difficult or obscure is not necessarily to brand it unreadable or condemn it to oblivion; on the contrary, such a text invites a diversity of analyses precisely because of the indeterminate nature of its meanings.

La Chute is a tantalizing and tempting work in that it needs its reader to come into textual existence yet denies the reader the pleasures of interpretive mastery and control.[2] This has not stopped critics from accomplishing their task, but it has rendered that task more formidable and less comfortable. Despite the help of secondary material, readers are disconcerted by *La Chute* to the point of dizziness: one falls into the narrator's verbal maze and becomes entangled in the blanket of guilt that the *récit* weaves around the crimes of twentieth-century humanity. The question "Is *La Chute* readable?" can be understood not only on the level of textual complexity—allusiveness, intertextuality, mise en abyme—as a problem of interpretation, but also on the level of moral power: Are we as readers strong enough to stomach the discomforting negative truths uttered by the loquacious protagonist? Can we digest a text that causes so much trauma and pain? Are we able to contemplate the mirror image of ourselves held up by a mad lawyer who purports to tell *our* story?[3]

Jean-Paul Sartre eulogized Camus as a *moraliste* in the classical French tradition (see the first epigraph to this chapter). According to Sartre, the reason Camus's thought had to be confronted and respected—even if one disagreed with its lack of historical determination, as did Sartre himself—was that it expressed the necessity of examining the excesses and monstrosities of the times sub specie aeternitatis, within a grand perspective whose bounds were set by universally recognizable human values. In his writings, Camus addresses himself to the essential humanity of the reader, and he communicates his message with clarity. As Edouard Morot-Sir has observed in his assessment of Camus as philosopher-essayist, Camus's style is that of the moralist in that it subordinates form and expression to thought: "Camus the artist suppresses poetic flights of fancy: his text expresses a sober lyricism; the image serves to buttress a logical framework" (204). This general statement fits not only *Le Mythe de Sisyphe* (*The Myth of Sisyphus*) and *L'Homme révolté* (*The Rebel*) but also *L'Etranger* (*The Stranger*) and *La Peste* (*The Plague*)— yet how can we apply it to *La Chute*, a work whose rhetoric of *démesure* (excess)[4] stands in diametrical opposition to the contained lyricism of the moralist? One wonders if Sartre did not secretly admire *La Chute* precisely because it did not fit the category of *moralisme* as such; because it added considerable obscurity to the perhaps excessively clear schematic ideas of Camus the philosopher.

But for what purposes does Camus relinquish the disciplined stylistic control he exercised in the essays and récits preceding *La Chute*? Why does he assume, with Clamence, the mask of a strategic duplicity? There is a self-reflexive dimension in *La Chute* that is not merely autobiographical but textual. *La Chute* is, among other things, a mise en abyme of the act of reading, a meditation on the potential and limitations of the written word. In this sense, Camus is much closer to the modern experimentation of *écriture* than he is to "humanistic existentialism"—a term by which Paul de Man implies a subservience of form to content and a certain lack of deep literary self-consciousness in the avowed literary-humanistic enterprise of both Sartre and Camus (see the second epigraph to this chapter). The possibility exists that *La Chute* is not merely a text we have difficulty reading, but a text that *stages* the difficulty—or even the impossibility—of a controlled and masterful reading, and that it represents a turn away from the rigorous aesthetic sobriety of moralisme. This is the hypothesis that will subtend our progressive encounter with the vertiginous playfulness of Clamence's lamentations.

In the following pages I propose to enter the abyss of *La Chute* with Maurice Blanchot as guide.[5] My purpose will not be to uncover specific clues that would unlock and explain the secrets of a difficult work, for this task has been assumed and to a large degree accomplished by a number of critics.[6] Rather, I shall proceed in an indirect and consciously circuitous manner in order to determine not what *La Chute* says or declares under the cloak of a discernible symbolism, but rather its potential for the elaboration of a theory of literary interpretation, how it functions within a network of barely audible intertextual echoes, and how its confessional mode relates to its narrative form. My point of departure will be the elucidation of Blanchot's suggestive but metaphorically elusive critical vocabulary.

BLANCHOT AND THE METAPHOR OF DIZZINESS

In the volume of collected essays entitled *L'Amitié* (*Friendship*) are two provocative studies of Camus's work that first appeared in *La Nouvelle Revue Française*: "Le Détour vers la simplicité" ("The Detour toward Simplicity") and "*La Chute*: La Fuite" ("*The Fall*: The Escape"). In the first article Blanchot attempts to locate the source of Camus's power as writer. Some of his observations correspond closely with generally received assessments of the author, but there is a certain opaqueness in Blanchot's descriptive terminology that introduces an enigmatic aura into an otherwise crystalline discourse. Toward the beginning of his argument, Blanchot asks a question that he answers in a highly personal and apparently impressionistic way: "And yet, what does Camus want, in the act of writing? To find again the simplicity that belongs to him, the immediate communication with happiness and unhappiness, yet perhaps something more (or less), another kind of simplicity, another presence" (216). Not only are the phrases "an*other* simplicity" and "an*other* presence" not definable in this initial context, but the remainder of the essay does nothing to explicate their significance. Rather, Blanchot leads his reader through a labyrinth of commentary destined to illuminate the dangers of misreading Camus. It is only in retrospect, after the meanderings of a complex logic attain some degree of immediate coherence, that one can link the idea of an "other" simplicity to the general problematics of textual interpretation.

Throughout Blanchot's analysis, the reader recognizes a constantly recurring structural principle, that of "centrality." We are told that the unique quality of Camus's itinerary as writer resides in a dogged determination to remain faithful to an original or central discovery. His career is not a progression of changing literary experiments, but an attempt to say the same thing in differing forms. Thus, it can be said that the theme of *indifference* (i.e., the silent force that brings together human beings in a communion beyond existential conflict) and the philosophical idea of *l'absurde*, which are the nodal points of the early works *L'Etranger* and *Le Mythe de Sisyphe*, never cease to inform the author's thoughts, never disappear from his subsequent work. Yet the drama and the pathos that characterize the later years of Camus's artistic activity derive, ironically, from Camus's misreading of his own deeper motivations—a misreading that parallels the early misinterpretations of critics. Thus, when Camus becomes involved in political journalism during the fifties, he is forced to reexamine his earlier writings as if they were a sum of declarations that could be reduced to a series of clear statements. But this form of *engagement*, however necessary or admirable in the political arena, is in fact a vast simplification. In wishing to disengage himself from his philosophy of the absurd, Camus must treat the term *l'absurde* as a fixed concept—precisely the mistake made by readers who have not understood the fragility of the undefinable center that is the secret locus of Camus's inspiration. Blanchot makes an important distinction: "The absurd is not absurdity; between the two words there is a great distance. Absurdity is a concept: it defines the meaning of that which has no meaning. The absurd, however, is neutral:[7] it is neither subject nor object; it belongs neither to the subjective nor the objective; it is that thing [*Cela*] which eludes significance, like the Divine" ("Le Detour," 220). If Camus's originality is to be understood as the uncovering and development of a central obsession with l'absurde, then his success as creator of fictions can be measured by the degree to which he respects the neutrality and nonapprehensiveness of the center itself, by the manner in which he forges a "silent" language appropriate to the *dérobade* (elusiveness) of meaning.

According to the interpretive framework of Blanchot, then, it would seem that what fascinates Camus, what compels him to continue writing the same thing under varying guises, is the desire to be within proximity of a properly inexpressible source—not to attain simplicity and the absoluteness of *présence*, but to hover around their periphery, to make the detour of an artistically productive avoidance. This desire is thematized clearly in many of Camus's works, but it appears most poignantly in *L'Etranger*, where the ideal of presence or simplicity is incorporated in the figure of the mother on whose death the events of the récit focus. In Blanchot's terms, the condemnation by society of Meursault's apparently unfeeling reactions at his mother's funeral can be best understood as a fundamental misinterpretation of the essential emptiness that characterizes the mother-son relationship.

> Meursault carries within himself the truth of his mother. Like her, he is almost speechless, thoughtless, thinking as close as possible to that initial void/lack [*manque*] which is richer than any thought, speaking on the level of things, their muteness, of the pleasures they give, of the certainties they reserve. From the beginning to the end, his destiny is linked to that of his mother. The trial he will endure consists of *transforming into a crime the pure lack/void* [manque] that brought them together and, at the same time, of *turning into a crime the integrity of their relationship*, that insensitivity thanks to which, without oral communication, they lived far from each other yet near to each other, in indifference, but with that form of disinterest which is the way of access to the only true solicitude. (223; my emphasis)

L'Etranger as text is thus an interiorized fable that presents both the other (mute) simplicity and the dramatic process by which the brute strangeness of simplicity is *transformed* and *reversed* into crime; it narrates the violence of misreading whereby a *pur manque* (pure lack, pure void) is clothed in the pathos of explicit (mis)representation.

Blanchot's reading of *L'Etranger* goes against the grain of traditional critical approaches in that it does not adhere to the surface of related events and their moral or existential significance but instead demonstrates how fiction as such originates from an unnamable primal source. It is not the message of the récit that matters so much as the way in which a message can be attached to a central void, or expressivity derived from the inexpressible. This raises a question whose technical importance is obvious and whose theoretical potential will be the focus of a later development in this chapter. If there were no misreading, no *reversal* of probity into crime, would there still be anything resembling a text? Is it not true that *L'Etranger* is read and appreciated because of the dramatic possibilities inherent in such a violation of simplicity? In *Le Mythe de Sisyphe*, Camus defined the authentic *oeuvre absurde* as a work that "furnishes no answers" (187). But can a text exist without drawing false conclusions from the unanswerable questions it asks of itself? Is it possible, in other words, to conceive of a literary form that would not turn the neutrality of l'absurde into the conceptual rigidity of absurdity? To encounter this problem in its complexity, we must turn to *La Chute*.

As is often the case with Blanchot, the essay "*La Chute*: La Fuite" is written on such a high level of reflective abstraction as to seem completely distant from the object of its scrutiny: the critic makes no attempt to deal with the significance of biblical and literary allusions that make Clamence's confession a disconcertingly complicated intertextual web; he is ostensibly unconcerned with the récit's formal identity; and he has little to say about the exacerbated eroticism at the core of the protagonist's strategy of self-evasion. In other words, the themes and problems that lend themselves to explanatory analysis and that have produced an impressive sum of criticism concerning the "hidden meanings" of La Chute lie untouched by Blanchot. But it would be a mistake to assume hastily that this refusal to enter into the detail of textual structures implies that Blanchot is really writing his own personal obsessions rather than reading Camus. There can be no doubt that "La Chute: La Fuite" is the fragmentary expression of an implicit theory that runs through L'Amitié like the Goethian "red thread," but one would falsify the precise nature of Blanchot's insight into Clamence's provocations were one to disregard what his essay says, sotto voce, about how *not* to interpret La Chute.

It is by now well established in the critical literature that La Chute is on one level an autobiographical/confessional text, Camus's poignant discovery of his own human fallibility.[8] Blanchot is sensitive to the thinly veiled personal element present in La Chute; he finds, for example, in the phrase "Was that not, in fact, Eden, my dear Sir, a life of unmediated contentment? That was my life" a statement more appropriate to Camus the man than to the ever-devious Clamence (L'Amitié, 233). He refuses, however, to interpret the récit in a uniquely psychological vein—that is, according to the stance adopted by the vast majority of critics. Prophetically aware of how La Chute will be read in succeeding years, Blanchot evokes the temptation of reducing Clamence's discourse to a drama of consciousness: "People will no doubt find in this story the rigid movement of a self-satisfied man who, by dint of indulging his virtuous and contented ego, gives himself over in the end to the force of dissatisfaction and destruction that also resides in the ego" (229). This is a concise summary of the book's plot—the process by which a self-satisfied lawyer, defender of widows and orphans, ends up as "judge-penitent" in an Amsterdam bar, with the avowed purpose of coercing all of humanity to share his own guilt. But Blanchot does not see in Clamence the illustrator of La Rochefoucauld's psychology and does not believe that La Chute is essentially a didactic text whose goal is to "teach dissatisfaction, the uncomfortable truth and necessary anxiety." Instead, he sees in the récit "the grace of irony—that gives us only what it takes away from us" (230). This irony can also be called *attirance* (magnetic attraction) or *fuite* (escape)—words that convey both the capacity of the text to draw the reader into its rhetorical spins and turns and also its potential to escape the imprisonment of semantic identification. What the protagonist relates is thus mere ornamentation—however brilliant and seductive—that hides the general "escaping" movement of his discourse.

As in his interpretation of L'Etranger, Blanchot in explicating La Chute inverts the traditional priority of content over form and demonstrates the insubstantiality of content itself: in so doing, he questions the usual reading that defines *La Chute* as a text about guilt. What, in fact, is the nature of Clamence's need to confess? "His confession is but a calculation. His guilty man's story is made of the hope of believing himself to be guilty, because a true crime would be a verifiable event in which he could anchor his life, a solid point of referential certainty [*repère solide*] that would allow him to limit his course" (230).[9] Just as the representatives of social order had transformed the pur manque of the bond between Meursault and his mother into a crime, Blanchot would have us believe that Clamence misreads the fuite in which he is caught and tries to turn it into a certainty (*certitude*) or solid reference point (*repère solide*). This misreading inscribed in the text mirrors the misanalyses of critics who take the confessed material seriously (literally) rather than inquire about the origin of confession as such. Once again, Blanchot's remarks suggest the structural scheme of a central void around which false interpretations can be formulated without limit; in the case of *La Chute*, however, the center is not defined as an enigmatically nonpresent presence but as a fleeing motion that lends itself to an allegorical correspondence with the temporal process of reading.

In the final paragraph of "*La Chute*: La Fruite," Blanchot touches upon the theoretical implications of the récit's dialogic form. Although the goal of the protagonist is quite obviously to implicate the reader in his own personal degradation, to draw him into the tightly constricted space of an individual discourse, the textual process of fuite is precisely the opposite: it forces Clamence into a strange realm of transindividual generality that surpasses his egocentric limits; it thrusts him into dizziness (*vertige*):

> We fall. We console ourselves for this fall by determining, in our imagination, the point at which we presume to have begun falling. We prefer to be guilty rather than to be tormented for no crime. . . . Everything must fall, and everything that falls must drag along with it in its fall, in an indefinite movement of growth, all that tries to remain. From time to time, we perceive that the fall far exceeds our measure and that we must, in a sense, fall more than we are capable of falling. *Here begins the dizziness through which we divide ourselves*, becoming, for ourselves, companions in our fall. (234; my emphasis)

Dizziness is an apt metaphor to describe the situation of all readers when confronted with the semantic proliferation of texts; and dizziness is the condition of literary dialogue, which originates when the indescribable otherness of the text is recognized and respected. To read himself, Clamence was obliged to create or locate his double—the silent interlocutor who, it turns out, is also a lawyer and perhaps the imaginary projection of the protagonist. And although this doubling is the crucial process by which the récit presents itself as an object to be understood, it necessarily renders comprehension in the sense of mastery impossible because it is born of vertige. Clamence's wish to control the order and meaning of his speech takes on a pathetic quality. His attempt

to violate the laws of dialogue and his desire to *be* the crying voice of a monologue present only unto itself mimic the hubris underlying the literary critic's
"natural" tendency to neutralize ambivalences and make definitive the interpretation of literary works.

THE GAME/PLAY: HERMENEUTIC THEORY AND TEXTUAL PRACTICE

From the preceding review of Blanchot's critical essays arise two major questions. First, is it legitimate to read into the critic's reflections on falling and
dizziness a genuine theory of literary interpretation, and if so, can that theory
be expressed in a more objective, less metaphorical formulation without los-
ing its pertinence and meaningfulness? Second, to what extent does *La Chute*
actually perform the textual dizziness of which Blanchot writes, and is it possible to localize with any degree of precision the moments at which the récit
succumbs to the démesure of the fall? In asking these questions and attempting to find their answers, I assume that what Blanchot has to say about Camus
constitutes an abstract design whose textual objective correlative is the narrative called *La Chute*; that is, I assume a demonstrable correspondence between
the remarks of the critic and the text he analyzes. It must be admitted, however, that this may not be true. In characterizing Blanchot's method, Paul de
Man has contended that the insights of the interpreter, however rich in general significance, do not necessarily make for a change in our view of the
author being studied:

> When we read him [Blanchot] on one of the poets or novelists he happens to choose
> for a theme, we readily forget all we assumed to know up till then about this writer.
> This does not happen because Blanchot's insight necessarily compels us to modify
> our own perspective; this is by no means always the case. Returning afterwards to the
> author in question, we will find ourselves back at the same point, our understanding
> barely enriched by the comments of the critic. Blanchot, in fact, never intended to
> perform a task of exegesis that would combine earlier acquired knowledge with new
> elucidation. The clarity of his critical writings is not due to exegetic power; they seem
> clear, not because they penetrate further into a dark and inaccessible domain but
> because they suspend the very act of comprehension. The light they cast on texts is
> of a different nature. Nothing, in fact, could be more obscure than the nature of this
> light. ("Impersonality in Blanchot," 62–63)

Although it is certainly true that Blanchot's task in writing about other literary creators is not principally one of exegesis in the traditional sense of that
term, I would argue that the suspension of comprehension seen by de Man
as the ultimate effect of Blanchot's style is in fact an invitation to descend
further into the textual abyme, where fiction and analytical essay mirror each
other and elucidate each other's darkness. Keeping this in mind, I will now

examine the origin and meaning of dizziness in *La Chute*. As a first stage of clarification I propose to identify the vertiginous process of transsubjective generality according to its theoretical potential and in the detail of its contextual functioning.

If Blanchot's metaphorical scheme of dizziness were translated into a philosophically coherent, discursively elaborated hermeneutic theory, it would resemble and even repeat the model of Hans-Georg Gadamer that relates artistic creativity to a game or play (*Spiel*). In the second part of *Wahrheit und Methode* (*Truth and Method*),[10] Gadamer distinguishes between the classical use of the term *Spiel* by Kant and Schiller—both of whom anchored the game analogy in the state of mind of a freely creating subject—and his own post-Heideggerian view according to which the game is nothing less than "die Seinsweise des Kunstwerkes selbst" ("the mode of being of the work of art itself"). For Gadamer, it is not the subject who controls the game, but the reverse. In fact—to play with words—the subject of the game is not the subject (or subjectivity), but the game comes to be represented *through* the activity of subjects or players. The game as such fulfills itself much as a musical composition does—through performance or "realization"—and affects its performers in a similar fashion: by transforming them, by actively modifying their being:

> The playing of games fulfills its purpose only when the player becomes caught up/ wrapped up in the playing [*wenn der Spielende im Spiele aufgeht*]. Not the game's relationship to seriousness, but only seriousness in the act of playing allows the game to be itself entirely. He who does not take the game seriously is a spoil-sport. The mode of being of the game does not permit that the player relate to the game as to an object. The player certainly knows what the game is and that what he is doing is "only a game," but he does not know what he thereby "knows" [i.e., he does not know what this "knowledge" has taught him]. (97; my emphasis)

A complete reading of the section on games would show that Gadamer's presentation is parallel to Blanchot's less explicit reflections in that the perceiving or interpreting consciousness relates to the game being played (or the book being read) as an individual subject relates to a generality whose rules determine his mode of existence. Gadamer insists that the player is bound by or wrapped up in the game (*der Spielende geht im Spiele auf*), and because the game surpasses the player's limited powers, it is a sign of bad faith to treat it as a mere object. Most important, Gadamer's model, like Blanchot's metaphorics of dizziness, indicates both the inevitability of the subject's cognitive relationship to the game he plays and also the limits of this relationship. To paraphrase Gadamer and his predecessors in the field of hermeneutics, one might say that the player has a foreknowledge of the meaning of the game, or, more precisely, of the boundaries that determine the game's potential significance; but at the moment of his dramatic *Aufgehen im Spiel*, he loses the capacity to know what he knows and, in a strangely literal sense, "loses himself" in the playing. The truth of the game takes on the form of an ironical reversal in which the manipulator of figures is himself manipulated. In Gadamer's succinct terms, the fascination of game playing is that the game becomes *master* of the player ("daß das Spiel über den Spielenden *Herr* wird") (102).

The central conflict of *La Chute*—Clamence's immoderate attempts to dominate by assuming the mask of a strategic immersion in guilt—is related in psychological terms, but its implications for a theory of reading are apparent once it becomes clear that Camus is speaking Gadamer's language. The third chapter of *La Chute* is a long discourse on *mastery* as such, but it reverses the ideal form of Gadamer's model in that it shows Clamence's refusal to be controlled by the game and his exasperated attempts to invent the rules himself. This defensive narcissism is especially evident in the passages dealing with love or sexuality. In his repeated scenes of seduction, the protagonist admits: "Je satisfaisais encore autre chose que ma sensualité: mon amour du *jeu*. J'aimais dans les femmes les partenaires d'un certain *jeu*"(1504; my emphasis) ("I satisfied even more than my sensuality: my love of *games* [of playing, acting]. I loved in women the partners of a certain *game/play*"). As long as Clamence is in charge of the game, eroticism has all the comforts of ritual habit. In this respect his conception of love repeats that of the Proustian narrator-hero, for whom pleasure is equivalent to the absence of pain—which in turn presupposes the anesthesia of habit and ignorance of the beloved's true activity. As in Proust, because the attachment of self to other is nothing more than the projection of self-love, the most adequate metaphor to express the loving relationship is that of imprisonment: "In the end I became attached to her in much the same way as I imagine a jailer relates to his prisoner" (1506). Furthermore, because the subject both needs the confirmation of outside approval and also denies the very right to existence of the outside as such, the women with whom Clamence shares spare moments must be "vacant" and "deprived of an independent life" (1508). On the psychological level, therefore, a subject incapable of relating to the *other* as existential reality creates a game in which it is possible to refuse the *other's* identity by fictionalizing it or otherwise rendering it harmless. This happens not only in the realm of eroticism, where a jailer tries to control the secretive essence of a prisoner, but also in the political-historical arena, as Camus demonstrates in a short parable on man's need for figures of authority. Readers of *La Chute* will remember the starkly illuminated episode in which Clamence tells how he came to be "pope" in a prison camp (1536–39). Having accepted, in jest (*par plaisanterie*), to play the role of a holy man who will share the miseries and assume the collective destiny of a group, Clamence eventually uses his power for his own selfish interests and acts out of a personal survival instinct. As he tells it, with a significant metaphor: "Disons que j'ai bouclé la boucle le jour où j'ai bu l'eau d'un camarade agonisant" (1539) ("Let us say that I came full circle the day I drank the water of a dying comrade").

The anecdotal material chosen by Camus to illustrate the problem of imprisonment—whether literally, as in the war context, or figuratively, as in the sensuality of love games—is so interesting in itself, so full of allusions to the crises of our modern age and to the private life of the author, that the temptation is to overlook the possible implications of imprisonment as metaphor—that is, how the term expresses *authorial* desires and functions in the literary sense. I am not suggesting that the matter of Clamence's confessions is of itself indifferent. It is only too clear that social decadence and political crimes need to be examined in themselves, and Camus's récit elaborates on these themes in a provocative way. But I would contend that what concerns Camus at the level where the act of writing reflects upon itself is also "imprisonment"— defined as the manipulative control exercised by an author over his own work. If this is true, then there is a special meaningfulness in Clamence's admission that he came full circle when he drank his comrade's life-giving water. Read as an allegory of reading, this statement translates into the inauthentic appropriation by the author of that which is not his by rights but which, when removed from its proper place, produces the life of his text. In other words, Clamence represents the writer who refuses to engage himself in the hermeneutic circle but pretends to close off the infinite regress of the turning circle itself.

THE BAUDELAIRIAN INTERTEXT: VERTIGINOUS LAUGHTER AND LITERARY LANGUAGE

To what extent can it be demonstrated that Clamence's actions emblematize the predicament of all writers in their efforts to achieve mastery over reality through form? Can it be shown, through concrete textual analysis, that *La Chute* stages the drama of authorial appropriation, thereby performing the conflict between self and transsubjective dispossessing generality found at the heart of Blanchot's dizziness metaphor and Gadamer's game model? If these questions are to be answered, we need to identify what Camus is obliged to "steal" in order to enliven his text; that which, in becoming part of his récit, risks expropriating it in a dizzying circle of uncontrolled relations. The most immediate response, if we view *La Chute* as the story of its own constitution, is that the force against which the author struggles is that of the *other texts* he has woven into the fabric of his own discourse. As has been noted, critics of Camus have long recognized the intertextual effects of Clamence's story and have written on the numerous biblical and literary allusions. But their studies most often assume the inviolable uniqueness and aesthetic unity of *La Chute*, so that whatever new information they uncover generally serves to consolidate the thematic coherence they had already presupposed to exist. Of course, it is possible to condemn Camus for an "excessive" borrowing,[11] but this judgment only serves to confirm the prejudice that a work of art need stand on its own, detached from and indifferent to the subversive potential of the texts it cites. In the following section of this chapter, I propose that the intertextual ramifications of *La Chute* be reexamined in their expropriative power; that is, I suggest that Camus's text is not so much a self-originating creation as a reading of other texts whose central theme is the bizarre movement of *vertige*. *La Chute* is vertiginous precisely insofar as it repeats or falls into dizziness.

The discovery that precipitates Clamence's decision to abandon Paris and a successful career is that his own apparent altruism is in truth the mask of a deeper self-love and will to dominate. When he becomes judge-penitent in the shadowy demimonde of Amsterdam, he simply allows the mask to stick and assumes a permanent stance of duplicity: he recognizes his guilt, but does penance while implicating others in his crimes, so that in the end he can judge all of humanity. One does not rid oneself easily of other people, however, and at times Clamence's relations with the outside world become exaggerated and frustrated to the point of violence. In the latter stages of his confession, by an ironic reversal, the protagonist attempts to convince his readers that the human solidarity whose precariousness he had formerly experienced is in fact possible, if it is clothed in the form of cruelty. This reversal is indeed interesting and produces some rather startling textual effects, but it is by no means original with Camus. The wording used by Clamence in the following passages indicates that he is quoting from one of Baudelaire's most disconcerting and disorienting prose poems, "Assommons les pauvres!" ("Let Us Bludgeon the Poor!"):[12] "With courtesy, and with a truly emotional sense of solidarity, I used to spit every day on the faces of the blind"; and later, in the same vein, "I planned to puncture the tires of wheelchairs, to go cry 'Dirty Pauper' under the scaffolding where workers were toiling, to slap infants in the underground" (*La Chute*, 1520).

If we turn now to Baudelaire's poem for enlightenment on the problem of cruelty as such and for illumination of its role in *La Chute*, we find more (and less) than we had bargained for. The argumentation adopted by the first-person narrator of "Assommons" resembles closely that of Clamence: both begin in a state of disillusionment about the possibility of social and spiritual equality among human beings. Having read numerous tracts "where the art of making people happy is celebrated" ("Assommons," 304–5), the poet has his own idea, which consists of attaining solidarity through mutual violence: by standing Christian morality on its head, he decides that the reciprocity of bludgeoning is the only authentic method of achieving the respectful exchange generally called "brotherly love." The tone of the poem is decidedly ironic, and the scene in which the poet and the beggar exchange blows is told with relish and a joyful accumulation of bloody detail whose immediate effect is to shock the reader and involve him deeply in the representational expressivity of a subject's will to power. Yet the very triumphant voice of the poet, coupled with the fact that he has presented his case as a rigorously demonstrated, logical theorem, make one question the truth-value of such an inflated ego's apotheosis in rhetoric. (As the beggar turns around to strike him, the poet exclaims: "Oh miracle, oh delight of the philosopher who verifies the excellence of his theory" [306]). Most important, one is led to wonder about the motivations behind the "idée supérieure" that drove the poet from the solitude of his room to the encounter with the beggar.

The origin of the poet's feeling of superiority is not original: it cannot be located in some primal psychological discovery; it is not the essence of a pure drama of solipsism. Superiority is born of reading; it is the defensive reaction of a subject to the books against whose ideas he wishes to construct his own philosophy. In the first paragraph of "Assommons" the poet criticizes "all the lucubrations of all these entrepreneurs of public happiness—of those who counsel poor people to become slaves, and of those who persuade them that they are all dethroned kings" (305). Like the English psychologists whom Nietzsche ridicules in the opening pages of *The Genealogy of Morals*, the "entrepreneurs of public happiness" make an easy target for a writer whose ostensible theme is the inversion of traditional Christian values, the radical questioning of morality in its usual guise of self-effacement and self-annihilation. But the condition of possibility of this inversion is the neutralization and elimination of the "mauvaises lectures" (305) ("bad readings, bad texts") to which the poet has subjected himself; hence the metaphors of digestion and swallowing that are used to express the act of reading itself ("I had thus digested— swallowed, I mean—all the lucubrations"). Here, to swallow a bad text is to render it impotent by assimilation. But one senses that the poet is only partially successful in his efforts, in that he is caught up in "a state resembling dizziness [*le vertige*] or stupidity" (305) that drives him from his room for fresh air and sets the stage for the episode of solidarity proving. It then becomes possible to read the poem as a whole on a deeper level than its thematic content immediately exhibits. In fact, the self's parading and basking in the feeling of its power are implicitly undercut by the first paragraph. The poem constructs itself in a movement of forgetfulness of its own origin, in the refusal to read the vertige from which it emerges and simultaneously wishes to escape. The poet's error is to leave his room in the first place and to conceive of his own superiority, when in fact his situation *as* poet is to be engaged in the movement of dizziness, wrapped up in the corpus of texts that traverses and negates the closed limits of his body and mind.

The Baudelairian intertext is not so much a convenient framework of themes and images that Camus uses to buttress his fictional argument as it is the allusive/elusive movement through which *La Chute* falls into the metaphorically expressed story of its own constitution as text. Quotations from

Baudelaire's work are not the signs of an intellectual heritage that Camus can interiorize and call his own, but they stand in the récit as trapdoors opening into the abyme of the poet's most daring literary provocations. Perhaps the most consequential but least obvious allusion to Baudelaire occurs in a deceptively trivial and seemingly realistic anecdote: Clamence explains how he has suddenly lost control of his usually rapt audience in the law courts, to the point of becoming the object of a general laughter:

> My fellow humans were no longer, in my eyes, the respectful audience to which I had become accustomed. The circle of which I was the center was breaking, and they were placed in one line, as at a trial. . . . Yes, they were there, as before, but they were laughing. . . . I even thought, at that time, that people were trying to trip me. Two or three times, in fact, I stumbled, for no reason, in entering public places. Once I even fell flat on my face. (1513)

The hidden source of this passage is "De l'Essence du rire," Baudelaire's philosophical and moral meditation on laughter. In this essay, the aesthetician of L'Art romantique grounds laughter in the ego's sense of superiority. If I laugh at someone who falls on the pavement, it is because I am assured of my own ability to avoid obstacles: "I do not fall; I walk in a straight line; my footing is strong and assured. I would not commit the foolish error of not seeing a broken-up sidewalk or a paving-stone that blocks my path" ("De l'Essence du rire," 248; Baudelaire's emphasis). But what is the origin of superiority as such? The answer is drawn from Christianity: one feels above others because one has lost the original innocence of Eden. Laughter is therefore Satanic in essence. In stating that "human laughter is linked to the accident of an ancient fall [chute ancienne], of a physical and moral degradation" (245; my emphasis), Baudelaire provides Camus with the title of his book as well as the theological vocabulary that critics most often examine independent of its contextual relationship to the theme of laughter.[13]

At stake in "De l'Essence du rire" is the same dramatic opposition between egocentric domination and the fall into transsubjective generality that generated the ironies of Gadamer's hermeneutic game-theory, Blanchot's metaphorics of dizziness, and Baudelaire's "Assommons les pauvres!" In fact, at a crucial stage in the development of his essay, Baudelaire enters into the problematics of vertige. In comparing what he calls the comique significatif (whose mode of functioning is double, based on the contrasts between mask and reality that constitute social comedy) to the comique absolu or grotesque (whose appearance is that of a closed unity "that must be seized by intuition"[254], Baudelaire finds himself at a logical impasse. Because the comique significatif involves the duplicity of theatrical hypocrisy, it can be analyzed into its component parts and understood; the grotesque, on the other hand, can be verified only by laughter itself, not by a discourse on laughter. To describe the comical at the absolute of its power, the writer necessarily resorts to metaphor, but not to just any metaphor. In his lively and impressionistic re-creation of an English pantomime, the theoretician is reduced to a radical impotence with regard to the overwhelming energy of the grotesque, his prose becoming a series of punctuated exclamations hovering in dizziness:

> And everything was expressed, in this singular play, with fury; it was *the dizziness of hyperbole* [*le vertige de l'hyperbole*]. (258; my emphasis)

> Immediately dizziness entered the scene; dizziness circulates in the air; we breathe the dizziness; it is dizziness that fills the lungs and replenishes the blood of the heart.
> What is this dizziness? It is the *comique absolu*; it has seized/dispossessed us all [*il s'est emparé de chaque être*]. (260; my emphasis)

The most striking example of the excessive or "hyperbolic" manner in which the individual actor-player is appropriated by the absolute comical is provided by the figure of Pierrot, who is guillotined on the stage with a complete lack of deference for the classical French *bienséances*. Undaunted by the loss of his head, he picks it up and pockets it, consumed by the monomania of his compulsion to steal. The violent laughter that moves through the audience proves that the effect of the absolute has been intuited, while on the level of theatrical staging, the scene as such represents the image of human intelligence working overtime, attempting to recuperate the irrecuperable. Pierrot is the appropriately absurd symbol of the philosopher or aesthetician who believes he can overcome existential loss by the willed mastery of a possession beyond the limits of the knowable, while the laughter that in truth possesses him (*s'empare de lui*) designates the flimsy foundation of his project.

The word *vertige* enters Baudelaire's critical vocabulary when the inexpressible absolute must be expressed. Its repeated use in the essay on laughter indicates the impossibility of the literary theoretician's desire to conceptually imprison the object of his study: there will always be a dizziness in the original text that the analytical treatise can only repeat. According to Baudelaire, the theoretician is not a detached, objective observer in control of his material, but a body agitated, dispossessed; hence the network of digestion and elimination metaphors already noted in "Assommons les pauvres!" At the beginning of "De l'Essence du rire," Baudelaire states that his purpose is simply to "communicate to the reader certain thoughts that have come to me often. . . . These thoughts had become for me a kind of obsession: I wanted to *relieve myself* [*me soulager*]" (244); and in his characterization of Maturin's *Melmoth the Wanderer*, "ce rire glace et tord les entrailles" (249) ("this laughter freezes and twists the entrails"). The situation of the critic vis-à-vis the text(s) he reads is that of an individual who is traversed by the food that descends through and departs from his body. To swallow the "lucubrations" of writers is not to interiorize them permanently but to allow them access to our own inner sanctum, where they are free to operate upon us with abandon. The act of reading is that process by which a body opens itself to the outside and submits to the rule of the other.

The proximity of laughter in its physiological function to literature as such is one of Blanchot's major insights in *L'Amitié*. In fact, his definition of laughter as that which requires "the abandonment of personal limits, because it [laughter] comes from afar and, passing through us, disperses us to the winds" (193) is a shorthand version of what he has to say about "the truth of literary language" in his article on Louis René des Forêts's *Le Bavard* (*The Chatterer*), a book that may have influenced *La Chute*.[14] What Blanchot writes concerning the fascinating power of des Forêts's curious monologue applies also to Clamence's excesses of *bavardage*:

> *Le Bavard* fascinates and upsets us. But this is not because it represents, symbolically, the inane chatter one finds in our world, but because it makes us realize that, once engaged in the movement of chatter, the decision to get out, the pretension to be free from it belongs to it [chatter] already and that this immense preliminary erosion, this inner void, this contamination of words by muteness and of silence by words, designate perhaps the truth of all language, and particularly of literary language, that truth we would encounter if we had the strength to go to the end, and the resolution to abandon ourselves, rigorously, methodically, in all cowardice, to dizziness. (*L'Amitié*, 146)

If laughter and the truth of literary language coincide, it is because they both designate or mean the movement of decentralization by which a body or text loses mastery over its functions. According to Blanchot, it is easy to underestimate the importance of this strange process because the work of art also seems to "represent" (i.e., to *refer* to the problematic world in which we live). It is tempting to see in *Le Bavard* or *La Chute* the symbolic expression of our modern age's "inane chatter," and it is more difficult, more disconcerting, to follow the text's fall into self-referentiality, into the domain where fiction turns into itself, generating itself in the dizziness of its noncoincidence with the apparent *repère solide* (solid reference-point) from which its representational reading is derived.

In the case of *La Chute*, it is especially difficult to arrive at that end point where there is a giving up to vertige, because Camus himself seemed unwilling to abandon authorial control. In the passage from Lermontov's *Hero of Our Time* used as the epigraph to the American edition of *The Fall*, Camus calls his work "a portrait, but not of an individual; it is the aggregate of the vices of our whole generation in their fullest expression."[15] This would indicate that we as readers should interpret *La Chute* as the indirectly stated discourse of a Zeitgeist, that Clamence's confessions originate in a definable guilt that is in fact our guilt. But such a reading presupposes the absolute solidity of a central point around which the récit constitutes itself through an internally verifiable, logical coherence. Is guilt a given, the base upon which Clamence's story is well anchored, or is there a story of the origin of guilt which, in telling how *La Chute* unravels itself from the center, thrusts the narrator into the démesure of dizziness? To encounter this question directly is to read the dramatic scene in which Clamence stands by passively while a woman apparently drowns.

THE MISREADING OF "GUILT": THE ORIGIN OF NARRATION

Like Dante's Hell, the narrative of *La Chute* is constructed concentrically around a point that supports the entire verbal edifice. However, whereas the movement of the pilgrim and his guide in the *Inferno* is a downward spiral toward the figure of Satan, and therefore toward a direct physical confrontation with the embodiment of Evil, *La Chute* is best described as a series of circles receding outward from an origin that is subsequently lost from view, much like the immediately disappearing pattern made by a pebble thrown into water. The pebble itself, or cause, is quickly forgotten in favor of its effect—the rippling waves it produces. Similarly, critical readings of *La Chute* have focused on the way Clamence defers his account of guilt causation and on the self-revelations that result from the later strategic use of confessional discourse. The passage that produces guilt is either paraphrased transparently or repressed by the critics, in an interesting mimicry of Clamence's own repressions. To *read* what happened on the November night of the protagonist's "cowardice," however, is to analyze the rhetorical disruption that inhabits the exact center of *La Chute*:

> On that night, in November, two or three years before the evening I thought I heard laughter coming from behind me, I was crossing the Pont Royal to the Left Bank, to return to my apartment. . . . On the bridge, I passed behind a human form, bent over the parapet, that seemed to be looking at the river. From a closer remove, I could discern a slender young woman, dressed in black. Between her dark hair and the collar of her coat, one could only see the back of her neck, fresh and moist, to which I was not insensitive. . . . I had already moved away by some fifty meters, when *I heard the noise*, which, despite the distance, seemed to me extraordinarily loud in the nocturnal silence, *of a body falling into water*. I stopped in my tracks, but without turning around. Almost immediately, *I heard a cry, repeated several times, which also seemed to follow the river's course*, then suddenly was extinguished. The silence that followed, in the now frozen night, seemed to me interminable. I wanted to run yet could not move. I was trembling, I think, from the cold and the shock. I said to myself that I had to act quickly and I felt an irresistible weakness overcome my body. I forgot what I thought then. "Too late, too far" [*"Trop tard, trop loin"*] . . . or something in that vein. (*La Chute*, 1509; my emphasis)

The most apparent effect of the episode is to inculpate Clamence, to condemn him for lack of action. He has seen a woman, heard a suspiciously revealing noise, and has not shown the slightest sign of altruistic behavior. He has allowed a suicide to occur, the critics tell us. But what is the textual origin of this "death"? A literal reading of the passage reveals only a series of juxtaposed perceptions: the protagonist sees a woman who appeals to him sensually and then he hears the sound of a body falling followed by a cry. The rhetoric of Clamence and the logic of referential anchoring cause us to combine these elements into a coherent picture: we conclude quickly that it is the woman seen on the bridge who falls and that her death is Clamence's crime of passivity. The text is persuasive enough to render all this believable and pathetic. On the purely literal level of the discourse's immediate significance, however, the dramatic center is nothing more than the enigma of an *invisible absence* that, through a subject's erroneous interpretation, becomes clothed in the language of guilt.

By reading *La Chute* from the center outward, by respecting the unbridgeable gap between falsely perceived cause and invented effect, we necessarily reverse the priorities implicit in the usual interpretation of the récit as illustration or clarification of the main character's obsessions. The initial moment of the woman's fall is not in itself a referentially verifiable given, a proven event that supports and justifies the meanderings of the protagonist's talk; it is, rather, the act of separation of the center from all conceivable analytical explanations which, paradoxically, grounds the text and allows it to function without limit. Clamence loses the substantiality of the knowing subject, as his own origin is not in self-knowledge or even self-debasement—which comes only later, after he has forged a language of guilt to cover the nothingness of the center—but in the *cry* of his Latin name ("clamans"), in the recognition of the inevitable lateness of his words: "Trop tard, trop loin." His exclamation, which adds to the pathos of represented events—the woman is gone, perhaps already drowned—is simultaneously an expression of his language's freedom to create, quite literally, from nothing.

The psychological coherence of Clamence's discourse and the clarity of his confessional voice arise from a misreading of the dizziness that is the textual movement of *La Chute*. It has been my purpose to show that Camus's enigmatic récit, although it may have been consciously (authorially) conceived as a text about our modern imprisonment in guilt, became, in the actual writing, the dérobade by which narration reveals its ironic relationship to the subject matter or message it conveys. Because *La Chute* hides its significance in the abyme of intertextuality, its repetition of the dizziness process performed by the texts it "reads" remains enclosed in darkness; and when it illustrates the logical contradiction on which its central drama is based, it does so with such blinding clarity as to go unseen. This chapter is a bringing to the light of what Blanchot had said with a certain secretiveness. In rendering explicit his interpretation of Camus, I have been obliged to name and rename the generality in which the writer is swallowed up and that can be called "dizziness," "game/

play," "laughter," and "the truth of literary language." No doubt this naming is the result of a fundamental tendency in language to say what is beyond words, to create a coherent metaphorics where there is nothing but a void demanding interpretation. But the naming is inevitable and productive of meanings. If Clamence had not identified his crime and assumed the cloak of guilt, there could have been no representable actions or matter for confession, but only the hovering around an absent center whose proper expression is silence.

Chapter Two

REAPPEARING MAN IN ROBBE-GRILLET'S

TOPOLOGIE D'UNE CITÉ FANTÔME, 1976

TO WHAT EXTENT is Robbe-Grillet's novel *Topologie d'une cité fantôme* (*Topology of a Phantom City*) readable? How does this puzzling work open or close itself to the act of interpretation? Of what significance are the numerous allusions in its pages to other works of Robbe-Grillet, to contemporary art, to Greek mythology? These questions all point to the twin problems of reference and meaning in the text, bringing up a difficulty that is by no means new, yet quite persistent, in the criticism of Robbe-Grillet's novels: the enigmatic status of the object or apparent symbol that seems to call for the reader's active deciphering yet at the same time eludes his grasp by the very solidity of its hermetically sealed surface.[1] As Roland Barthes observed in his introductory essay to Bruce Morrissette's *Novels of Robbe-Grillet*, this ambivalent status of the object led, from the very start, to two diametrically opposed views of the author: for some, Robbe-Grillet was an objective describer of phenomena, a *chosiste* interested in demystifying the Romantic treatment of the exterior world as reflection of a privileged individual consciousness; for others he was a humanist who reinfused a modern meaning into the myths and signs of the past.[2] To choose between these interpretations in a definitive way is rendered especially hazardous by the fact that Robbe-Grillet seems to endorse the first in his early theoretical writings ("In future novelistic constructions, gestures and objects will be *there* before being *something*. . . . Henceforth . . . objects will lose their inconstancy and their secrets, will give up their false mystery"[3]), whereas his principal interpreter, Morrissette, derives a substantial thematic continuity from the study of objects and actions as if they were vehicles of a deeper significance than their surface exhibits.

Morrissette's early essays not only show the coherence of images, allusions, and motifs, but they tend to organize around a single center, to coalesce as if drawn together by the magnetic power of a transcendental signifier. Thus, the detective novel *Les Gommes* (*The Erasers*) is to be explicated from the focal point of the Oedipus myth; *Le Voyeur* (*The Voyeur*) becomes a series of variations on the figure-of-eight design that signifies murder; and *L'Année dernière à Marienbad* (*Last Year at Marienbad*) turns on the unique pivot of "persuasion" as the psychological power of hypnotism. Yet the further one reads in Morrissette's *Novels of Robbe-Grillet*, the more apparent it becomes that Robbe-Grillet's later works, beginning with *La Maison de rendez-vous*, escape theoretical and critical organization to such a degree that the critic, no longer capable of finding a center, must speak instead of the novel's perverse capacity of decentralization, must admit that even "modern critical criteria of narrative identification . . . appear outmoded by comparison with these unprecedented fictional structures" (260).

Such an admission of the limits of interpretation in the analysis of contemporary novels does not imply that critical discourse as such will wither away and die but merely changes the outward appearance of a given reading: it now describes absences and impossibilities, without revealing the "true" presence of a temporarily hidden significance. This brings criticism closer to its essence (the essence it would prefer to forget), which is the repetition and reorganization of that which has already been written rather than the more exalted idea of discovery, unless one wishes to use the latter term for the uncovering of an already exhaustively mapped and charted area. In the case of Morrissette and Robbe-Grillet, however, a curious reversal of the traditional roles of critic and author/creator has taken place. It is now abundantly clear that Robbe-Grillet has read Morrissette as carefully as (if not more playfully than) Morrissette has read him, and he considers his interpreter's theories to be of such importance as to quote and develop them at length in his recent works, especially *Topologie*.

As Françoise Meltzer has noted, the origin of the terms *topologie* and *générativité* (of the chapter heading "Dans la cellule génératrice") are to be found in Morrissette's articles "Topology and the French *Nouveau Roman*" and "Post-Modern Generative Fiction: Novel and Film."[4] By incorporating the terminology of his critic, Robbe-Grillet seems to affirm both the novel's capacity to "generate" itself as well as its existence as a map of imaginary, interpenetrating surfaces. The dictionary definition of *topology*—"science that studies mathematical reasoning without reference to concrete significance"—is immediately applied and made to function in the novel, where a succession of *espaces* (spaces) develops in a formalized geometrical progression that *is* its own meaning by abolishing the reassuring outside of a recognizable referential reality. As the chapter titles would indicate,[5] *Topologie* is an experiment in the self-enclosed self-sufficiency of a pure fictional construction whose raison d'être might well be the desire to realize Flaubert's dream of a novel about nothing. Yet this attempt to achieve an absolute distance from the outside as such takes on the bizarre form of a parody of modern formalist literary criticism; indeed, it is hard not to think of Jean Rousset's "boucles" (loops), "vrilles" (spins), and other geometrical shapes in *Forme et signification* when one reads *Topologie*. In a reversal that Flaubert might have appreciated for its irony—but perhaps not for its disconcerting implications—the work that sets out to remove itself absolutely from a slavish adherence to the exterior world cannot escape the *textual referent* of a contemporary corpus of writings and, paradoxically, imitates the skeletal framework of a structural schema.

Robbe-Grillet's more recent works have become increasingly resistant to critical probing precisely because their formal arrangement, in itself purely abstract and beyond analysis, has tended to assume more importance for the novelist than the more traditional fictional tools of plot, character, chronological succession, etc. In fact, Morrissette does not hesitate to say that the various "themes" chosen by Robbe-Grillet are selected for their banality, presumably so that they will not interfere with the architectonics of the novel.[6] But Morrisette's analysis does not account for the monotonous regularity with which themes of sadism, violence, "perverse" eroticism, and the like, return to haunt the pages of Robbe-Grillet's writings. The reader may well conclude that the conspicuous repetition of these elements details a powerful obsession.[7] Even if one adopts a perspective similar to that of the novelist himself, who insists that his discourse *on* the themes of sex and violence is more important than the themes themselves,[8] the fact remains that the very insistent presence of such themes in the text represents a signal that the reader cannot easily ignore. Granted the hypothesis that the old distinction between form and content ("that old sunken ship—the scholastic opposition between form and content"[*PNR* 48]) has been overcome in a novel that conceives itself to be pure form based on the design of a topology, the so-called themes would have to be devoid of all substance, the energy of their signifying potential neutralized. Those objects that appeared to symbolize or to point in the direction of a meaning beyond their immediacy would have to be emptied of all metaphysical and psychological content.

The question this chapter proposes to deal with is the following: Does *Topologie* really fit the model of the self-enclosed, self-perpetuating generative novel, or are there elements that cannot be accounted for within the confines of a fiction that develops in self-referential isolation? A preliminary discussion of the object as it functions in the novel will be followed by reflections on two major aspects of *Topologie* that serve to problematize this question: the notions of spectacle and discovery, which oppose each other in the constitution of the novel's order as space (theater) to time (the temporal unraveling of a criminal investigation); and the seemingly contradictory presence of man (the human being) in a text whose theoretical status as self-referential topology depends upon the neutralization of subjective consciousness and the absence of interpretive intrusions.

Throughout *Topologie* runs a complex system of objects that eventually form a clear and coherent thematic network. One can trace the relative positions and uses of the pebble, easel, fragmented Greek temple, cards, watermelon, bowler hat, mannequins, eggs, etc., across a wide variety of contexts. But at first glance these objects entertain curious relationships of chance contiguity, making it difficult, if not impossible, to assign them a well-defined significant role in the novel's development. At the beginning of *Topologie*, for example, a pebble lies just outside the building in which are housed the uncountable virgins who alone seem to have survived a holocaust. Some visiting women (tourists who observe the imposing structure that does not necessarily give the appearance of a prison) arrive, one of whom considers this pebble attentively. Later on, it is found inside the prison, the point toward which a stream of blood is flowing; yet soon afterward, the narrator tells us that the entire scene, including the pebble, is in fact an allegorical tableau contained within the game of cards being played nearby (30–37). Objects relate to other objects in diverse game-patterns; they fuse and merge, separate, negate each other, or, as in the case just mentioned, engulf and are dissolved by each other in a mise en abyme.

Robbe-Grillet's elaborate manipulations of representational space remind one of certain techniques in modern painting, and not without reason: the novel *Topologie d'une cité fantôme* evolved from a joint project by the author and Paul Delvaux entitled *Construction d'un temple en ruines à la déesse Vanadé.* The original work out of which the novel grew included eleven etchings by Delvaux as well as what was to become the first section of the novel. Considered in the light of this collaboration, the physical aspect of the sacrificial virgins with their long, blond hair, the persistent scene with the Greek temple as background, the man with the bowler hat, etc., all become explainable and reducible to the outside model of a given series of paintings (which, however, as imaginary representations, are no more explainable than the text that describes them and send us into the void of a representation to the second degree). Yet it would be a mistake to assume that all allusions made by Robbe-Grillet to painting point in the unique direction of Delvaux. Robbe-Grillet no doubt also intended the reader to think of de Chirico and Magritte—the deserted city squares, Greek landscapes, and mannequins of the former, and two specific works of the latter that are not difficult to recognize in the text: "L'Echelle du feu" ("The Ladder/Scale of Fire") and "L'Assassin menacé" ("The Threatened Assassin").[9]

The chain of objects in *Topologie* does not in itself become a key that unlocks determinate meanings in the novel, even if the various series are pursued in all directions; one finds, rather, that each object is capable of appearing in any given espace, so that the general movement is one of constantly changing juxtapositions in an infinite proliferation. Robbe-Grillet is obviously experimenting with the idea of surprise relationships, much as the surrealists did in their collages and their *jeux du cadavre exquis*. The strange beauty of the best surrealist art arises from the incongruity of elements that, taken in combination, produce an uncanny effect. Yet the playfulness of surrealist technique in poetry and the representational arts is only a surface playfulness: the aim of the games, jokes, and aesthetic shock in general is to reach the spectator/reader in the depths of his or her unconscious and release the pent up thoughts and desires that had, until that moment, remained embedded in the shadows of the self. Magritte viewed the combination of objects as a means of knowledge about and intuitive penetration into a world whose true interconnections generally escape the untrained eye. He invented what he called "problems": "He brought objects together in such a way as to demonstrate an evident relationship which, subjected to reason, they bear to one another, even though until that moment such relationship had remained concealed from the consciousness."[10]

In *Topologie*, given an atmosphere of surrealism, objects come into contact with other objects and with inconsistent, negative outlines of people or characters: there would seem to be, on the surface, no a priori justification to privilege the human over the inhuman, or vice-versa. All elements chosen by the author appear equally neutral or equally charged with meaningful connotations, depending on the attitude or critical stance of the reader. How can one affirm that David Hamilton, the male protagonist, carries more significant weight than a watermelon or a card game? In fact, Robbe-Grillet loads the dice to make the reader more easily accept the opposite: David Hamilton evolves, generatively, out of juxtaposed letters whose arbitrariness is apparent from the start and is also, incidentally, the name of an influential music critic quoted by Morrissette in his article "Generative Fiction."[11] The watermelon, on the other hand, is invested with unmistakable, contextually clear symbolism (sex, blood, fragmentation through ritual cutting with the connotation of sacrifice). It would seem, then, that the novel could be read in the same way that one interprets the structural composition of a painting, assuming that whatever action takes place, being based on "ignoble, even worn-out fictional situations," is in itself a matter of indifference. The novel would then become less a temporal movement of duration than a flattened set of intermingling spaces that render meaningless any discussion of progress or change. The relationship of space to time in *Topologie* is not so easily dispensed with, however: certain surface signs (such as the use of espaces in lieu of chapters) point to a negation of time, but it is only a detailed analysis of crucial articulations in the text that will allow us to determine whether the theory of the novel as topology or generativity accounts for its complex praxis.

The text begins with the inner monologue of an absent voice (*subject* would be too positive a term) describing a state between wakefulness and sleep, similar to the prelude that opens Proust's *A la recherche du temps perdu*. Just as in this novel, Robbe-Grillet's "Incipit" prepares the way for the development of the work by presenting several of the most important themes: the city in its atmosphere of hazy indefiniteness; the paradoxical copresence of destruction, ruins, and a group of virgins apparently living in a cell block; the sacrificial rites to which these girls are destined; and the act of writing itself. This last theme signals itself in a dramatic way, concluding the passage on a note of affirmation: "I now write the word CONSTRUCTION, *trompe-l'oeil* painting, imaginary construction by which I name the ruins of a future divinity" (13). Important in this statement is the relationship of creation to annihilation: the voice assumes an authorial tone and posits an act of nomination that gives birth to the negativity of "ruins." The logic of paradox becomes readable, however, if one understands that the ruins in question are strictly a literary or fictive creation and have no ties with reality. Robbe-Grillet is not referring to some outside topography, but is inventing a purely imaginary topology. The sentence is quite similar to Mallarmé's definition of evocative naming: "Je dis: une fleur! et, hors de l'oubli où ma voix relègue aucun contour, en tant que quelque chose d'autre que les calices sus, musicalement se lève, idée même et suave, l'absente de tous bouquets" ("Crise de vers," 368) ("I say: a flower! and, beyond the forgetfulness to which my voice has relegated all floral shape, as something else than the known calyx, musically arises, sweet identity itself, the absent of all bouquets"). The poetic flower or novelistic construction separates itself completely from the natural referent while continuing to point toward it as an absent origin; and the divinity mentioned by Robbe-Grillet is "future" in the sense that it will come into (factitious) being only when it is named by the author.

Robbe-Grillet's city achieves its identity through a series of permutations developing from the letter G. Generativity in this sense illustrates the constructive possibilities of *l'arbitraire du signe*, with special emphasis on the power of the signifier to build its own chain of words which only later (*après coup*) attain some degree of meaning. Thus the letter G yields:

vanadé—vigie—navire
danger—rivage—devin
noyer—en vain—carnage
divan—vierge—vagin
gravide—engendra—david

(49)

It may be perplexing that the originating letter was stated as G rather than V, but then it is no more strange, in the end, that David G. should become David H. or "David Hamilton" through the logic of liberated signifiers. It would be a major error to think that Robbe-Grillet takes this word list as seriously as might his critics: he insists upon the humor inherent in the artifice of his game by prefacing this series with an ironic description of a *divan vide* (empty couch; motivating the "natural" but [con]textually aberrant question, "How is a child born of an empty couch or bed?"—linguistically, of course, da vid, gra vide, divan vide . . .) and by following it with an intentionally farfetched story based on an overwhelming repetition of v sounds ("La vierge— le poste de vigie—Vanadium—navire—rive—voiles" [50]).

Most important, the scene motivated by the chain of signifiers designates itself as visual drama or theater in the strongest sense. The passage is not just a parody of origination myths (David is born from the union of water and blood); it is, more fundamentally, a satire on the idea of theatrical representation as revelation. Thus, the narrative that emerges from the V series serves to explain that which had previously remained enigmatic in the text: "Therefore we now know that this invisible side of the scene, in this representation on the playing-card, was not emptiness [le vide]: it was the sea, into which the violated virgin hurls herself" (52). But this is absurdly superfluous knowledge, or rather, it cannot be knowledge at all because its origin is the pure arbitrariness of letters, divorced from significance. It is as if Robbe-Grillet were writing a parody of his well-intentioned but misguided critics who feel the need to infuse a meaning based on the logic of mimesis into even that which designates itself as representationally meaningless. The irony is all the deeper when one juxtaposes the claim of the narrator—"ce côté invisible n'était pas le vide" ("this invisible side was not the void")—to the word Vanadium itself, which, as a group of letters, is the insubstantial frame of nothingness (le vide: Va nad(a) ium).

Although the generative chain of signifiers accounts for fairly large sections of the first espace, it is clear that the novel as a whole is based upon a tonal alternation between meditation and action (erotic reverie and police investigation), much like the change of atmosphere that one finds in a musical composition made up of slow and fast movements. The erotic passages bring into play many of the techniques of experimental description used previously by Robbe-Grillet and contain both the voyeurism of an observing eye and the infinite horizon of Kafkaesque corridors one immediately recognizes as the author's own. The addition of constant allusions to Delvaux's painting enriches the descriptions somewhat but does not erase their tediousness and uninteresting banality. The fourth espace is especially disappointing: the point of view shifts to that of a nearly blank female consciousness (we enter the mind of one of the virgins), whose meanderings are expressed in an exaggerated, cloying style. The third and fifth parts of the novel, on the contrary, possess an intricacy that invites analysis. Both revolve around a series of murders mysteriously associated with the sacrificial rites performed in a Greek temple. One is necessarily reminded of Les Gommes, and Robbe-Grillet confirms the reader's impression by alluding to this novel toward the beginning of the "Mise au point" that introduces the third espace:

> What I notice immediately, toward the right and farther back, is the changed letter on the oriflamme of the ship anchored against the quay along the river. I seize my binoculars in order to verify this important detail of the staging of the scene (or even, of the text). I adjust them to my eyes and I slowly turn the center wheel to focus precisely on the image of the inscription, although this particular problem, the erasing [le gommage] of a letter and its replacement by the following sign in the alphabet's order (here, the erasing of a G in favor of an H), has been treated exhaustively in the first novel I published long ago. (98)

The entire investigation takes place under the aegis of a persistent irony. The narrative voice pretends, from the very start, to value above all things the clarity of knowledge: "Ah! ah! I see that things are getting complicated. If we don't want to fall into a trap, it would be appropriate, now, to clarify a certain number of details that have remained imprecise or contradictory" (93). But this sudden interest in rational understanding represents a radical departure from the ill-defined attitude of the narrator up until now, to such an extent that it appears difficult to reconcile in any way the first half of the book with what follows. This is primarily due to the completely opposite functions assigned to the objects in the investigation chapters. The same pebble, stiletto, watermelon, crumpled paper, and mannequins are to be found, but they are no longer simply *there*, merely present as the objects in a Magritte or Delvaux painting. The magical atmosphere born of a surrealistic use of objects has given way to a more traditional, heavily symbolic textual functionalism that infuses meaning into things. Thus, the pebble and stiletto, previously asignificant circulating elements in a serially constructed narration/description, now become the accompaniment and instrument of murder (102–3); in other words, they find their accomplishment through the temporal process of the investigation in the now fully explained and illuminated crime.

It is the gaze of the inspector, like that of the structuralist literary critic, that retrospectively assigns significance to that which seemed neutral and dead. The novel suddenly takes on the appearance of a converging thematic web of signs: all crystallizes in the crime. Robbe-Grillet's fascination with the Oedipus myth (which, according to the language of Sophocles, is the retrospective deciphering of *traces* and *signs*) leads him to thematize the dramatic notion of revelation. But this revelation is presented in the text from the standpoint of a geometrical formalism. Using the coordinates of the locations in which the first three crimes took place, the police (i.e., investigating literary detectives) deduce the "existence of a fourth location, which is the fourth side of a perfect square" (113). From this discovery it is not difficult to find that the center of the square, or *schéma générateur initial*, is occupied by an old watchtower that provides further clues as to the identity of the murderer (in the end, the narrator himself, like Oedipus, has blood on his hands). In a sense, Robbe-Grillet's intellectual links with Morrissette parallel his relation to the Oedipus myth: he cannot do without the critic who discovers the secrets of his novels' composition, just as he cannot do without mythological or symbolic references as such, but he can place both within an ironical parenthesis and deal with them through a paradoxical combination of adherence/attraction and distance/repulsion.

Robbe-Grillet's implicit parody of Morrissette as the detective with bowler hat who discovers the center of the generative signifiers has its more serious side: the novelist is engaging indirectly in a theoretical reflection on the implications of literary criticism. He points out the same dilemma that had been the focal point of Derrida's early essay "Force et signification"; namely, that the act of analysis or uncovering of structures necessarily involves a spatialization of that which is essentially temporal, a neutralization of the text's *force* in its reduction to *form*. In this sense, Morrissette the detective is metaphorically guilty of a crime. The blood is on his hands for the killing of the chain of signifiers whose textual existence is inseparable from uncontrolled proliferation. On the level of time, the discovery of crimes that leads to (or is equal to) the committing of crimes is always too late with respect to the action it seeks to understand. Robbe-Grillet further parodies the impact of the critic's contribution by making his so-called discovery the utter simplicity of the letter *V*, which, as we have seen, cannot be privileged over *G* or *H* or any other letter. The critic, like the archaeologists of *Topologie*, is condemned to reconstruct (falsely, fictionally, arbitrarily) that which is dead from the fragmentary evidence of an alphabet.

The ultimate revelation of the Oedipus myth, presented by Sophocles as a crisis leading to simultaneous self-knowledge and recognition of human frailty, takes on the form of an unmediated vision in a paradoxically illumined darkness. It is the unmediated or transparent quality of this final understanding that is manifestly lacking in Robbe-Grillet's novel. The crimes of the third espace, interrupted by the erotic dreams of the fourth, reappear in an extraordinarily theatrical conclusion that, with its mythological allusions and obscure prophetic forebodings, was obviously intended to mirror qualities of antique drama. Murder is once again inseparable from the notion of religious sacrifice, and we are told that the protagonist, David, has "incestuous and fratricidal tendencies" (185). But the moment of the crime's description has a pictorial quality that needs to be analyzed for itself. The adolescent girl who is murdered has a "double" in the guise of a mannequin reminiscent of de Chirico's paintings; and, more important, the scene itself is a near reproduction, with just slight variations, of Magritte's "L'Assassin menacé." The major elements of Magritte's painting are all to be found on pages 184 and 185 of *Topologie*: the murdered naked girl, the club and fisher's net, and the phonograph that, according to the narrator, has reproduced the cry of the victim. The one major change in the novelistic description is that the three male figures looking in on the scene from the outside have been replaced by a feminine outline wearing a "vaporous bathing gown" and holding a red rose—but this could be a reminiscence of Magritte or Delvaux.[12] The crime is thus not to be interpreted as a subject's inner illumination but rather as the mediating textual function of a representation that itself signals, en abyme, another picture.

Topologie d'une cité fantôme can be read on one level as a novel about fictional composition, as a text that tells the story of how texts originate. The sections that develop out of a pure play of signifiers would then illustrate certain recent theories of narration, notably generativity and topology. But the construction that the authorial voice wishes his book to become does not fully correspond to the pure, isolated, self-enclosed unit referred to by Robbe-Grillet in his essay "Du Réalisme à la réalité." Indeed, the dream of building on an empty foundation "something that can stand on its own, alone, without having to depend on anything beyond the work" (*PNR* 177) presupposes the possibility of a creation ex nihilo in the strongest sense of the term, whereas *Topologie* begins as a collaboration, as an act of pointing to its outside, of referring to paintings, literary texts, theoretical treatises. The models of topology and generativity are mechanisms that function within a larger textual movement that is constantly exceeding the bounds of its own representation, constantly calling into question the idea that a novel could exist in a self-enclosed space. *Topologie*, in its praxis, is an exploded text, a *texte éclaté*, a grouping of words and structures that destroy the artificially imposed limits of the closed book's horizon.

Critical analysis of the novel, by revealing the evolution of Robbe-Grillet's thought, necessarily leads to a confrontation with some of his early and somewhat dogmatic theoretical statements, and questions especially the hypothesis on which the essay "Nature, Humanisme, Tragédie" is based: namely, that it might be possible to speak of "something that addresses no sign to man" (*PNR* 58). We have seen that precisely those objects at first limited to the emptiness of their surfaces later acquired a contextual significance during the police investigation: even the series of words in *V*, far from merely being there, led to a hyperbolic, mythological, genesis story. In both cases, an overabundance of meaning floods through the flimsy edges of supposedly neutral, formal elements in an explosion of irony. This return or reintroduction of meaning as *excessive* energy can only be understood in the light of the duality man/object. Robbe-Grillet's demystification of an exalted and dangerously simplistic idea of humanism is accompanied by theoretical reflections on the status of objects in the imaginary realm of fiction. The novelist wishes to give back to the object that which man had stolen from it: its simple, irreducible, nonsymbolic presence. This accomplished, Nature could return to the business of being herself, having lost the phantoms of meaningfulness that man had injected into her. But the problem, both practical and theoretical, for the writer who intends to adhere to such a demystified view of things is that he or she must attempt to limit and carefully define the entire problematic matter of subjectivity. The novelist must not interfere with the outside or other; hence the insistence, in Robbe-Grillet's early essays, on the neutral gaze of the eye and its quasi-scientific attention to surfaces. To leave objects as they are requires a difficult, perhaps impossible, renunciation: one must seek to describe them without touching them, so that the emptiness of things does not recover a false substance through interpretation. Out of respect for the purity of a surface narration, the narrator must cease to be, except *for* his art. In emptying himself of himself, his goal is to *be there*, as close as possible to the level of objects, as nothing more than his vision.

If "Nature, Humanisme, Tragédie" is more powerful, more demystifying and demystified than most of Robbe-Grillet's theoretical writings, it is because it reveals the tenacity of misleading, illusory connotations that subtend the three central categories of its title and shows, in a more transparent way, what Heidegger had written in his *Letter on Humanism*: that all humanism is (hides, pretends not to be) a metaphysics. But to criticize humanism as the mask of metaphysics does not allow one to shelve the problem of man. Even if (especially if) one strives to construct a theory that would exist in its purity without any dependency on the human being, there arises a moment in which one must *refer* to a human presence. This is the case in *Topologie*, where a strictly formal theory of generativity/topology coexists with the reemergence of an interpreting consciousness. Derrida has shown how, in philosophical texts, anthropologism or anthropocentrism is first criticized and relegated to a secondary status, so that the notion of purity can be thought in its essence; but then, in a second movement, when the philosopher searches for examples of the general law he has developed, the only example to be found is man. We arrive at the logical impasse where "the example is always already the totality of what it exemplifies."[13] Man: an irreducible, continual functioning of subjective consciousness whose nature is to interfere and who, in eliminating himself for theoretical purposes, becomes the totality of what he describes. In this perspective, the abolition of purity by the intervention of man can be called irony; and man "himself" can be observed in the literary text as the surprise surfacing of the particular into the abstract design of the general.

Robbe-Grillet once wrote: "La condition de l'homme, dit Heidegger, c'est d'être là" (*PNR* 121) ("Man's condition, according to Heidegger, is to be there"). But the *présence* whose importance is so obvious in Robbe-Grillet's theoretical writings is doubled by another force, which might best be compared to Heidegger's *Dasein*. It is not a matter of "being there" in the literal sense (*da sein*), but of being insofar as one questions: "Dieses Seiende, das wir selbst je sind und das unter anderem die Seinsmöglichkeit des Fragens hat, fassen wir terminologisch als *Dasein*" ("This entity which each of us is himself and which includes inquiring as one of the possibilities of its Being, we shall denote by the term *Dasein*").[14] Robbe-Grillet's theoretical reflections, like Heidegger's thinking, remove man from the center of things as usurping tyrant or master. But the complicated textual work performed in *Topologie* also brings back the haunting shadow of a human figure. Man is reinstated as the one element in the fictional scheme that, like Magritte's "Assassin" bending over a phonograph, heeds the resonance of signs.

Chapter Three

NARRATIVE LEVELING AND PERFORMATIVE PATHOS IN

CLAUDE SIMON'S *LES GÉORGIQUES*, 1981

O NLY RECENTLY has Claude Simon gained international acclaim beyond the limited scope of literary connoisseurship and academic scrutinizing. Even more than was the case for Samuel Beckett, whose novels are not widely read but whose theater has reached a large audience, the awarding of the Nobel Prize in Literature to Claude Simon resulted in a suddenness of recognition, a dramatic leap from obscurity to the limelight, that puzzles the reading public as much as it gratifies his patient critics.[1] For the sociologist of literature, this gap between the unrelieved darkness of a writer's toil through four decades of novelistic production and the retroactively found, stark, media-induced star status of an unassuming and quietly brilliant artist has its own nontrivial significance within the increasingly problematic relation of "high art" to the "masses." On a lower level of generality, the gap between work and reading-public should be considered a challenging phenomenon by the literary critic, one of whose primary functions, traditionally, has been to mediate between these two poles, to be a Moses to the multitudes, bringing the esoteric tablets down into the public domain by deciphering their significance and social relevance.

In the case of Claude Simon's novels, the risk of insufficient or even failed mediation is exacerbated by two ironically interwoven facts: (1) his works are found to be difficult or even unreadable by a number of cultivated but nonspecialized readers;[2] (2) the specialists who do read Simon often interpret his writings as if, despite certain inevitable textual complexities, they were eminently decipherable, containing a pleasing inner luminescence within their opaque shell. For the moment, I shall assume the truth-value of neither of these two positions but shall proceed on the assumption that each issues a challenge to the reader of Simon, whose task it is to determine the readability or intelligibility of intricate fictional constructs.

In the present chapter, I shall examine *Les Géorgiques* (1981) (*The Georgics*), one of Simon's richest and most highly articulated texts—a work that, in its repetitions and recapitulations of the writer's previous texts, stands as an impressive *summum* or "totalization"[3] of his most essential novelistic preoccupations. Like *La Route des Flandres* (1960) (*The Flanders Road*), *Histoire* (1967), and *La Bataille de Pharsale* (1969) (*The Battle of Pharsalus*), *Les Géorgiques* is the narratively elaborate encounter of a human consciousness with the forces of Nature and History, the staging of a dramatic confrontation between the desires of an individual will and the cosmic forces that overwhelm it and render its efforts both puny and comical. At the same time, *Les Géorgiques* can be analyzed as an experiment in fictional form in which theoretical problems of the highest level of abstraction take precedence over thematic content.[4] In this sense, the novel of 1981 extends the questions of form and representation raised more rapidly and cryptically in *Les Corps conducteurs* (1971) (*Conducting Bodies*), *Triptypque* (1973) (*Triptych*), and *Leçon de choses* (1975) (*The World About Us*).

The major interpretive difficulty to be faced by the uninitiated nonspecialist reading *Les Géorgiques* is clear enough: How is it possible to understand a discrete work of literature that is composed by references to its own "past" in other texts by the same author and in texts of other writers to such a degree and with such recurrence that the boundaries between it and its antecedents are virtually abolished? For the specialist, the problem is of a different order but also thorny and potentially embarrassing: *Les Géorgiques*, precisely *because* it "totalizes" so many of Simon's works over such a long period of the author's literary production, retroactively confuses the neatly drawn categories established by the critics to delineate the evolution of his writing style. Most important, the slippery, protean essence of *Les Géorgiques* reintroduces a problem that seemed to have been solved in one authoritative branch of the critical literature: namely, that Simon's texts were progressing from the dramas of consciousness and the crises of representation to a "pure," "self-generated" movement of liberated signifiers.[5]

Increasingly, it had appeared to theoretically oriented critics that the subject of Simon's novels was no longer the ambient reality (however distorted by the mirror of literary mimesis) in which we as humans live, but rather the act of writing reflecting upon itself, the literariness of the literary, in the infinite regress of a purely textual mise en abyme. As the text turns inward upon its own generation, the referential function of literary language becomes problematized. In the words of Ralph Sarkonak, one of Simon's most distinguished recent critics:

> The technique of *mise en abyme* has as its primary function to call into question referential illusion as such, for in turning inward upon itself, the text presents itself openly as what it is, namely a human artifact, in all that distinguishes it from the extra-textual. . . . In unmasking itself for what it is, the text underlines the only reality that counts, that of language, including its mimetic capacities *and* limits. . . . Traditional referential *mimétisme*, which does not cease to function however enveloped it might be in the textual *abyme*, becomes a kind of *plus value* or supplement which the text cannot bypass or do without even though it never ceases to unveil the "weaknesses" of the representational mode. (83)

In the pages that follow, I shall address the related issues of meaning, intelligibility, and readability in *Les Géorgiques*, with special emphasis on the delineation of the novel's narrative levels and on the essential problem of textual self-reflexivity as it relates to the referential function of literary language. At stake will be not only what distinguishes a given text from the extraliterary realm to which it points or erases its pointing, but also the problematic nature of literary reference as such.

Les Géorgiques consists of five untitled chapters of unequal length preceded first by a short liminary quotation from Rousseau's *Confessions*[6] and then by a six-page passage in which the narrator describes an artist's drawing of two nude figures in the late-18th-century "Academic" style. The narrator's careful prose depiction of the artist's study of an older man seated at his desk writing (while apparently issuing an order of some type to a younger man) plunges the reader into a highly stylized pictorial/literary abyme whose "code," to use the narrator's own word, is not a matter of indifference: "It is evident that the interpretation of such a drawing is dependent upon the existence of a code of writing assumed by each of the two parties, the drawer and the spectator" (*Les Géorgiques*, 13). The problem for the reader of *Les Géorgiques* is that the code for this drawing and for the novel that relates to it in an increasingly deep but always oblique way is not available; there is no pact or shared set of assumptions that unites novelist and reader in a common understanding. As the narrative unfolds, it is true that the older man in the drawing seems to foreshadow or foretell the protagonist—the "colossal" General whose activities during the Revolution and Napoleonic Wars occupy center stage at crucial points of the novel—and the younger man may prefigure the later unnamed character whose regiment retreats through Belgium in 1940 and who, we learn near the end, is the most recent in the line of the General's descendants (438–48). However, these identifications are based upon the flimsiest of broadly sketched analogies and derive from the reader's natural desire to endow empty form with imagined substance: it is comforting to assign definite identities to the unnamed Academic figures, comforting to clothe their nakedness with retrospectively discovered, significant potential. Once the man and the youth become X and Y, identified characters, the enigma of their pure appearance disappears; the novel solves its own riddle by the progressive filling in and coloring of the initial sketch; *Les Géorgiques* as story becomes the transmutation of drawing into painting.

As we shall see, the temptation of this type of reading, whereby initially shadowy figures become endowed by the interpreting consciousness with increasingly opulent significance, is inscribed within the text and is, as such, unavoidable. Yet it is worth noting that in the conclusion of the first scene the narrator is unable to discern with any certainty the exact nature of the relation linking the two figures. It would appear that the older man, seated at his writing desk, is commanding the youth to leave the room, "with a gesture both negligent and imperious, like that of someone who dismisses an inferior or an importunate person" (17), but it is impossible to establish a clear causal or temporal linkage in the events that precede and follow this frozen moment in time, and it is notably impossible to determine at what point the letter (no doubt delivered by the Apollonian youth/messenger and now located on the General's desk) has been, is being, or is about to be read. At the outset of *Les Géorgiques*, Claude Simon scenically represents the literary act as the delivery or transmission of messages, but leaves the content of the delivered message invisible, unknowable, describable only in the hypothetical mode:

> It remains to be seen whether this gesture (this dismissal) takes place before the addressee takes cognizance of the tenor of the letter (which the other figure with the slightly mocking expression despite his respectful attitude seems already to know), or during his reading, or afterward, so as to preserve his solitude to read it once again, since, while he continues to wave his hand indolently, the seated man does not lift his head, his gaze still intent, as if hypnotized, on the unfolded sheet of paper. (17)

The enigmatic representation of the act of reading as "hypnotized" state raises one very practical question for the reader of Simon's novel: To what extent is *Les Géorgiques* intelligible as text? As is the case for Faulkner's most difficult works, the intelligibility of *Les Géorgiques* rests on the possibility of distinguishing among narrative levels, and the act of establishing distinctions must be constant in this case, as Simon alternates, sometimes disconcertingly, among three main temporal/spatial milieus:

(1) The glorious days of the French cavalry; the Revolution and the Napoleonic Wars as experienced by the General; the General's public and private life as revealed in his letters.

(2) The ignominious defeat of 1940 as experienced by the member of a decimated latter-day cavalry unit.

(3) The Spanish Civil War in 1937, as experienced by an Englishman engaged in the Republican ranks.[7]

These three levels, which mirror and complement each other thematically, are in turn juxtaposed to the cycles of Nature, to the rhythms of life, death, and rebirth. The General appears not only as a hero and survivor of multiple strategic incursions but also as an owner of large properties who is obsessed with the proper cultivation, fructification, and storing of their multiple crops. His letters, whether military or private, are all desperate orders and commands proffered from great distances and destined to alter the facts and face of the earth.

As the novel progresses, the narrative layers or levels not only become increasingly distinct and recognizable in their specificity but also begin to relate to each other in fundamental, mutually illuminating ways. At first, the only obvious link between the unnamed protagonist's story in 1940 and the General's peregrinations is the men's common belonging to the French cavalry (at radically different stages of its usefulness, to be sure). In the last chapter of the novel, however, the narration centers on a family drama, the matter of a disputed inheritance. We discover that the young protagonist who participated in the Meuse campaign of World War II is related to the General by blood: the decrepit grandmother of the modern man, described in her museum-like house in the last two chapters, was the great-granddaughter of the General. Thus, not only does History repeat itself in the mode of farce, with the once-proud French cavalry being blown to bits by German tanks, but the latest in the line of sons repeats his ancestor's actions—but in the mode of retreat.

It is significant that the modern protagonist learns of his ancestry in a discussion with his uncle Charles: here, Simon refers us back to his earlier novel *Histoire*, in which Charles's nephew returns to his childhood home for an inheritance and relives his past experiences during a twenty-four-hour period richer in memories and fantasy than in the mundane events of the narrative present. It would appear that the modern protagonist of *Les Géorgiques*, the man addressed in the second person (*tu*) by Charles, *is* in fact the central figure of *Histoire*, the man who, regressing through memory, imagines his own birth in the novel's powerful concluding pages. Thus, *Les Géorgiques* is not just the story of family relations but is simultaneously the staging and activation of an intertextual relation in its repetition and rewriting of *Histoire*.

Once the family tree of the General is revealed in its intricate ramifications, once the temporal abyss that separated the Napoleonic era from World War II is bridged by the continuity of an individual bloodline, the mysterious quality of events apparently unrelated and metonymically juxtaposed in the first four chapters dissipates, and the illumination of a retrospective, metaphorical, totalizing process seems to rescue the novel from semantic fragmentation. This movement toward significant wholeness, this filling in of deepening meanings, takes on full force once the principal characters of the family drama have been identified *by name*. The Napoleonic General known to the reader as "the colossus" or "The Commander" in the earlier sections is named in the context of the inheritance dispute (382), and we learn, during Charles's explanations of the family tree, that the General, Jean-Pierre L.St.M., has a brother, Jean-Marie L.St.M., who has been condemned to death for desertion and emigration (440–41). The act of naming creates a clear distinction that separates the brothers, in the mind of the reader, into two opposing forces, personally and politically irreconcilable in their absolute difference. In short, one major effect of the concluding pages of *Les Géorgiques* is to make it possible for the reader to pin an identity on the pronoun *he* (*il*) at each of its occurrences, whereas in the beginning pages of the novel that *he* seemed to refer to a multiplicity of actants who could have been either different characters or diverse manifestations of one transhistorical personality, in the mode (the literary wake) of Joyce's HCE: Here Comes Everybody.

The kind of reading I have been delineating suggests that *Les Géorgiques* is a layered novel, a rich work of accumulated narrative levels that possesses disconcerting qualities but that can be deciphered, that is intelligible once the initial indeterminacy of the pronoun *he* resolves itself into distinguishable characters with identifiable, individuated traits. In this view, to read *Les Géorgiques* is to unravel the chaotic temporal and spatial juxtapositions of the opening pages, to stretch out, clothes line style, the heterogeneous, piled-on elements of the beginning. To read = to render distinguishable = to make intelligible = to differentiate signs through an intellectual apprehension of semantic spacing (*espacement*). As I have already suggested, the type of reading expressed in the preceding, simplified equation not only produces useful elucidative results when applied to the novel but also inheres within its significant potential. Claude Simon has structured the progression of his narrative to induce the reader to work toward solving identities and separating levels. At the same time, however, it is possible to discern an opposite movement within *Les Géorgiques*, a movement that tends toward the flattening of differences, the melting down of separate entities and identities, a rhythmical, repetitious establishing and reestablishing of *sameness* that I shall call *La Loi du Même* (The Law of Sameness/The Rule of Analogy). It is this law, along with its implications for the act of reading and the intelligibility of the Simonian text, that I shall examine at this juncture.

As in *La Route des Flandres, Histoire*, and *La Bataille de Pharsale*, one of the major themes of *Les Géorgiques* is the stylized ceremony of death and destruction brought on by war. Although Simon does choose to describe specific moments of historical conflict, his essential message is that war, as fundamental expression of human violence, is infinitely repeatable and always the same. Thus, in the narrator's description of the latter-day protagonist's retreat through the devastated landscape of Belgium, we read:

> But these were the same paths, the same frozen ponds, the same silent forests that had been crossed by successive hordes of pillaging incendiaries and assassins, beginning with those that had come from the depths of Asia, then men with red beards dressed also in armor, like crustaceans, floating their banners decorated with savage or fantastic beasts, with wild boars, bears, salamanders spitting tongues of fire, armed with spurs, talons, sharp beaks, and later armies with feet enveloped simply in rags, and after that still others, and always the same valleys, the same hillsides climbed, cleared, decimated, climbed again, decimated again, simply because this was the best passage that one could find from East to West. (136)

According to a later passage, war is the "common denominator," not just in the usual sense of an inhuman violence perpetrated equally on the participants of both sides of a conflict but also in the cruel ironical sense of an event that collaborates with Nature in affirming the eternal cycle of birth-death-rebirth. The passage that follows centers on the experiences of the English gentleman fighting in the Republican cause in Spain in 1937, but these experiences, despite their specificity to the Spanish context, gain their ultimate significance by being universally applicable to the "chemical" process of war—a process of organic transmutations that mirrors and expands the reflection on the historical continuity of war quoted above from the Meuse retreat/World War II context:

> [He had] arrived at this level of total destitution both material and moral where even valor, courage no longer mattered . . . but the patient obstinacy to solve the elementary problems of survival, the mind exclusively preoccupied with the necessity of fighting incessantly against the dirt, cold, and vermin, of protecting oneself from the rain or from machine-gun fire, of cleaning one's weapon, of mending one's tattered garments impregnated with those stubborn odors that brought everything down to organic or chemical common denominators: those of the filth, of the mud where he flattened himself, of the ammoniacal sweat glued to the flanks of the donkeys whose burdens he unloaded, of things emanating from or extracted from the earth only to be later reabsorbed by it, to return there in the form of excrement, rusted metal, sulphur and coal exploding with the savage and innocent violence of matter in whose embrace he now lived in a kind of symbiosis. (347)

The juxtaposition of these two passages illustrates not only the sameness of the theatrical phenomenon called war but also the interchangeability of its dramatis personae: the male protagonist or *il* who fights for Napoleon; the *il* who flees German tanks; the *il* from Eton plunged into the labyrinth of the Spanish Civil War—is it really so crucial to distinguish among them, if they all live the same life and the same *corps-à-corps* with death? Those passages in *Les Géorgiques* that stage the conspiratorial relatedness of war to the processes of natural change (and such passages are numerous) thematize with great clarity and power the insufficiency of a reading that would emphasize exclusively the intelligibility of perceived differences. In fact, although Simon and his narrator would not state the matter so baldly, it is our human tendency to establish distinctions (i.e., our tendency to indulge in clichés such as "our world is no longer as it was before," or "the geopolitical situation has changed"), our inability or unwillingness to collapse levels of time and memory, that causes us to repeat the errors of our ancestors, to turn their presumed heroism into our own inept disasters.

There is no small irony in the realization that the reader's efforts to establish intellectual distinctions, characters' identities, and narrative levels may run counter to the willed confusion of the novel, and that the dizziness or hypnotized vague awareness with which one encounters the phenomenal presence of the work's signifying surface at the outset of the interpretive endeavor may be closer to the difficult negative truths the text expresses than any triumphant intellection of retrospectively revealed thematic relations. *Les Géorgiques* is a multileveled fiction, but it is also a leveling of fiction, *un roman à niveaux*

multiples, mais aussi un nivellement du roman. In describing the mental confusion of the old grandmother whose blood links the Napoleonic Commander
to the *il* of the Meuse retreat, the narrator evokes the historically cumulative
process of *leveling*:

> As if . . . she felt a sense of solidarity, linked by an obligation stronger even than her
> moral convictions, some nurturing umbilical cord (of which the three orgasms, the
> three ejaculations of semen through which the family name had been conserved until
> her birth, constituted the relays), to that man [the obsessive ancestor] for whom one
> might imagine she mourned (or felt shame) . . . living out a kind of posthumous
> existence buried in this *grisaille* in which, for the old woman, were confused in one
> unique perspective of past or imminent catastrophes the smallest events of life or the
> most painful, conferring one same apocalyptic dimension on all that could constitute
> some motivation or pretext for alarm, so that everything was indifferently placed on
> the same plane, leveled [*de sorte que se trouvaient indifféremment placés sur le même*
> *plan, nivelés*]: the colds of the children, the defective operation of a water heater, the
> illness of a friend, the accounts of her steward, the pruning of the ivy, the execution
> of the imperial family of Russia, the disappearance of a pillow case or the composi-
> tion of the menu for the next day. (194–95; my emphasis)

Etymologically, the word *niveau* comes from the Latin *libella*, meaning
plumb-line or surveyor's level. But libella was so close to *libellus*, which means
little book or diary in classical Latin, that gradually libella became libellus in
the popular Latin of the Middle Ages. The two words collapsed into one and
were subsumed by the masculine form of the noun, such that, in a sense
curiously appropriate to the topic at hand, the instrument of leveling merged
with, collapsed into—"became"—a letter, a libel, a diary, a book.[8]

In *Les Géorgiques*, the principles of the land surveyor and the primacy of the
book (the coupled themes of reading and writing) combine with and are incorporated into the figure of the General, whose essential activities are engineering military strategies, perusing classical authors, and composing letters
and diaries. According to uncle Charles, the General "was a man of organizational genius, an artilleryman, a specialist of alloys and mixtures, of the fabri-
cation of gunpowder and of differential calculus" (446). Because he was a
member of the artillery, "that corps of over-educated dialecticians" (ibid.), he
never enjoyed Napoleon's complete confidence. His analytical and orderly
mind might serve military designs temporarily, but his independence and creative urges were perceived as potential threats by an establishment that thrives
on respect and unquestioning loyalty. A soldier by duty and through the vaga-
ries of history, the General stored his passions elsewhere—in the cultivation
of the earth, the raising and training of horses, and in literary pursuits. In the
words of Charles:

> And horses. With *The Social Contract* and Virgil it seems that horses were his passion.
> At bottom, like all that *petite noblesse* and despite his knowledge of mathematics, he

was a peasant. Hence the constancy with which he watched over his acres of land by epistolary means, hence the sameness of the style he used so naturally to command Jourdan to hold the passages of the Rhine and Batti to close off the pastureland. All these letters during all these years . . . . A veritable agricultural treatise. Something as cyclical, as regular as the return of the hands of a watch on the same numerals of the dial, month after month, season after season, while he was running all over Europe with his cannons, his trajectory calculations, and his interminable inventories of *matériel*. Although if one thinks about it, the two things [organization of an estate and military strategy] are not so contradictory. I mean as far as the qualities necessary in both cases. I mean that eternal beginning again, that indefatigable patience or no doubt passion that makes one capable of coming back periodically to the same places to engage in the same labor: the same meadows, the same fields, the same vineyards, the same hedges to trim again, the same fences to check, the same cities to besiege, the same rivers to cross or to defend, the same trenches periodically open under the same ramparts. (446–47)

In this passage, Simon's Loi du Même emerges in a new light. The eternal repetition of the same does not necessarily entail the disappearance and destruction of the individual under the leveling force of Nature, provided that individual knows how to live with Nature in a cooperative, nonconfrontational way. It is significant, of course, that the General's favorite literary works concern the ordering of mankind in the polis and the ordering of man's activities within the natural context: Rousseau's *Social Contract* is mentioned explicitly, and the work of Virgil to which Simon alludes here without needing to name it is *The Georgics*, the Latin poet's second great work, the purpose of which was to sing the praises of agricultural organization.

In effect, Simon's text opens into a double abyme at this juncture, as both the author's novel and the General's collected letters ("a veritable agricultural treatise") constitute a rewriting of Virgil's poetic admonitions. In this sense, the General can be taken as an allegorical figure of the Writer as such, and his efforts to order his own limited universe through epistolary advice and persuasion can be seen to reflect the role of all artists of the written word. Thus, at a crucial moment of the novel, the moment of Charles's "revelations" to both narrator and reader, the text turns into itself and offers a parable of what Ralph Sarkonak has called "the adventure of the writer in the act of writing" (63). From this observation, it is only one short step to the conclusion that Claude Simon's text is really about other texts—his own previous novels, Orwell, Rousseau, Virgil, etc.—and that whatever apparent representational function the novel might seem to have is, in fact, only an unavoidable secondary effect, "a kind of *plus value*, a supplement which the text cannot bypass or do without even though it never ceases to unveil the 'weaknesses' of the representational mode" (Sarkonak, 83). If this is true, then *Les Géorgiques* seems to present itself (in the same vein as Robbe-Grillet's *Topologie d'une cité fantôme*) as a self-generated text and appears integrable into the evolutionary scheme of the novelist's works as classified by the theoretically minded critics cited earlier. According to this interpretive grid, the key to understanding and unlocking the mysteries of Simon's novel is recognition, by the critical reader, of the pure, self-generating mobility of signifiers that lies beneath the surface of an apparently representational medium. Once the uninitiated reader understood the central importance of such notions as *mise en abyme*, *self-generativity*, and *pure fiction*, the doors would open and *Les Géorgiques* would become intelligible, readable.

Perhaps the most attractive feature of this kind of textual *allegoresis* is its very high level of abstract generality. If the General becomes the figure of the Writer, it is possible, even justifiable, for the critic to write eloquently about Claude Simon's special theoretical position as new novelist. However, the unlocking of the textual abyme, which has as its point of departure the discovery of a hidden, deep, self-representational level of discourse, results in a draining and impoverishment of the text's concreteness. In the particular case of the General and his figural role as Writer, a reading of *Les Géorgiques* that emphasizes self-generation and antirepresentational tactics at the expense of the novel's mimetic signaling does so at the risk of misreading or even *not* reading the concrete nature of the General's writing activities.

Far from exemplifying the ideal of a self-referential pure fiction, the General's writings, whether military or domestic, all convey the impossible but literarily seductive desire of abolishing the barrier between sign and referent. Especially in his lifelong correspondence with his female servant and *intendante*, Batti, the General's mode of discourse can be best described, in the terminology of speech-act theory, as that of performative utterance.[9] Indeed, each message the General sends from the battlefields and Napoleonic administrative centers throughout Europe to his home is a complex weaving and unweaving of orders; each message is the act of a will that attempts, repeatedly, to force letters and words into deeds. Simon's text is a massive orchestration of the special pathos of the performative utterance, in that it dramatizes the desire of the scribe to efface distances, both spatial and temporal, so that the word of the code might merge immediately with the action it symbolizes or signifies. At the other end of the exchange, Batti enacts the reader's frustrations as clumsy decipherer of signs and inept symbolizer:

> This dialogue carried on for years through hundreds of letters that converged from all over Europe toward the same point and the responses that came back, the sheets covered with her [Batti's] awkward yet diligent handwriting, in which she tried, pathetically, her face contorted, to convert into words meadows, ditches, young seedlings, foals, hours of labor, woodlands, hours of walking, paths, receiving several weeks later from one of those places whose names she copied laboriously (Turin, Milan, Hannover, Mittelhagen, Barcelona) the letters sealed in wax which she opened or rather decoded, trying to see in what he [the General] called the blue division, the green division, the pink division, those poplars, acacias, fields, those vineyards dispatched, so to speak, by the mails on rectangles of paper covered with small signs

from which (in the manner of those microscopic Japanese flowers which, thrown into water, swell up, unfurling unsuspected petals) now materialized anew the exacting earth, the hills, the valleys, in turn green, russet, dried-out or muddy under changing skies, the slow meandering of clouds, the dew, the thunderstorms, the frosts, in the immutable alternation of immutable seasons. (461–62)

The materialization of the world from within cryptic signs, the metamorphosis of coded language into the elements of nature, with its strong Proustian overtones ("in the manner of those microscopic Japanese flowers"),[10] establishes unambiguously the degree to which Claude Simon's writing engages in the problematic of what theoreticians call the "referential illusion." What fascinates Simon is the quasi-magical power of the performative to reverse or neutralize the differential *espacement* of written language, to reinstate the illusion of a vocal proximity and transparence, so that Batti now seems to "hear" the brusque commands of her master:

While continued to come and go in her [Batti's] head the words, phrases, orders, advice, reproofs, as if she could hear the familiar voice itself, obstinate, tyrannical, imprinted with that calm rudeness, that inflexible moderation which seemed to be his ruling principle whatever the circumstances, dictating to the successive and indifferent secretaries who copied them in successive registers bound in faded blue both battle plans and instructions for sowing-time, letters to ministers of government, instructions for the cultivation of potatoes, proposals for advancement or decoration, reports of accomplished missions: *I think that what remained of rotting hulls in the division of plum trees is long since ploughed-under, in case this has not been done you will have it taken care of immediately so that the cold weather can burn the earth and after the month of May all divisions will be active and bear fruit.* (464; Simon's italics)

In this passage, Simon's prose enacts what might be called an apotheosis of the performative. Not only is the General's writing full of those performative utterances (orders, volitive advice, directives) possessing an especially high level of illocutionary force, labeled "exercitives" by Austin,[11] but even the General's use of an apparent constative is a strong performative in disguise: "I *think* that what remained . . . is long since ploughed-under" is in fact the reissuing of an original order under the guise of a retroactively uttered assumption. "I *think* that" signifies: "I urged you once before; if you did not obey my command then, do obey it now."

The linguistic code of *Les Géorgiques* is that of the performative and, more precisely, of the exercitive. One need only read Austin's list of principal exercitive verbs to realize the extent to which Simon's novel is permeated by this mode, the degree to which the General lives out the potential of these various actions: "appoint, dismiss; demote; name; order; sentence; levy; command; direct; urge; pray; bequeath" (Austin, 154–55). Logically enough, the exercitive category as established by Austin carries out the polysemic potential of the original Latin verb *exerceo*, five of whose major meanings relate directly to the General's functions in the novel:

(1) to train by practice, exercise [the General and his horses]

(2) to cultivate land [the correspondence with Batti concerning the General's properties]

(3) to wield power or authority [the General's mode of action, domestic and military]

(4) to administer, enforce a law [again, both domestic and military]

(5) to tax, exact, levy [in Napoleon's army, directly and literally; by metaphorical extension, the General's efforts to maximize the economical utility of his land]. (*OLD*, 1:640)

The preferred mode of utterance of a high-ranking member of the army (*exercitus*) is not descriptive, as the constative language of description can only recreate, in the terms of pale reflection, what is already there. The General is the victim of a particular hubris, a hubris he shares with poets: namely, the will to create, out of the obscure depths, what is *not yet there*. His performatives are, in effect, volitive subjunctives, calls into being from the human will, commands that seek to usher in and define an unknown and unimaginable future.

Viewed from the perspective of poststructuralist literary theory, the General's constantly reiterated attempts to abolish the distance between word and deed, to materialize the linguistic resources at his command, can be interpreted as naïve and erroneous—as pathetic, doomed efforts to bypass the essential spatial/temporal *différance* of language and to reinstate a transparency between sign and referent that is both unsophisticated and nostalgically regressive. Not only has the General (like Simon himself) "not read Derrida,"[12] but his every utterance seems to *reverse* the hard-earned truths of antilogocentric deconstructive discourse. My contention in this chapter is not that Simon uses *Les Géorgiques* to engage openly (constatively) in a theoretical dialogue, but that his novel, in its manifest reliance on a performative mode of expression, forces its reader to reflect upon the question of literary reference.

As I illustrated earlier, there seems to be a double movement within the narrative structure of *Les Géorgiques*: on the one hand, toward the establishing of levels, categories of time and space, and the possibility of coherent intellectual distinctions; on the other, toward the erasing of all conceptual boundaries and a disconcertingly generalized blurring of spatial and temporal domains into the sameness of cyclical historical repetition. There is an undeniable playfulness in this technique that consists of dismantling the castle of carefully placed cards erected by the serious reader in search of narrative coherence (and we are all such readers, whatever our degree of engagement with contemporary literary theory), but there is more at stake here than a gratuitous *jeu de langage*. In tearing down the very possibility of the acts of distinction and categorization, Simon is questioning, in the most radical way available to him as writer of fictions, the coexistence of the analytically sophisticated constative logic of theoretical discourse and the naïve and magical performative power of literary language as practiced by his General—that "mad" tactician of words.

Underlying much current poststructuralist criticism is one tenet that remains stable and unquestioned: the *difference* between the literary and the extraliterary, the *distance* between textual artifact and extratextual reality.[13] The strongest challenge posed by Simon's Loi du Même to poststructuralist theory is in its analogical equation of the literary act to such extraliterary pursuits as war, love, death, and, in *Les Géorgiques* particularly, agriculture. The common thread that unites such apparently disparate human activities, and that brings together the issuing of commands for cultivating the earth and the performative pathos of the written word, is the urge or the will to create order in the face of recurring chaos. This theme has its deepest source in the text of which Simon's novel is a repetition or rewriting, Virgil's *Georgics*. At the beginning of his poem, Virgil explains the mythical origin of agriculture *and the arts*:

> For the Father of agriculture
> Gave us a hard calling: he first decreed it an art
> To work the fields, sent worries to sharpen our mortal wits
> And would not allow his realm to grow listless from lethargy.
> Before Jove's time no settlers brought the land under subjection;
> Not lawful even to divide the plain with landmarks and boundaries:
> All produce went to a common pool, and earth unprompted
> Was free with all her fruits.
> Jove put the wicked poison in the black serpent's tooth,
> Jove told the wolf to ravin, the sea to be restive always,
> He shook from the leaves their honey, he had all fire removed,
> And stopped the wine that ran in rivers everywhere,
> So thought and experiment might forge man's various crafts
> Little by little, asking the furrow to yield the corn-blade,
> Striking the hidden fire that lies in the veins of flint.
> Then first did alder-trunks hollowed out take the water;
> Then did the mariner group and name the stars—the Pleiads,
> Hyads and the bright Bear. . . .
> Then numerous arts arose. *Yes, unremitting labour*
> *And harsh necessity's hand will master anything.*
> [*Labor omnia vicit*
> *Improbus, et duris urguens in rebus egestas*].
> (*Georgics* 1:121–38; 145–46; my emphasis).

Like the biblical story of man's expulsion from Paradise and his initiation into the toil of the fields (Genesis 3:17–19), the mythological explanation given by Virgil emphasizes both an original "sin" (here, sloth or laziness) and a divine order that changes the nature of the relation between the human individual and a now-hostile environment. There is a clear break between an inaccessible "before"—the time of a communal sharing of resources in which no boundary lines cut the earth into fragmentary, privately cultivated parcels—and an alienated "after"—in which those resources necessary for survival and for happiness are no longer immediately available but lie hidden away underneath enveloping and obscuring barriers. The creation of the arts is born in necessity and in labor;[14] to create a work of art is analogous or equal to the tilling of the resistant soil or the extraction of minerals from the hard rock. In each of these activities, the individual is impelled to expose or decrypt a natural object or an entity or a code in order to restore a lost state of harmony. And in performing these actions, the alienated individual swims against the stream of history in an impossible effort to reverse the course set by a god's original act of will.

In Simon's novel, the "golden age of Saturn" (*The Georgics* 2:533–43) and the history-engendering command of Jupiter have no place of memory in the post-Revolutionary secular world, but the General's letters to Batti, in their volitive and performative rage, *repeat* the original command of the god, but in the specific mode of the written word. For Jupiter's designs, between command and act, volition and epoch-making change, no distance, no time, no word need intervene. For the General, and for Simon, to imbue words with the power of altering the material world, to color the earth in the hues and tones of the sign, is to deny the undeniable differential logic of language and to grant literary discourse a referential magic and an illocutionary force that it does not, *in fact*, have. But the power and the pathos of the performative rest not in the analytical verifiability of the factual but in the sameness of that constantly recurring inaugural projection of the word on the world that we read (but do not precisely or theoretically understand) as literature.

Chapter Four

THE SELF AS REFERENT: POSTMODERN

AUTOBIOGRAPHIES, 1983–1984

(ROBBE-GRILLET, DURAS, SARRAUTE)

ONE OF THE SURPRISES of the 1983–1984 literary season was the near-simultaneous appearance of autobiographies by Nathalie Sarraute, Marguerite Duras, and Alain Robbe-Grillet. These three writers, whose profound stylistic and theoretical divergences I propose to examine, were designated (somewhat too categorically and conveniently) in the fifties and sixties as new novelists or nouveaux romanciers. With the exception of Duras, whose fictions and films exuded, from the very beginning, a haunting personal and thinly veiled confessional quality, it seemed strange, uncanny, that three practitioners of abstract technical innovations should decide to publish highly readable self-portraits twenty to thirty years after the scandalous impact of their earlier work.[1] In the numerous review essays and interviews with the authors that appeared shortly after the publication of Sarraute's *Enfance* (1983) (*Childhood*), Duras's *L'Amant* (1984) (*The Lover*), and Robbe-Grillet's *Le Miroir qui revient* (1984) (*Ghosts in the Mirror*), there was widespread speculation concerning this apparent shift or turn in stylistic procedure, the immediate result of which was a considerable gain in readership. It was as if the turn toward the autobiographical mode implied, of necessity, an increase in communicability, a new and much-appreciated opening of the previously arcane and recondite. Reviewers hostile to the theoretical and ideological underpinnings of revolutionary writings exulted in what seemed to be a return to traditional values of discursive clarity and (relative) narrative simplicity, whereas those critics who had accompanied and in some cases actively encouraged the innovative struggle of the new novelists through three decades of patient labor in the face of incomprehension now found themselves obliged to demonstrate that the autobiographies were in fact only an apparent departure from the earlier formal experimentation; that, on a deeper level, they were a continuation and elaboration of the same fundamental problems that occupied the central position of the authors' fictional constructs.[2]

In fact, the stylistic turn toward autobiography could be neither an abandoning of formal complexity in favor of a supposed transparent proximity of voice nor a seamless, continued weaving of a previously begun textual pattern. Each writer faced and solved concrete technical difficulties inherent in the choice of first-person expression in a highly personal way—the three solutions are widely divergent yet interesting to juxtapose—but each writer exhibited a similar degree of caution toward the greatest temptation of the genre: the tendency toward structuring the text as the progressive revelation of the truth of a self whose experiences transcend the personal realm and extend to the universal level of essential human nature.

In *Le Miroir qui revient*, Robbe-Grillet has constructed a hybrid text that includes both a literary self-portrait in the conventional sense (in this case, a series of exactly described scenes of childhood and adolescence, of family influence, of developing political and artistic awareness) as well as theoretical reflections on the act of writing and a fragmented group of freely imagined, discontinuous narratives centered on the ambiguously real/imagined character Henri de Corinthe.[3] Whether *Le Miroir* is about Robbe-Grillet himself or the nature of postmodern fiction or the enigmatic Corinthe is an open question, and the first-person narrating voice, constantly doubting its ability and even its right to represent the scenes of the past *as* remembered reality, does nothing to dispel the reader's interpretive quandary. As John Sturrock has correctly observed, Robbe-Grillet's "mirror" has nothing in common with Stendhal's;[4] the images reflected in the former are not only cloudier and less defined but also very possibly the unreal figments of an aroused and unreliable imagination.

In *Enfance*, Sarraute has created a dual narrative consciousness, a dialogue between two opposed *instances narratives*. The first voice remembers, or at least attempts to bring into recollection, the dispersed fragments of the past, while the second voice, acting very much like a censor,[5] questions the precision, verisimilitude, and possible hidden motives of the remembering self. This technique allows Sarraute to avoid the pitfalls of excessive narrative assertiveness and to remain true to the cautious search for the hidden undercurrents of human thought that has characterized her writings from their origins in the labyrinthine meanderings of *tropismes* and sous-conversation.[6]

In *L'Amant*, Duras tells the story of her childhood and adolescence in a series of fragmentary paragraphs whose chief quality is not narrative completeness but a subtle, poetically evocative character. The entirety of her text of remembrance is centered on the crucial *traversée du fleuve*, the day in which, at age fifteen and a half, dressed in the incongruous but erotically significant combination of a man's felt hat, high-heeled shoes, and a near-transparent silk dress, the young Marguerite Duras crosses the Mekong and meets the Oriental man, the elegant Chinese gentleman in the black limousine who has appeared in several of the author's earlier texts[7] and who will initiate the young girl into the secret pleasures of lovemaking. In a sense, *L'Amant* is the most focused, the most centered, of the three autobiographies in that all the major themes of the work can be derived from, or subordinated to, the formidable dominant force of desire.[8] At the same time, however, the author herself cautions the

reader against confusing the undeniable, retroactive clarifying quality of certain passages in the autobiography with the full illuminating force of a discovered, hidden truth. L'Amant will be the uncovering of previously hidden and
masked facts of the writer's existence, but it does not claim to "tell the whole
story," as the story of one's life as faithful depiction of recovered reality is
radically impossible:

> The story of my life does not exist. It does not exist. There is never a center. No path,
> no line. There are vast places where one pretends that there was someone, this is not
> true there was no one. I more or less already wrote the story of a very small part of
> my youth. I mean, enough to perceive it faintly, I am speaking of precisely this part,
> the crossing of the river. What I am doing here is different, and the same. Before, I
> spoke of the clear periods, of those that were illuminated. Here I am speaking of the
> concealed periods of this same youth, of certain hidings or buryings [enfouissements]
> that I may have carried out on certain facts, on certain sentiments, on certain events.
> (14)

The cryptic metaphorical qualities of Duras's cautionary remarks make it
difficult for the reader to translate the preceding passage into a coherent theoretical statement on the nature of autobiographical writing, yet it is certainly
tempting to see in these comments more than a personal reference to her
previous works of fiction and their relation to the present attempt, in L'Amant,
at self-portraiture. On a higher level of generality, what Duras has to say about
her own difficulties in recapturing even fleeting moments of her past life contains, suggestively and implicitly, an undeniable theoretical potential whose
riches might be mined by the literary critic as decryptor of textually self-
reflective enfouissements.

Duras begins the passage with a series of negations: there is no story of her
life; there is no center; no way of access to her past; no "line"; no well-defined
subject or anchor in the search for origins. The logical result of these negations
is that the narrative she constructs must itself be broken, woven around obscure empty points of loss and forgetfulness, in order to correspond to the
broken emptiness of the past. The fragmentary construction of L'Amant is no
mere parti pris esthétique but rather the necessary extension of an original,
existentially founded negation. In saying that L'Amant is both the same as and
different from her previous works, Duras poses the problem of the generic or
modal identity of the autobiographical project in a particularly acute way: her
text will be both fiction and "true confessions," both imaginary and focused on
remembered reality. More precisely, however, Duras asserts that the autobiographical mode of writing is a centering on the moments of the past that had
been overlooked or censored by the fictional works, a dwelling on certain
fundamentally meaningful but hidden nodal points or enfouissements. It remains to be seen whether to write about obscure and hidden moments can be
accomplished in the light of day or within the ambient darkness of the buried

past itself. The nature of Duras's writing in its concrete stylistic manipulations may be less a matter for abstract theoretical generalization than for careful rhetorical analysis, for close reading.

Reduced to its most salient features, Duras's meditation on the problematics of autobiographical textuality touches upon three points that occupy a central position in the autobiographies of Robbe-Grillet and Sarraute as well:

> (1) *representation*: the impossibility of a linear, explicative, and all-encompassing narrative discourse that accounts for the past in its essential totality; the difficulty of constructing a narrative that hovers around and remains in proximity to the targeted enfouissements without violating their dark complexity;
>
> (2) *modal identity*: the autobiographical text is both the same as and different from the fictions that it rewrites and transforms; it is a hybrid form; and
>
> (3) *status of the subject*: in one of her lapidary comments—"There are vast places where one pretends that there was someone, this is not true there was no one"— Duras poses the question of the identity of the self-contemplating subject in its most radical form: if fictive texts, based upon the logic of imaginative verisimilitude, or *faire-croire*, cannot hide the patent fact of their lying, will the autobiographical text restore the identity of the subject, or rather dwell within its empty form?

Whether read essentially as a personal statement on her own past as it impinges on her current project, or as a series of interrogations pregnant with universal critical/analytical possibilities, Duras's reflections on autobiography open up a theoretical space that can serve as a horizon for all three texts under scrutiny here.

For the literary historian who should cast his gaze on the contemporary production of autobiographical writings, the negativity of Duras's formulation ("no story of my life; no center; no 'line'; no person") is less an idiosyncratic expression of a personally felt nihilistic philosophy than a highly symptomatic statement representative of a generation of writers whose misfortune it is to come after (to write in the shadow of) Proust, Gide, and Sartre. Because all three writers analyzed in this chapter are acutely conscious of their status as latecomers in the already well-ploughed field of the novel, aware that, in their quest for fictional innovation, they must write otherwise than their nineteenth- and early-twentieth-century predecessors,[9] it can be assumed that they might feel similarly constrained and (negatively) defined by the personal and aesthetic triumph of *A la recherche du temps perdu*, the confessional fullness of *Si le Grain ne meurt*, and the ironically formulated but narratively achieved clarity with which Sartre illuminates the unfolding of his impulse to write in *Les Mots*. In the simplest and boldest of terms, the question is: What remains to be written by and for and within the self? Duras's answer cannot be stated in a peremptory way; and even if we formulate it provisionally, and too abstractly, as "nothing," we know from both Duras and Beckett the degree to which writing from nothing and around the guarded enfouissements of absence and silence does not signify the death of meaning or threaten the generation of prose. If the autobiographies of Duras, Robbe-Grillet, and Sarraute inhabit a theoretical space and evolve, as creative works, alongside the parallel development of seminal discursive texts, it is not in the direction of Proust, Gide, Sartre, or even Leiris[10] that we should look for structural patterns and theoretical underpinnings, but rather toward Roland Barthes—the "late Barthes" who, as *romancier manqué* expulsed from the Elysian fields of Proustian memory-retrieval, wrote the quintessential postmodern autobiography that is simultaneously a theory of the literary self-portrait and a portrait of contemporary literary theory: *Roland Barthes par Roland Barthes*.[11]

In introducing Barthes's innovatively indirect[12] mode of self-reflection here, I do not suggest that Duras, Sarraute, and Robbe-Grillet are indebted to his idiosyncratic style, nor would I affirm that the thematic content of their diverse writings owes him anything; rather, it is the strong theoretical impact of *RB*, its categorically and conceptually precise formulation of the possibilities and limits of literary autobiography within the postmodern intellectual horizon, that can serve as a convenient frame for the analysis of our three authors. Put in the simplest terms, Barthes's aphoristic remarks confirm and extend Duras's suggestive but only implicitly theoretical passage and provide, in a schematic way, what might be called a postmodern *état limite* for the depiction of the self in writing. The following five statements from *RB* express Barthes's autobiographical credo in succinct and provocatively absolute terms:

(1) I do not say: "I am going to describe myself," but "I am writing a text, and I call it R. B." I do without imitation (description) and I rely on nomination. Do I not know that, *in the domain of the subject, there is no referent*? (60; Barthes's emphasis)

(2) The dream, then, would be: neither a text of vanity, nor a text of lucidity, but a text with uncertain quotation-marks, with floating parentheses (never to close the parenthesis is, quite precisely: to drift). (109–10)

(3) All of this should be construed as said by a character in a novel—or rather by several characters. For the imaginary, inevitable material of the novel and labyrinth of the jagged fortifications in which he who speaks of himself goes astray, this imaginary is taken up by several masks (*personae*), placed at intervals according to the depth of the scene (and yet *no one* behind). (123)

(4) His work [that of Roland Barthes] is not antihistorical (at least he hopes not), but always, obstinately antigenetic, because the origin is a pernicious figure from Nature (from Physis). (142)

(5) [On the Act of Writing as Neutrality] Figures of the Neutral/the Neuter [*le neutre*]:[13] white writing, exempt of all literary theater—Adamic language—delectable insignificance—the smooth—the empty, that which is without contour—Prose (the political category as described by Michelet)—discretion—the vacancy of any "person," if not cancelled, at least rendered unlocatable—the absence of an *imago*—the suspension of judgment, of judicial procedure—displacement—semantic drift-

ing [*la dérive*]—bliss [*la jouissance*]: everything that evades or thwarts or renders absurd all ostentation, mastery, and intimidation. (136)

The problems of representation, modal identity of autobiographical prose, and the status of the subject, which had surfaced in Duras's *L'Amant* as open interrogations, are revealed discursively and theoretically here *as* problems— that is, as objects of possible knowledge, as questions for which a solution might be found. For Barthes, the three issues are interrelated in a logically demonstrable way: because, in the realm of the subject, there is no referent (I cannot imitate or describe myself), literary representation becomes a game of masks and of textual/intertextual drifting, in which the infinitely regressing theatrical *persona* replaces the *person* (the target of traditional autobiography, the seat of authenticity) in a climate of vertiginous and noncontrollable fiction. Autobiographical writing, even in this radically ludic conception, re- mains a search, continues to be "historical" in its narrative deployment of moods, tastes, and intellectual evolution (part of the value of *RB* for the Barthes scholar resides in the author's retrospective analysis of his seemingly mercurial but motivated shifts from Marxism to structuralism to a generalized semiotics to the "pleasure of the text"); but it is not "genetic," it does not attempt to situate one origin or set of origins that could account for or ground the subject. Barthes's own solution to the nontrivial problem of "appropriate style"—how to write an autobiography that avoids the pitfalls of the ascertain- able referent, the temptations of the grounded subject, and the seductions of the genetic, explanatory source—is to theorize writing as Neutrality: as white, smooth, empty vacancy of self, as suspension of judgment, as *jouissance*.[14] Whether this theory begins to account for the complexity of Barthes's late style is not a matter for the present chapter; important for our purposes is the fact that a style can be theorized *as* the answer to the problems inherent in the representation of the self.

As we turn to the rhetorical analysis of the recent writings of Robbe-Grillet, Duras, and Sarraute, I propose to keep as a reference point not only Barthes's cogent theoretical remarks concerning the "antireferential," intertextual, fictional/"imaginary," and "antigenetic" characteristics of postmodern autobi- ography but also his evocation of writing as Neutrality. I will be concerned not only with matters of theoretical convergence or coincidence but also (perhaps especially) with each individual author's creation of a *style of writing*—a rhe- torical armature of words—with which to confront the absences, displace- ments, and masks of the self.

LE MIROIR QUI REVIENT

Written in spurts between 1976 and 1983, periodically abandoned in favor of the fictional works *Souvenirs du triangle d'or* (1978) (*Recollections of the Golden Triangle*) and *Djinn* (1981), *Le Miroir qui revient* is a project about which

Robbe-Grillet did not hesitate to express his reticence and profound doubts, both in the interviews that followed the publication of his autobiography and in the book itself. As he explained to Jean-Pierre Salgas, *Le Miroir* in its initial conception was to be a volume in the "Ecrivains de Toujours" series published by the Editions du Seuil[15]—the small-format *par lui-même* monographs, popular with both students and the general public, that house succinct critical interpretations of major authors accompanied by photographs and other documents relating to the writers' lives and social/historical milieus. The original purpose of the series (transparently expressed by the phrase *par lui-même*) was to make accessible to the nonspecialized reader the equivalent of an intellectual autobiography—an autobiography that was never written by the author but that took form, after the fact, thanks to the organizational and analytical talents of an important critic in the field. A crucial exception to this pattern occurred when Roland Barthes was asked to write his own self-portrait for the series. Having already completed a *Michelet par lui-même* in 1954, Barthes then found himself in the uncanny position of textual doppelgänger when he undertook to "compose himself" in *RB*. As Robbe-Grillet affirmed in his exchange with Salgas, it was the overwhelming popular success of *RB* that prompted the Seuil editors to ask him for a similar volume; and it is the temporary failure of Robbe-Grillet to produce that volume that stands at the origin of the composite work entitled *Le Miroir qui revient*.[16] In Barthes's vocabulary, *Le Miroir* is, on the surface at least, an excellent example of textual drifting (*dérive*): a writing project that does not achieve closure, that drifts from point to point without attaining domination or totalization of its liberated imaginary material.

The major problem facing any reader of *Le Miroir*, regardless of critical persuasion, is that of the origin and raison d'être of the text's remarkable stylistic fragmentation and thematic diversity. The fact that *Le Miroir* is, by traditional standards, an incomplete, "failed" autobiography is not simply grist for the mill of those establishment critics who have been hostile to Robbe-Grillet throughout his career, not merely confirmation of the latter's personal admiration of and theoretical allegiance to Barthes's aesthetics of fragmentation. To say that *Le Miroir* stages and practices more fundamentally and systematically the "vacancy of any 'person'" and the "absence of an *imago*" formulated by Barthes than does Barthes's own text is no doubt partially true and underlines a neat specular symmetry between the two autobiographies: *RB* as successful (complete) theorization of the failure of the self to constitute itself in writing; *Le Miroir* as unsuccessful (incomplete) textual *praxis* illustrating the success of that theory.[17] At the same time, however, there are elements of *Le Miroir* that cannot be reduced to or even compared with Barthesian theoretical tenets and that seem to derive from a more traditional or classical conception of autobiography as search in and through subjective memory for the formative events of a life and an artistic vocation. The pages in which Robbe-Grillet describes his father, mother, and sister; his family's apparently bizarre but consistent far-right politics; his remembrance of early episodes of sadism and continued erotic interest in very young girls; his meeting and marrying Catherine; his evocation of the Service du Travail Obligatoire in Nuremberg and his progressive realization of the horrors of Nazism; his clear and un-equivocal revelations concerning the anecdotal origins of key episodes in his fictional works—each of these passages is grounded in a precise attention to detail, to the minute components of the slices of remembered time that coa-lesce into what remains vivid and illuminated after the massive disappearance of the past into forgetfulness. In each of these cases, the act of writing aims at a moment of the past and constitutes itself as the targeting or attempted mir-roring of that moment. This representational or mimetic thrust that charac-terizes some but not all of the text makes *Le Miroir* a schizoid nonunity; it mixes with the Barthesian, irresponsible free-play of signifiers, the patient and melancholy labor of referential truthfulness:

> The project of relating my life will present itself to me in two different and opposite ways. Either I persist in trying to encircle it in its truth, pretending to believe that language is competent (which would mean that it is free), and in this case I can never make of it more than a *received life*. Or else I will replace the elements of my biogra-phy with *opérateurs* [imaginary constructs], which belong openly to ideology but on which and thanks to which I can act. The second method produces *La jalousie* or *Projet pour une révolution*. The first, alas, produces the present work. (18; Robbe-Grillet's emphasis)[18]

At the outset of *Le Miroir*, Robbe-Grillet describes his project as an uncom-fortable "alternative": either he writes a traditional autobiography (with the assumption that the language he uses is an instrument competent enough to track down the truth of his past), or he substitutes for the remembered events of his life the imaginary constructs that inhabit and engender his fictions—in which case, the autobiography as such disappears. It is important to empha-size the Manichean absoluteness of this opposition, which is typical of Robbe-Grillet's theoretical statements on literature and crucial to an understanding of the rhythmical alternations of *Le Miroir* as textual structure. If *Le Miroir* is a schizo-text, if it is divided between evocations of a life that is recognizably that of the author and fanciful, dreamlike fragments reminiscent of the writer's late fiction, it is because Robbe-Grillet finds himself in a theoretical double bind from which he can imagine no exit. The stylistic fragmentation and thematic diversity of the book that derive from this double bind are an *embarras de richesses* that embarrass the critics, who imitate Robbe-Grillet in alternatively preferring the mimetic "true" account or the formally complex fictional opera-tion.[19] It would seem, on a theoretical level, that one of the major functions of the text is to block its own potentially unitary or unified interpretation. The question that remains is whether the praxis of *Le Miroir*—its rhetorical struc-ture and effects—corresponds to or works out this theory.

Near the conclusion of his reflections, after a long section of condensed and somewhat over-simplified modern literary history (the result, perhaps, of extended periods as guest professor in North American academic institutions), Robbe-Grillet focuses on a structuring or operational principle that may be useful in deciphering *Le Miroir*: he describes the use, in his own texts as well as those of Dostoevsky and Flaubert, of what he calls a *creux générateur*—an empty space around which the text organizes and mobilizes itself.[20] It is this void or absence that not only allows the literary work to move (according to the laws of displacement and dérive) but that also allows for the reading situation as such. Robbe-Grillet explains his theory by alluding to a well-known Oriental *jeu de société* based upon strategies of escape and encirclement:

> The text lives thanks to the holes that move through its web, just as a territory in the game of go [*weiqi*] remains alive only if one has taken care to arrange within it at least one free space, one vacant square, what the specialists call an open eye, or a liberty. If on the contrary all the sites determined by the interlaced lines are occupied by stones, the territory is dead, and the enemy can take control of it by a simple operation of encirclement. (214)

Translated allegorically, the total occupation of all territory that creates the opportunity for simple encircling by the enemy is the stable but deathlike appearance of the literary text that allows itself to be consumed by a reader to whom the author has given the power of masterful understanding but not the freedom of active collaboration in the interpretation of the text's devious, unstable potential. In granting priority and unequivocal preference to textual freedom, to the freedom of displacement and the undoing of possessive encircling moves, Robbe-Grillet espouses a clear theoretical position, but he does so belatedly, twelve pages before ending his book. The question that logically arises is whether any part or aspect of *Le Miroir*—episode, character, dramatic scene, authorial analytic discourse, symbol, or metaphor—enacts (or has enacted) the peculiar movement of the creux générateur, whether any portion of the failed autobiography has illustrated and confirmed its own birth in fictional play.

The most obvious focal point around which the remainder of the text revolves is the enigmatic figure of Henri de Corinthe, who is presented, alternatively, as a friend of Robbe-Grillet's family and as a legendary character who emerges from the mists of the Bay of Biscay to occupy the most sustained and self-contained fictional narrative of *Le Miroir* (89–103). Henri de Corinthe appears at both the beginning and the end of *Le Miroir*: the initial question that opens Robbe-Grillet's reflections concerns the identity of this character ("Who was Henri de Corinthe?" [7]), and the final paragraph of the volume alludes to his funeral. At other points in the autobiography, Corinthe plays the part of the exotically fascinating visitor who brings with him to the simple house of the Robbe-Grillet family an air of the mysterious otherness of the outside world (in this sense, his relation to the young Alain mirrors that of Swann to Marcel in *Combray*) and also that of the politically active and historically significant man of intrigue whose secret missions elude the analytic attention of the young writer Robbe-Grillet (in this sense, Corinthe assumes the mediating function of the Marquis de Rollebon in Sartre's *La Nausée*, as is explicitly stated in *Le Miroir* [173–75]). The originality of Corinthe *as* figure is precisely that he assumes the attributes both of the Sartrian Rollebon (he incorporates the difficulty or impossibility of a historically precise imprisonment ["encircling"] of the real world within the synthesis of a "competent" writing) and of the protagonists of many of Robbe-Grillet's fictions, whose empty symbolical appearances as "phantoms" permeated with unmistakable mythological and legendary qualities invite interpretation but also frustrate precise identification. Corinthe is everywhere in the text—at its beginning, its end, in its interstices as sought after *créature de fuite*—but primarily in its middle, in the sequence that gives the autobiography its title. In placing the "miroir qui revient" episode at the center of his book, Robbe-Grillet poses the Barthesian problem of sources and origins (the historical versus the genetic) in a playful and elaborate staging whose articulations I now propose to examine briefly.

The sequence of the "returning mirror" is divided into four separate parts and can be summarized as follows:

(1) Henri de Corinthe rides on horseback one moonlit night on the Brittany coast when he hears an indecipherable sound that he initially interprets as the beating of wet clothing on wooden boards. Although there is a local legend that tells of nocturnal washerwomen ("lavandières de nuit"[90]) from the spirit world, Corinthe sees no one near the old-fashioned and worn wooden apparatus. He continues along the coast and sees a large and heavy mirror in an elaborate frame, which, Sisyphuslike, he manages finally to bring from the water onto the sand of the beach ("At the cost of inordinate effort he managed nevertheless to accomplish this absurd labor"[93]). In the mirror he perceives not his own reflection but that of his lost fiancée, Marie-Ange, who had drowned near Montivideo and whose body was never found (94).

(2) A customs officer retrieves him from the beach and takes him to a nearby pub, where Corinthe recovers his strength (94–97).

(3) Corinthe returns to the site of his discovery, where now the mirror can no longer be found (98–100). What Corinthe does encounter is the wooden laundry apparatus now surrounded by heather on whose branches hang a woman's silken undergarments covered with blood (100–101).

(4) The narrator hypothesizes that Corinthe's horse may have seen his own image in the mirror rather than that of his master's fiancée, and that this vision, a harbinger of certain death, transformed the animal into a "demon" or "spectre" (102) whose hoof sounds became, from that time on, silent.

Reduced to the series of discontinuous actions here enumerated, the episode of the returning mirror resembles a dream in its apparent arbitrariness, in its metonymical juxtaposition of heterogeneous objects. The mirror, horse, woman's clothing, and blood, uncanny and impossible specular reflections, form an ensemble that seems to point to the working through of a crisis in identity tinged with sadism, but the elements cannot be combined easily into a coherent, significant whole.[21] The temptation to translate Robbe-Grillet's narration of arbitrary encounters into the necessity of a psychocritical, allegorical metanarration is unavoidable, but the text itself is full of warnings to the reader that emphasize the hazards of such a project. At the end of the second section, for example, we read: "There remained, finally, a . . . troubling possibility: that these three elements—the horse, the mirror, and the horseman—found themselves assembled at this same precise point of the beach by pure chance, that is, without there being the slightest link among them, either of causality or of possession" (97).

At numerous points in the story, the primary narration of events conveyed by Corinthe's progressive and repetitive encounters with the various apparent dream-symbols is interrupted, both by authorial intervention and by the related thoughts of the participating characters—notably the customs officer and Corinthe himself. At stake in the majority of these interruptions is the question of verisimilitude: How plausible is it for washerwomen to be working on the beach at midnight? wonders Corinthe (90–91). How can one understand the simultaneous presence on the sand of an elegant exhausted gentleman and an abandoned mirror—was there perhaps a shipwreck? imagines the customs officer (96–97). As the story continues, the moments of such punctuated commentary increase in frequency to such a degree that the récit as such breaks down and becomes purely hypothetical in nature. From the third section on, the repeated use of the expressions "peut-être," "sans doute," "il est possible que," "on peut imaginer que," "c'est peu vraisemblable," and "on raconte que" make of the episode not so much a fictional/symbolical construct that promises meaning (however obscure and polyvalent) to the reader, but rather the very movement by which the text, in revealing the fragility of the conventions on which it is based, unravels itself and *disappears* as meaningful totality. Like the mirror in the story, Robbe-Grillet's autobiography sends back an image to the reader that may or may not be his own, that may or may not hold a cryptic significance, but its chance presence on the open "shore" (its readability) is less constitutive of its structure than is its inevitable disappearance into the depths, its return to the status of undifferentiated, shipwrecked debris.

If the "miroir qui revient" sequence is taken to be the creux générateur of the larger surrounding text to which it gives its name, one must conclude that Robbe-Grillet's self-portrait as a whole cannot escape the most radical force of fiction as self-effacing hypothetical questioning and that the fiction/autobiography alternative as formulated by the author cannot be neutralized or overcome in some higher synthetic unity. The nature of the relation—logical and textual—between the mirror episode as such and the fragments of the text devoted to the writer's life is undecidable: the most one can assert as reader is that the hypothetical narration that coalesces around the figure of Corinthe motivates the self-reflexive quality of the text, which mirrors its own constitution and disappearance more consistently and more unrelentingly than the evanescent "person" of Alain Robbe-Grillet. If this fragmentary, self-dissolving volume does not solve or resolve itself, it is because Robbe-Grillet as theorist has decided to live within the double bind he describes as the constant, life-defining tension between order and freedom (expressed literarily as the conflict between autobiographical competence and the fictional free-play of textual self-generation):

> The problematic experimentation with novelistic material and its contradictions imposed itself on me quite naturally . . . as the most suitable field for the staging, in its permanent imbalance, of this fight to the death of order and liberty, this insoluble conflict of rational classification and of subversion, otherwise called disorder. (133)

For Robbe-Grillet, because there is no possible evasion from the order/disorder alternative, there is also no glimpse of an encompassing (encircling) writing style such as Barthes's dreamed-of Neutrality by which one might arrive at a dimension of expression beyond judgment and ethical ambiguity.[22] *Le Miroir qui revient* remains a double text—of conceptual imprisonment and imaginary freedom—in which not even the author's occasional professorial tone of discursive rationality is capable of gaining access to the fictional projections, the figures of creative fantasy, whose open significant potential escapes his control.

L'AMANT

Like *Le Miroir qui revient*, *L'Amant* is an autobiography whose final form is not the completion or realization of its original conception. Initially planned by Duras's editor as a commentary on photographs that would have been visible to the reader and decipherable as reliable documents illuminating the author's life, *L'Amant* became, in the words of Francine de Martinoir, a text woven around a central forgetfulness, a hidden, invisible skein of repressed memories that, *as* absence or lack, engendered the fullness of the récit: "It is a photograph that had not been taken, an invisible snapshot, forgotten, hidden, which provoked a strong resistance in her memory [that of Duras] and which is at the origin of this story, of all the other stories" (92). At the outset of her account, Duras insists upon the paradoxical quality of the *traversée du fleuve*— an event that her previous fictions (de Martinoir: "*All* the other stories") had actively avoided, but from which they had derived both thematic content and narrative organization. Quite precisely, the crossing of the Mekong and the meeting with the gentleman from Cholen constitute a photograph not taken. Duras emphasizes, with great explicitness, that the photograph was omitted or forgotten rather than merely removed from the totality constituted by the images of her past; and it is the original incomprehension of the event's future existential resonance that lends it an *absolute* meaning:

> A photograph could have been taken, as another could have been elsewhere, under different circumstances. But it was not taken. The object was too slight to provoke it. Who could have thought of that? It could have been taken only if one could have prejudged the importance of this event in my life, this crossing of the river. Whereas while this crossing was taking place, one could not even imagine its existence. God alone knew. That is why this image, and it could not have been otherwise, does not exist. It has not been detached, taken away from the total. It is due to its not being taken that it owes its power, that of representing an absolute, of being the author of this absolute. (16–17)

In Robbe-Grillet's theoretical vocabulary, the untaken photograph is a creux générateur—a central void that allows the remainder of the text to be generated. The difference between all of Duras's previous writings and *L'Amant* is that the fictions were the unconsciously motivated dérive formed by an original repression, whereas the autobiography is a conscious focusing on the source of fiction as such. This means that the author's apparently simple and direct narration of her initiation into lovemaking is, simultaneously, a metanarration that sets out to unravel, with the analytical precision afforded by hindsight, the knot of passion and unfulfilled desire that is coterminous with the very possibility of fiction for Duras. *L'Amant* is fascinating both to the general public and to specialized interpreters of the postmodern novel for similar, or at least parallel, reasons. The casual reader sees in the autobiography the clarification of a personal confession and concludes, from the straightforward, erotically explicit love story, that he or she now understands the creative personality of a writer whose reputation for obscurity may have been exaggerated. The critic finds in *L'Amant* a neat recapitulation of Duras's entire literary production and has the intellectual pleasure of retroactively reordering and reinterpreting the repetitive obsessional themes of the fictions, now that the ultimate source of these themes has been uncovered by the author herself.[23] A text dependent upon the negativity of an original emptiness for its narrative deployment is received by readers of widely divergent backgrounds and persuasions as an expression of explanatory openness, of significant fullness. One finds in *L'Amant* not only the story of physical ecstasy, of sensory completion and exhaustion, but also the allegory of accomplished meaning: *la plénitude des/du sens.*

Because Duras seems to invite us to see in her autobiography the movement of authorial reflection by which the hidden source of her urge to write becomes illuminated, it might appear inappropriate to frame an analysis of her work in the theoretical terms envisaged by Barthes. Indeed, is not *L'Amant*, in its confessional directness, in its power as unraveling and unveiling discourse, the kind of text that not only eludes theoretical conceptualization but also dissolves it? If we refer to the essential problems of postmodern autobiographical writing as formulated by Barthes, we find (1) that Duras's text is by no means predicated on the undermining of the real referent; the popular appeal of *L'Amant* is based on its illusion of proximity to reality; (2) that the unmistakable presence of intertextual allusion to the author's previous fictions within the recapitulative autobiography is less a matter of "uncertain quotation-marks" than of cumulative thematic richness; the fact that *L'Amant* is a rewriting of *Un Barrage contre le Pacifique* (*The Sea Wall*), for example, results in the mutual clarification of both volumes rather than in textual uncertainty or undecidability; (3) that the voice narrating *L'Amant* is that of the person Marguerite Duras, who now sheds the masks (personae) behind which the enfouissements of her fictions had been covered; and (4) that the result of the three preceding, anti-Barthesian points suggests that Duras's autobiography may owe a great deal of its rhetorical power to its depiction of a genetic conception of origins and sources. Duras may be indulging in what Barthes condemned as the "pernicious" practice of mythologizing the figure of the origin as *natural* beginning from which all subsequent effects and developments can be derived and understood. Without affirming in a peremptory way that Duras's mirroring of self is exclusively genetic in its structure, one can see, nevertheless, that the author's inversion of Barthes's principles results in a mode of description, a style, that is as far from Neutrality as one can imagine. The equation of desire and writing in *L'Amant* does not produce jouissance in the specific Barthesian sense (i.e., deferred pleasure, suspended gratification), but rather a form of writing whose erotic aura lies in its capacity to approach and encircle its object without depriving it of its essential resistance to descriptive and thematic enclosure. It is the mutual implication and determination of the erotic impulse by/with the concrete practice of autobiographical writing in its stylistic particularity that stands at the center of Duras's text as "absent photograph" of passionate excess and that will be the nodal point of the brief analyses that follow.

At the center of *L'Amant* is the dramatic scene of the *traversée du fleuve*, which announces and symbolically expresses the crossing from childhood to womanhood accomplished in the act of love. The one-and-a-half-year liaison of the young Marguerite Duras with the Chinese gentleman is simultaneously the story of personal development, of self-discovery through and within erotic adventure, and the account of a progressive liberation from the constraints of an unusually painful and complex family romance. With her father absent from the family drama, Marguerite defines herself in relation to a mother whose *originalité* as described in the early pages of the book is, in fact, the sign of an evolving, increasingly visible madness, and to two brothers, one of whom is prone to violence and crime (called "the assassin" by Duras), and the other, of gentle disposition (called "the hunter" [*le chasseur*]), who seems to be the object of Duras's subtly expressed but not entirely repressed incestuous desires.[24] The minutely described scenes of lovemaking in the apartment of the Chinese gentleman do not take place in a vacuum, therefore, but occur illuminated against the dark background of the family's emotional imbalance and financial hardship.

One of the reasons for the popular success of *L'Amant*, no doubt, is its peculiar blend of exoticism (the almost Faulknerian degeneration and impoverishment of the family unit within a lush but morbidly suffocating tropical environment) and stark realism: we know from the beginning that Marguerite will accept money from her lover and that, in pursuing her far-from-unnoticed amorous adventures with a rich Oriental, she risks certain ostracism as "the young whore" mistrusted, then disdained, by her hypocritically *bien-pensant* colonial countrymen. In the universe of *L'Amant*, the loss of Marguerite's virginity is the breaking of a double taboo: the one set up by the mother in the way of her daughter's pleasure and precocious accession to womanhood, and the one established by the social milieu in which she lives. Crossing, breaking, moving beyond, or, as Duras puts it, "aller jusqu'au bout de l'idée" ("to go to the end/limit of the idea")—these are the actions that convey the capacity of Eros to abolish barriers and overcome separations.

In one of her several descriptions of the Chinese gentleman's apartment that becomes the lovers' refuge, Duras emphasizes the proximity of the room to the noises and smells of the outside world: the two spaces—the one of protected intimacy, the other of feverish, crowded activity—appear to coexist in a state of balanced interpenetration:

> I remember well, the room is dark, we don't speak, it is surrounded by the unceasing din of the city, embarked on the city, in the movement of the city. There are no glass windows, there are blinds and shutters. On the blinds we can see the shadows of people walking along the sunny sidewalks. . . . The bed is separated from the city by these slatted shutters, these cotton blinds. No hard material separates us from other people. Yet they ignore our existence. We, however, perceive something of their life, the totality of their voices, of their movements, like a siren that would send off a broken, sad, and monotonous shrieking. (52–53)

The passage as a whole is constructed rhetorically on a series of contrasts: between the silence of the lovers and the strident noise of the street; the immobility of the lovers and the chaotic movement of the crowds whose shadows are visible from inside; and, especially, the lovers' knowledge of the *totality* of the outside world's activity and the ignorance in which this world lives vis-à-vis the very existence of the young girl and her Chinese protector. The enclosed chamber can be taken as the poetic figuration of the womb ("*aucun matériau dur* ne nous sépare des autres gens"; "*no hard material* separates us from other people") and is a privileged location in that, unaffected and untouched by the mundane relations of the street, it nevertheless allows the purified essence of the outside (its "shadows") to penetrate its haven and be enveloped in a totalizing act of perception. The lovers not only have each other in a silence beyond the necessity of words, but they also possess knowledge of the expansive outside world, here depicted as the locus of a clamorous, fragmented *appeal* to the understanding: "like a *siren* that would send off a broken, sad, and monotonous shrieking." The room is therefore not only a protective womb but also the place where the dispersed, individually insignificant sounds of the world are gathered and recuperated in a meaningful whole.

The atmosphere of tranquil harmony that emanates from Duras's description of the room is based on the ultimate envelopment of the outside by the inside, of the street's disorder by the perceptual ordering of phenomena in the consciousness of the lovers. The street "passes through" to the lovers, not in the strident threat of its concrete reality, but in its aesthetically transformed outline. The blinds and shutters act as a one-way filter that preserves the room's quietude from contamination while guaranteeing the illusion of interpenetration between inside and outside. Such is the structural spatial pattern of the relation between the loving subject and the environment. Between the two lovers themselves a somewhat different pattern obtains, although the rhetorical movement of the text continues to depend on manipulations of borders, barriers, and limits to be overcome. Toward the end of the book, when Duras increasingly presents Marguerite and the man from Cholen in scenes that appear to be atemporal, detached from the contingencies of narrative progression and causality, she describes each as a *limitless* entity in relation to the other. When the Chinese gentleman observes the sleeping child he has transformed into a woman, he does not see an object over which he has possessive control, but rather an *être de fuite* quite similar to the Proustian Albertine:

> He looks at her. With eyes closed he looks at her again. He breathes her face. He inhales the child, with closed eyes he breathes her breathing, this warm air that emanates from her. He discerns less and less clearly the limits of this body, this one is not like the others, it is not finite, in the room it continues to grow, it is still without defined form, constantly in the process of becoming, it is not only there where he sees it, it is elsewhere also, it extends beyond sight, toward playfulness, toward death, it departs completely in bliss as if it were large, mature, it is without malice, frightening in its intelligence. (121)[25]

Similarly, when Marguerite observes her lover, she sees a man *and* the "beyond" toward which he transports both himself and her. Unlike the act of inclusive, enveloping perception as practiced by the lovers on the outside world from within their private domain, the amorous glance, *le regard amoureux*, is powerless to imprison or delimit the object of its desire. What Marguerite sees extends far beyond the perceptual realm and includes visions, fantasies, hallucinations—all of which *pass through* the infinitely open space of her passion. While embracing the Chinese gentleman, she "sees" both of her brothers, the dreaded assassin and the unconsciously longed-for hunter who, metamorphosed into a dream symbol emerging from the primeval forest, temporarily blends with the man from Cholen into one transpersonal figure of desire:

> I observed what he was making of me, how he was using me and I had never thought that one could act in this way, he went beyond my hope and in conformity with the fate of my body. Thus I had become his child. He had become something else for me as well. I began to recognize the inexpressible softness of his skin, of his sex, beyond himself. The shadow of another man also had to pass through the room, that of a young assassin, but I didn't know yet, nothing yet appeared to my eyes. The shadow of a young hunter also had to pass through the room but in this case, yes, I knew it, sometimes he was present in bliss and I said it to my lover from Cholen, I spoke of his body and of his sex as well, of his ineffable softness, of his courage in the forest and among the mouths of rivers haunted by black panthers. Everything went according to his desire and caused him to possess me. I had become his child. (122)

The space of desire—its "topography"—contains a series of recurring thematic elements and metaphorical manipulations that are subject to variation as they pass through the pages of *L'Amant*. The early description of the room/womb that shields the lovers from the street but translates the outside world's essence to their consciousness is constructed on the careful balancing of inside and outside: the room envelops and includes the world beyond within itself, thereby preserving its translucent boundaries. The later passages, in which the lovers' perception of each other initiates a meditation on the limitlessness of the beloved object, evoke an infinitely permeable space in which the barriers that separate entities and define the specificity of their realm of action have been abolished. No longer are there two spaces that interpenetrate; now there is one vast utopian topography of passionate excess in which all is possible.[26] The Durasian text here reaches its limit as boundless *lieu de passage*. The shadows that pass through the room are no longer those of the anonymous, unknowing crowd, but of Marguerite's two brothers. The family members against whose constraining power she must exert her willful defiance now metamorphose into the figures of the writer's fancy. The older brother, dispossessed of his violence, passes through the text only to disappear; the younger brother becomes the mythical huntsman whose androgynous sweetness repeats that of the Chinese gentleman; and the mother is replaced/negated by the maternal caring of the lover, who treats his beloved as a child ("I had become his child"). The text becomes the space in which Marguerite gives birth to herself; she herself emerges from the figural play of the text.

L'Amant is the story of erotic passion, of family drama, and also of a developing artistic vocation. To write is much more than a defense against the rigors and folly of the world and the family; it is, in Duras's words, Destiny. Just as the young woman's body was created so that it might be used, transformed, transfigured by a Chinese gentleman ("he went beyond my hope and in conformity with the fate of my body"), in the same way it was necessary that she turn to writing—in order to become herself. Whereas her lover and her adolescent friend Hélène Lagonelle seemed to possess the gift of life from outside or beyond themselves, Marguerite must search for her own "beyond" in artistic creation:

> I can no longer stand the thought of the man from Cholen. I can no longer stand that of H. L. [Hélène Lagonelle]. It would seem that their lives are full, that this complete-ness comes to them from outside of themselves. It would seem that I have nothing similar. Mother says: this one will never be happy with anything. I think that my life has begun to reveal itself to me. . . . I will write books. That is what I see beyond this instant, in the great desert in whose traits the expanse of my life appears to me. (126)

For Marguerite Duras, the act of writing begins in the discovery of a lack or void (*manque*). The writer does not possess the fullness of life that seems to adhere naturally to other people; but this fullness comes from the outside and therefore is itself a masked, unperceived lack—a lack of authenticity. The affirmation of the will to write arises when the future artist sees beyond the moment and understands that within emptiness lies extensiveness—the space of textual lieux de passage. The texts of Duras are *prepositional exercises*, based upon complex and variable manipulations of linguistic moments of passage, all of which center on the possibility of crossing *through* and going *beyond* the limitations—both conceptual and concrete—imposed on the human percep-tion by the strictures of family, society, and good manners in general. Art is not polite, it is not aesthetically pleasing to the disinterested, contemplative mind. Like the musical phrases of Chopin heard by Duras as she makes her second decisive crossing (this time, of the ocean, as she navigates from Indo-china, the place of her childhood, to France, the space of her writing about and around this childhood), art is a bursting forth, an explosion, whose ec-static extension in the world is the answer to and expression of a primordial injunction or command:

> That night, lost among the nights and the nights . . . she [Marguerite Duras] had been there when that thing had happened, that explosion of the music of Chopin under the brilliantly illumined sky. There was not a breath of air, and music had spread throughout the black ship, like an injunction from the sky whose relevance was obscure, like an order from God whose import was unknowable. (138)[27]

ENFANCE

In Nathalie Sarraute's fictional universe, there is little room for the passionate excesses and portentous vocabulary of Duras, and even less for the theoretical assurance of the professorial Robbe-Grillet. From the very beginning of her patient analytical explorations of the human psyche in *Tropismes* (1939) and in the early novels *Portrait d'un inconnu* (1948) and *Martereau* (1953), Sarraute has been concerned with two essential problems: (1) the existence of a nearly invisible flux of preverbal communication (sous-conversation) between individuals whose actual, stated conversation stagnates within the tight boundaries of the commonplace; and (2) the difficulty of seizing that flux *in* its movement with a language of honesty and accuracy that itself avoids the pitfalls of easy categorization and neat definition inherent in the conversational as such. Sarraute's literary aesthetic combines Proust's attack on Sainte-Beuve's glorification of conversation at the expense of the *moi profond* with a Sartrian concern for establishing the authenticity of the human being within the superficial and alienating relations of the social environment.[28] Although it is true that the appearance of *Enfance* caused a somewhat similar stir to that of *L'Amant* (in that both volumes sold very well and seemed less difficult or obscure to the general public than the authors' preceding fictional works), there was near unanimity among critics familiar with Sarraute's career on one fundamental point: that the autobiography was the logical continuation of Sarraute's fictional experimentation, that it remained focused on the issues of tropismes and sous-conversation and on the painstaking creation of a literary language appropriate to the expression of these hidden but real phenomena.[29]

The subject of *Enfance* is that of its simple title: the world of childhood before puberty and before the full social integration of the protagonist. Unlike *Le Miroir qui revient* and *L'Amant*, whose narrations extend to adolescence and to formative erotic and sexual incidents, Sarraute's autobiography stops abruptly when Nathalie is about to enter the lycée, and the only experience depicted in the volume that contains strong sensual overtones bordering on the sexually explicit occurs two pages before its conclusion, in a scene characterized more by a joyful, pantheistic fusion with nature than by passion in its Durasian mode.[30] The story of *Enfance* is the account of a childhood full of delicately remembered sense impressions, isolated scenes of family contentment and unhappiness, and words—beautiful, puzzling, or especially significant in their distant context. The subject matter of the book—the formative events of Nathalie's young life—contains enough dramatic, even melodramatic, potential for a traditional autobiographical narration composed of well-orchestrated *péripéties* and timely synthetic reflection on the lessons of the past; yet Sarraute consistently refuses to forge causal links among the fragmented moments of her memory. What the author presents fleetingly to the reader in a series of discontinuous scenes is the interrupted, multifaceted, cubist rendition of a story of progressive abandonment and isolation. Rejected in different ways by both her mother and her stepmother, caught in a difficult emotional triangle with a loving father and the young new wife whom he also loves, separated from her native Russia, sent into permanent exile from her home with no word of explanation, Nathalie discovers at a very early age both the fragile nature of human relationships and the necessity of self-reliance.

Throughout *Enfance* are precisely described moments of the author's childhood that contain, *in nuce*, the seeds of trauma and anxiety that never are exploited, that never come to fruition. It is as if Sarraute, even as a child, had been deeply suspicious of the melodramatic potential of such moments, as if she had wished, from the beginning, to void them of all pathos, to keep them alive in their existential intensity but without lending them a momentous, retroactively imposed prefigurative significance. When Nathalie steals a sack of candy from a *confiserie* after requesting the sweets unsuccessfully from her stepmother, not only is there no authorial probing into the hidden motivations for the dishonest act (we as readers must content ourselves with the appropriately naïve reasoning of Nathalie the child: "J'en avais envie" ["I wanted them"]), no Gidian luxuriating in the problematic of dissembling, masked behavior and antisocial risk taking, but the incident itself loses its significant intensity, *dies* as emblematic event once the young girl realizes that her father, in scolding her after the fact, is only pretending to be angry ("I feel that he is tired, that it is a fatiguing duty for him to appear angry" [149]). In the end, the potentially traumatizing confrontation recedes into obscurity: "These furious words pass through me and go somewhere else, beyond me" (150). Similarly, when a very young Nathalie is afraid of being alone in her dark bedroom, her father comes to be with her until she falls asleep; he sings her an old Russian lullaby until he thinks she is sleeping, but on leaving the room he notices her hand move and he returns until she no longer betrays her wakefulness. All the necessary elements are present for a rewriting of the Proustian Ur-trauma, the *scène du coucher* in Combray, but Sarraute—both child and adult author—does not oblige. In analyzing her childhood behavior, the primary narrator agrees with her dialoguing, censorious alter ego that the movement of the hand is playfully disingenuous, that her desire to keep her father close by for a few moments longer can be interpreted as a longing for comfort and protection; but she refuses to grant the scene prefigurative status as sign of her later abandonment by her parents. Sarraute concedes that it would have been possible, conceivable, for her to begin imagining a future parental betrayal (*trahison*)—"I recognize that everything appeared appropriately assembled for that to form in me"—but the truth of the matter is otherwise: she simply had a pact with her father that called for his staying with her until she fell asleep; if he left prematurely, he was at fault in breaking the agreement. We are far indeed from the coercive love-petitions and devious emotional blackmail of the young Marcel in his attempts to break the paternal pact by encircling and obtaining for his exclusive use his mother's doting attention.

Sarraute's consistent undercutting of the childhood trauma motif present in classical autobiographies extends even to the most sacred of all moments: the discovery, by the young person, of his or her talent at writing, the revelation of the literary vocation itself. In one of the more humorous incidents described in *Enfance*, Sarraute relates the scene of an early discomfiture, but without pathos and with an almost serene, Olympian detachment. Asked by her mother to show a cultivated friend (a Bergotte figure who never materializes as such) the "novel" she is composing as a young girl, she does so, only to incur the bemused but also rather cruel judgment: "Before setting out to write a *novel*, one must learn to spell" (82). Sarraute then explains that although this verdict caused her to abandon her efforts at fictional writing for years to come, it did not instill in her either anger or hatred toward her excessively rigorous literary critic; in fact, the absolute quality of the condemnation was a kind of "deliverance"—"a little like what one feels after having undergone an operation, a cauterization, a painful, but necessary, salutary ablation" (84).

So it is that the reader in search of a *creux générateur* within the pages of *Enfance* encounters a series of barriers and blockades. Sarraute does not seem particularly concerned with the modest intellectual pleasures of the theoretically minded textual interpreter in search of narrative origins and causes, nor does she furnish easily available ammunition for possible feminist or sociocritical readings of her work. She states, with disarming directness, that the passionate political and cultural discussions with Russian émigrés held in her father's Paris apartment included women as well as men and that "what strikes me now is that both morally and intellectually speaking, no one differentiated between men and women" (189). Similarly, her family's Jewish origins are not a source of stated anguish and not central to her identity as a child or as a developing writer: "I do not remember questions being asked of me [at school, concerning my Jewish origins], obviously ideas on racial or religious difference did not occur to anyone" (220).

In the entirety of *Enfance* there is only one moment of heightened emotional intensity that the author evokes *in* its intensity, without irony or self-deprecation: this occurs at the midpoint of the book, when Sarraute describes her despair at being "betrayed" by her mother. Nathalie, not quite nine years old, has just moved to Paris, to live with her father and stepmother, Véra. She has agreed with her mother (who remains in Russia) on a private code that will be understandable only to the two of them: if Nathalie says in her letters that she is happy ("Je suis heureuse"), that means that she is unhappy; only the phrase "Ici je suis *très* heureuse" ("I am *very* happy here") will signify actual contentment with the new family order. One evening, a few days after writing her mother using the "Je suis heureuse" formula, Nathalie is "amazed, astounded, striken" when her father reproaches her: "You wrote your mother that you were unhappy here" (112). The mother's betrayal, her breaking of the pact and opening of the secret code to the father, is the one event in the autobiography that the author singles out not only as being "traumatic" in the psychological sense but also as being full of consequences for the future:

At that moment and henceforth, against all appearances, an invisible bond that nothing has been able to destroy attached the two of us [my father and me] one to the other. . . . I don't know exactly what my father felt, but I, at that age (I was not yet nine), am certain that everything that revealed itself to me gradually during the following years, I was able to perceive it all, as a unit. . . . All my relations with my father, with Véra, their own relations, *have been merely the unwinding of what had been wound up there* [*n'ont été que le déroulement de ce qui s'était enroulé là*]. (113; my emphasis)

The affective power of this passage derives both from its completely atypical tone within the otherwise controlled and distant voice of the autobiographical subject and from the absoluteness of its affirmations. Sarraute sees in the one incident of betrayal the totality of the relations defining her broken family, now and forever. The incident is emblematic, it contains within itself the significance of future events, the "wound up" significance of what will later unwind itself in the progressive, discrete revelations of an existence. It is because of the mother's betrayal and failure in the ethical domain of pacts and codes that a lasting link is established with the father. It is because of the mother's flagrant and scandalous violation of the agreement that an invisible link can emerge with the father and that the daughter's perception of relations (*rapports*) in general can take place (take root). If Sarraute's autobiography differs so profoundly from those of Robbe-Grillet and Duras, it is because, unlike these two writers whose works derive from the irresponsible free-play of signifiers and the uncontrollable, unlimited excess of desire, her own writing, having refused the classical traumatic moments of the self-involved and self-loving subject, centers on the subtlety of the elusive, preverbal rapports that arise when pacts and contracts are born and destroyed. Sarraute's universe is that of the ethical, or rather, of the continual making and unmaking of ethical relations in a consciously *responsible* style of writing—some of whose characteristics I propose to examine briefly.

From the very beginning of her autobiography, Sarraute focuses on the events of her life in which the laws of the family are at stake—the issues of parental directives, permission granted or refused, the establishing of guidelines for the child's appropriate behavior. The two earliest memories described in *Enfance* (when Nathalie is five or six years old), in staging both the strength and the frailty of these laws, illustrate the magical or totemic power of individual words issued as warnings or commands. The first of these scenes takes place in Switzerland, at Interlaken or Beatenberg, in the foyer of a hotel where Nathalie is vacationing with her father. The young woman in charge of supervising Nathalie's comportment and teaching her German, seeing that the child for whom she is responsible is about to tear open the upholstery of an armchair with a pair of scissors, issues the warning: "Nein, das tust du nicht" ("No, you will not do that"). Nathalie responds initially with the words "Doch, ich werde es tun" ("Yes I will do it"), then with the more violent and descriptive "Ich werde es zerreissen" (12–13) ("I will tear it"). On a psychological level the significance of the scene is banal enough: a child is testing the limits imposed upon her by the adult world and seems to be as interested in the response of this world to her subversive action (reprimand, punishment mild or severe) as she is in observing the physical result of the upholstery tearing. But in Sarraute's explanatory remarks, we discover that (1) the child is not really fearful of punishment ("I know that there will be no punishment . . . or perhaps a mild reprimand"); and (2) her curiosity extends far beyond the concrete effect of the scissors (described in the last sentence of the passage almost as an afterthought: "I rip the back of the chair from top to bottom and I observe what comes out. . . . Something soft and grayish escapes from the fissure" [14].[31] What interests the child is the effect of words, or more precisely, their pressure and release within her consciousness. The words of warning—"Nein, das tust du nicht"—"weigh me down with all their power, with all their enormous burden . . . and under their pressure something just as strong within me, stronger yet, breaks free, rises up. . . . The words that come out of my mouth carry it along, *drive it in over there [l'enfoncent là-bas]*. . . . 'Doch, ich werde es tun'" (ibid.). Sarraute's metaphorical style reveals that the sinking of the scissors into the chair is merely the secondary extension of a more original *enfoncement*—that of her own language into the world: it is her words that carry the undefined "something" of her revolt outward. Nathalie's use of the future tense is performative in its force; it is a promise, a linguistic contract that replaces and displaces the warning of the *gouvernante* and whose antisocial consequences are clear to the child at the time: "'Ich werde es zerreissen'. . . . I am warning you, I am about to step over the threshold, to jump outside of this decent, inhabited, mild and sweet world, I am about to tear myself away, to fall, to sink into the uninhabited, into the void" (13).

Throughout *Enfance*, if the serious attention to and use of language is described as a fall, a dizziness, an encounter with the uninhabited void, it is because language in its magical essence projects the subject it possesses far beyond the boundaries of the "decent, inhabited, mild and sweet world" whose mode of communication is the superficiality of conversation and of the commonplace. This point emerges with great clarity in the second early scene (once again in a Swiss hotel, a year or two later). Nathalie, now suffering from a growth in her throat, has been told by her doctor and her mother not to swallow food until it becomes, through chewing, "aussi liquide qu'une soupe" (16). These words contain the same degree of power as "Nein, das tust du nicht" but produce the opposite reaction in Nathalie, whose literal interpretation of the directive, whose efforts to reduce all nourishment to an absolute, perfect liquid state, lead to painfully long mealtimes for all concerned and make of her the object of the other children's ridicule. Here, the mother's words of admonition take on the symbolical significance of a *gift*, a precious object to be conserved and hidden by the child in a place to which no one has access—her mouth:

> My mother herself . . . caused me to carry that along with me . . . "as liquid as soup" . . . it is from her that I received it. . . . She gave it to me to be guarded, I must conserve it piously, preserve it from all attack. . . . I come from far away, from a foreign place to which they do not have access, whose laws they do not know, laws that I can afford to flout over there, and I do occasionally transgress them there, but here loyalty obliges me to submit to their rule. (18–19)

What separates the child from the alienating otherness of social discourse and the realm of the commonplace is the purview of the law—understood as the spatial extensiveness from the mouth to the world, within which only the subject struggling with language has the power to effect authentic, rigorous change. Whether Nathalie reacts to the pressure of the outside with the enfoncement into reality of her utterance "ich werde es zerreissen," or whether she keeps the potent mana of the word enclosed within her lips—"aussi liquide qu'une soupe"—the same opposition obtains between self and other, between the banal and predictable regularity of the world and the "folly" of the young child inhabited by a coercive, otherwordly linguistic lawfulness.[32]

Much of the humor and the seriousness of *Enfance* derive from what lexicologists would term simple problems of definition, illustrated by Nathalie's attempts to match words with objects that do not fit the accepted, general patterns of meaning that exist in the world of those "others" who do not have access to the stringent laws of loyalty of the mouth. One of the most elaborately described, potentially traumatic scenes of the autobiography that remains suffused with a delicate and distinctly nontragic irony is that in which Nathalie, overcome by a sense of linguistic and moral honesty, is compelled to conclude that her mother is not as pretty as the doll she has been admiring in a store window (89–97). The totality of this complex passage, which deserves fuller analysis than can be undertaken here, is based upon the problem of identifying words with their referents.

The passage as such follows a very strict logic and is narrated according to the steps of the child's thought process as she makes her discovery. This logical movement proceeds as follows: (1) Before the attempted doll-mother comparison, the mother was incomparable in the eyes of Nathalie: "Far from all possible comparison. No criticism, no praise seemed to be able to adhere to her. It is thus that she appeared to me" (91). (2) Having seen the doll, which seems beautiful to her, Nathalie "takes hold of" the phrase "Elle est belle" and tries to *transport* it to her mother: "And I still do not know what compelled me that day to take hold of this 'Elle est belle' ('She is beautiful') that adhered so perfectly to that hairdresser's doll, that seemed made for it, to transport it, to try to make it hold, as well, on the head of my mother" (92). (3) As in the "ich werde es zerreissen" episode, Nathalie gives in to the pressure of her comparison and *opens up* her thought to her mother, who reacts severely: "A child who loves her mother finds that no one is more beautiful than she" (93). (4) The mother's observation itself now enters the child's consciousness, where it becomes, like the "aussi liquide qu'une soupe" phrase, "un paquet bien enveloppé" ("a well-wrapped package") whose resonant significance will engender a long reflective passage in which Nathalie concludes that, *because* she does not have the thoughts of a "real child," she *therefore* must be a "monster," a child who does not love her mother ("what I am: a child who does not love her mother" [94–95]).

The reader familiar with Sarraute's novels will recognize in this parable one of their major themes: the incompatibility of the logic of generality (the supposed feeling of *a* child, "*un* enfant") characteristic of conversational commonplace with the tentative, groping logic of the writer or would-be writer, who, armed exclusively with words against the inconsistent appearance of the world, can only resort to the indirect figuration of metaphorical discourse— the *transport* that brings words onto and into objects, that attempts, not without absurdity and pathos, to hold together the disparate elements that compose the universe in which we live and out of which fiction metamorphoses itself.

For Nathalie Sarraute, the description of childhood memories is fraught with as many difficulties as the composition of a fictional work, not only because of the resistance of a malleable and elusive subject matter and the inherent inaccuracy of human remembrance but also (especially) because autobiographical writing, like the writing of all imaginative works of art, cannot bypass or transcend the problematic confrontation of words with the world. Unlike Barthes, for whom postmodern autobiography begins with the abolition of description as such, with the assumption of the impossibility of picturing the self from the outside, as definable referential entity, Sarraute takes on the complex task of approaching the self and the meaning of its past experience through the indirect path of metaphorical discourse, without illusions, without the vain hope of achieving a pseudopictorial accuracy or analytical/conceptual closure. Sarraute and Duras are remarkably similar in their creation of what might be called a *prepositional rhetoric*—the elaboration of a style based on an imaginary topography in which the act of writing emerges as an extension into the world, a movement toward, into, and beyond the limitations established by the social sphere (for Duras, hypocritical barriers of a narrow, moralistic type; for Sarraute, the imprisoning conventions of the commonplace). This prepositional rhetoric arises as the concrete stylistic answer to the problem of self-representation. Because the self cannot be caught as itself, in one moment of understanding, it must be worked toward gradually, patiently; it is the gradual movement of writing as prepositional labor that opens up the distinctive imaginary landscapes of Duras and Sarraute.

Each of the three autobiographies under consideration in this chapter en-counters, in its own individual way, the issues of postmodern writing as elab-orated by Barthes, and each of these works refuses the ideological and meta-physical temptations of closure inherent in the traditional model of literary self-portraiture. For Robbe-Grillet, the result of this refusal is a double work—part fiction, part anecdotal remembrance—whose center (the "miroir qui revi-ent" episode) is consciously enigmatic, polyvalent in its potential significance, and therefore antigenetic in the Barthesian sense. *Le Miroir qui revient* focuses on two subjects, the author and human individual Alain Robbe-Grillet—whose distrust of traditional autobiography does not stop him from indulging in confession and personal revelation—and Henri de Corinthe, the fictional construct that functions as the text's creux générateur. What Duras and Sar-raute achieve, in radically different ways but in each case more powerfully, more effectively, than Robbe-Grillet, is not so much an achieved work (one that could be rated "superior" to that of Robbe-Grillet on narrow aesthetic grounds) as a rhetoric of passage, a style that responds to the problematic of literary self-depiction by *crossing through* the entirety of their texts. Duras's *traversée du fleuve* is the ostensible dramatic center of a text that is nothing but the linguistic tissue of a constantly repeated *passing beyond all limits*. Sar-raute's fixations on magically charged words, her discovery of the invisible links that attach people and bring together words and entities, produce a coherent topography of writing, a space of thresholds, linguistic and ethical crossings, that traverse not only *Enfance* but her fictional writings as well.

What Duras and Sarraute negate, through the very cohesiveness of their texts' rhetorical webbing, is the possibility of writing as Neutrality in the strict and complete Barthesian sense. Certainly, displacement and drifting (dérive) characterize *Enfance* and *L'Amant* as well as *Le Miroir qui revient*, but the theo-retical ideals of "white writing, exempt of all literary theater—delectable insig-nificance—the smooth—the empty" have no bearing on these works, each of which stages the problem of significance without abolishing its magnetic at-traction. Perhaps the greatest power of these complex autobiographies resides precisely in the challenge they pose to any literary theory that would attempt to solve the question of meaning by discursive statement, by unequivocal affirmation. To question the meaningfulness of a text is to engage in a rhetori-cal process that is itself far from "white" or "smooth" or "empty"; this engage-ment-*in* is prepositional and topographical in the sense I have elaborated. In asking the question of meaning, we move *toward*, and in so doing we both leave the realm of what is and enter the domain of what might be; and there, in that space of infinite fictional/hypothetical possibilities, remains the labor of writing, of transporting the words at our disposal toward and into the imag-inary figures of our creation. In the words of the young Nathalie, writing takes place in the extenuating and disquieting space of labor and magic. The prob-lems the writer approaches and confronts are "solved" only when the voice of the critical judge intervenes from beyond, from outside the text's topographi-cal extensiveness, to break its enchantment. In this sense, the temptation to achieve theoretical closure can be seen, with appropriate irony, as the *deliver-ance* of textual travail:

> I stretch towards them [the imaginary characters of my "novel"]. . . . I try with my weak and hesitant words to get closer to them, very close, to touch them, to manipu-late them. . . . But they are rigid and smooth, icy. . . . it would seem that they have been cut from leaves of tinselled metal. . . . however hard I try, nothing can be done, they remain always the same, their slippery surfaces gleam, scintillate. . . . they are as if enchanted.
>
> A spell was also cast on me, I am spellbound, I am enclosed with them, in this novel, it is impossible for me to escape. . . .
>
> And now these magical words . . . "Before setting out to write a *novel*, one must learn to spell" . . . break the charm and deliver me. (*Enfance*, 85–86; Sarraute's emphasis)

PART TWO

"PURE FICTION" AND THE INEVITABILITY

OF REFERENCE

In each of the first four chapters of this book, I have begun my analyses with the question of the readability or obscurity of the texts under consideration. In Camus's *La Chute* I encountered, under the surface of an ironical discourse on guilt and the crimes of twentieth-century humanity, a deeper ironical movement, a "fall into textual dizziness" that plunged the *récit* into a self-referential abyme. The difficulty or obscurity of *La Chute* consists of its vertiginous intertextual qualities as well as its convoluted weaving of a discourse "on" guilt around the *pur manque* of its central narrative moment. In Robbe-Grillet's *Topologie d'une cité fantôme*, on the other hand, a novel that announces itself as a practical working out of the self-referential theories of topology and generativity becomes subsumed within a larger textual movement in which the decrypting hermeneutic relation of man to his world takes precedence. The specific difficulty of reading *Topologie* emerges in the rhythmical *alternations* between self-referentiality and the novel's appeal to the world beyond its bounds. This kind of alternation is even more visible in Claude Simon's *Les Géorgiques*, an experimental novel that simultaneously points to the limits of narrative differentiation (layering, leveling) and also represents the protagonist (the General) as allegorical figure of the writer engaged in what I have called the *performative pathos* of projecting words upon the world. The hubris of the General consists of his desire to efface the barrier between sign and referent, to paint the world in the color of his linguistic commands.

The necessity of the reader's attentiveness to the specific modes of interplay between complex referential "pointing" and the textually self-reflexive in these three novels extends also to the postmodern autobiographies I analyzed in the preceding chapter. Such attentiveness proved necessary despite the superficial appearance of clarity or (relative) lack of obscurity in *Le Miroir qui revient*, *L'Amant*, and *Enfance*. The explicitly made *turn* toward the depiction of the self as referent did not entirely negate the self-generational force of the "returning mirror" episode in *Le Miroir*; and this turn produced, in the works of Duras and Sarraute, a distinct style, a prepositional rhetoric of passage through words toward the world that could not be confused with a transparent mimetic function. Language does not mirror its outside in photographic fashion, but moves toward it, passes through its interstices, produces an interwovenness of sign and referent.

As I make my own turn now—toward works of fiction by Maurice Blanchot and Samuel Beckett that can only be described as formidable in their demands on interpretation—I would like to keep in mind the issue of mimetic or referential "competence" (Robbe-Grillet) versus textual self-reflexivity that has predominated in the previous four chapters, but I would also like to add to it the matter of the possible relation between the referential function of literary language and what I propose to call the *ethics of fiction*.

The chapter devoted to Blanchot is perhaps the most ambitious synthetic essay in this book: in it, I attempt to bring together a discussion of the author's criticism with a reading of three of his sibylline prose fictions. At the center of my argument is Blanchot's own notion of critical "commentary," which he defines as an explanatory *betrayal* of the "transparent mystery" of the literary text. Yet this betrayal perpetrated by the critic, this "banging of the hammer," is not some aberrant form of behavior that could be corrected by a "better reading": it is, rather, the necessary correlative to the constitutive distances and displacements that reside within the core of the fiction itself. What Harold Bloom calls "strong misreadings" and Paul de Man calls "blindness" result from the inner constitution of the literary text, which is not conceived of by Blanchot as a straightforward, intentional activity or expression of a prior message, but rather (as we saw in his interpretation of Camus) as a verbose narrative web hovering around a founding void (vide, manque). Thus, not only is the practice of criticism a treacherous "surrounding" of an inexpressible emptiness by heavy-handed explanation, but the writing of fiction seems itself to be condemned to precisely this same enveloping function.

In the second half of my chapter on Blanchot, as I examine the structural particularities and semantic intricacies of his récits, I argue that the notion of a pure fiction (which finds its strongest theoretical exposition not in Barthes or in structuralist or poststructuralist ideology but in Blanchot) is not realizable—not because of some technical deficiency of style, but because of the inevitability of a containment or envelopment that is referential in mode. Even in a fiction that presents itself as essentially *relationless*, without a link to the world beyond its confines, there is a final *fall into worldliness*, which is also a fall into human time, a recognition of history and mortality.

In the final chapter of my book I juxtapose one of Beckett's late prose works—the short novel *Compagnie* (1980) (*Company*)—to his early play, *Fin de partie* (1957) (*Endgame*). In *Compagnie* I find an intricate combination of theoretical metadiscourse on the possibilities and limits of narrative fiction and a focused, referentially competent, directed meditation on the meaning of what it is to be human (much the same alternation as that which characterized Robbe-Grillet's *Topologie d'une cité fantôme*). In *Fin de partie* I analyze a similar split between an inward-turning movement of solipsistic meditation (Hamm's retreat from the world, his act of *recueillement* as private thinking) and the fragile promise of a human community in which the "taking in" (*recueillement* in the transitive sense) of one's fellow humans via the creation of a narrative circle or encirclement guarantees, within language, the permanence of an ethical dimension. *Fin de partie* is a play, a drama, but its reliance on the narrative function as that specifically human activity which distinguishes us from all other entities within nature is the reason for its inclusion, as exemplary text, in this book.

For Blanchot and for Beckett, the act of literary creation is not to be confused with a self-enclosed play of signifiers, however liberated. Although both write reflectively about textuality within their texts, the ideal of a pure fiction or "relationless narrative" is not achievable; even within those experimental works that seem most involuted, most semantically self-sufficient, there is an undeniable referential residue that calls for interpretation. The text in its praxis is not a linguistic structure that contains all else, but rather a created form that points both to itself *and* to the world outside from which it differs and from which it derives its ethical force.

In his compact and suggestive article entitled "Lifting our Eyes from the Page," Yves Bonnefoy reminds us that poetry, or language in its highest form of concentrated evocativeness, "is what attaches itself—and here is its specific responsibility—to what cannot be designated by a word of language; and this because what is beyond designation is an intensity, a plenitude we need to remember" (798). Poetry is a pointing toward, an intentional act, in which the poet's fascination with the absolute presence of the world *results in* the text; but the text itself, the object of idolatry of all critical and theoretical formalisms, is in fact only *that which remains* of the poet's labor:

> But even in a poem, words formulate; they substitute signification, representation, for this One, this unity faintly perceived, and therefore it is the sense of dissatisfaction that is the strongest. Dissatisfaction before this fact of textuality in which the fundamental intuition vanishes, but not without leaving something glittering in its wake. . . . The text is not poetry's true place; it is only the path it followed a moment earlier, its past. (ibid.)

The texts I have read and will have read in this book are the "glittering remnants" of a linguistic confrontation with the world, of a struggle that opposes the consciousness of the writer with the universe of experience and of emotion in which he lives. As readers, the only concrete place we have in which to pursue our meditation, our *recueillement* in the self-involved sense, is the page, the text itself. And yet, as Bonnefoy argues in a suggestive formulation, this document on which we expend so much interpretive energy, out of which we spin webs of theoretical abstraction, is not the "true place" of poetry but its past, its residue. Throughout my study, I have (will have) tried to indicate that the question of the place of the text is fundamental, *incontournable*. To interpret the difficult works of contemporary experimental prose that I have proposed for examination here is not to remain within the page, within the self-sufficient logic of proliferating signifiers, but to be willing to move between word and world, or, in Bonnefoy's excellent expression, to be willing to "lift one's eyes from the page." Like Blanchot, to whom the poet owes a (perhaps unconscious) theoretical debt, Bonnefoy sees in the act of reading and in the act of writing itself the movement of a fundamental, foundational betrayal. The inaccessible void that lies at the heart of things, the *vide* or *manque* in Blanchot's terms, the *One* of absolute *Presence* according to Bonnefoy, is that which fascinates us, that which causes us to write, to surround its inaccessibility with the always excessive signs and images that lie at our disposal as fabricators, artisans of the word. As illustrious example of the lifting of the eye from the page that is constitutive of all creative (mis)readings and (mis)writings, Bonnefoy cites the passage from Dante's *Inferno* (5:121–38) in which Paolo and Francesca are reading about Lancelot and Guinevere, but soon, inspired by the kiss "in the text," pause, themselves, to kiss:

> But something comes to them [Paolo and Francesca] from the text that encourages them to turn toward one another, and then "quel giorno più non vi leggemmo avante," they read no further. Was this reaction the result of the erotic suggestion in the Arthurian romance? Certainly not. It is the result of poetry's own will, which is the force in the words that moves them toward more than words, which is to say, poetry's potential for love, the appeal it throws out to the reader to go further than the poet toward unity. . . . In this passage where Dante's own emotion bursts forth, he has represented, "en abîme," the essence of poetry, except that he betrays it later, as every poet always does, by reducing this fundamental intuition of the other into devotion to a kind of icon. In *The Divine Comedy*, Beatrice is a symbolic figure, the keystone of meaning, but not the passionate look or trembling hand. (802)

All literary language that aspires to the concentrated expressiveness of poetry contains within itself, wrapped in the fold (the Mallarméan *pli*) of its self-reflexive abyme, the very essence of the poetical. At the same time, however, in a movement of betrayal that is necessary, inevitable, the fundamental intuition that lies at the base of all art becomes "reduced" to the status of icon. From the naked origin of the "passionate look or trembling hand," we *progress* toward symbolism, toward meaning, but this progress is, in fact, the foundational reduction of the theoretical gaze, that gaze which appropriates through abstraction, which inhabits all "strong texts" as they (re)read and (re)write one another.

Literary theory is not an artificially added-on appendage that we could do without in some hypothetical pure reading conceived of as transparent encounter with the surrendered significance of the text. Theory is part of texts as well as part of commentary, as both Bonnefoy and Blanchot illustrate in their own theoretical meditations. However, when theory becomes an end in itself, when it becomes a formalized and self-contained system, then the theoretician, the inventor of icons and symbolical maps, in enveloping the world within language, has, in fact, lost the world. In my book, and following the reading lessons of Blanchot and Bonnefoy, I am suggesting that we must pass through theory, recognizing both its inevitability and its "uselessness." In so doing, we leave open the true place of the literary, which resides *between* words and that element of extended space in which we live *and* write our books—that space that is always both beyond and more than words. If there is to be an ethics of reading, itself dependent upon an ethics of poetry or fictional creation, it cannot be housed within language as self-referential container but must arise in what Heidegger would have called the "ecstatic openness" of the appeal (*Ruf, appel*) from words to the world, an appeal that cannot be better expressed than in the words of Yves Bonnefoy:

> To sum up my idea of the kind of reading that tends toward poetry, I might have said that it asks us to lift our eyes from the page and to contemplate the world, that is always so unknown, always so virginal, so full of life—"vierge et vivace" as Mallarmé would say—and that written forms interpret but thereby conceal beneath the play of possibilities that each time are less than the world is. (806)

Chapter Five

BLANCHOT AND NARRATIVE

THE TITLE of this chapter is deliberately, perhaps provocatively, simple: "Blanchot and Narrative." According to the conventions of literary criticism and the usual telegraphic style of titles, such a phrase would seem to be the shorter, more economical equivalent of "Narrative according to Blanchot." But in the latter formulation, a relationship of inclusion is unequivocally established: I am stating, or at least suggesting as a hypothesis for subsequent confirmation, that a part of the immense whole defined as narrative in literary studies is to be found in the works of Maurice Blanchot. In consequence, the reader of an essay with this second title might expect (assuming the seriousness of its author) to learn something about narrative itself by gaining insight into Blanchot's ideas about or manipulations of its diverse laws. The starker, balder formulation "Blanchot and Narrative," on the other hand, leaves open the possibility that the two subjects connected by the conjunction "and" might not be related by inclusion or even analogical resemblance. If one leaves the title open in its semantic indeterminacy rather than make the conventional assumption (in fact, already an interpretation) that properties are necessarily shared between Blanchot and Narrative, then the subject at hand, in its presentation as mere juxtaposition, promises very little indeed, offers nothing to intellectual apprehension, remains on the far side of that preliminary movement toward understanding that titles so often generate.

If I have decided to keep the title in its first form, it is because I am not convinced that the points of intersection between Blanchot and narrative are easily established, or that the vertiginous moments at which Blanchot's texts descend into the narrative maelstrom lend themselves transparently to critical/analytical description. And it is small solace to realize that, as belated critic, one is in distinguished company—i.e., that a number of critics and philosophers who have brought Blanchot's writings into public view during the last twenty years with éclat and with an advanced level of interpretive awareness agree on two essential points: (1) that the author's works of narrative fiction are obscure or, at the very least, quite difficult to understand; and (2) that these same works are, properly speaking, indescribable. A very inauspicious double bind indeed: one can only pity the interpreter of postmodernism who thinks he has penetrated to a certain extent the obscurity of these fictions but who, because of their unbinding, dispossessing nature, is unable to recount the triumph of his insight. One is tempted to divide Blanchot critics into two groups: on the one side are those readers who choose to forget, repress, or ignore the ironical, violently disorienting force of the fictions and who succeed thereby in making statements about the author, in categorizing his literary achievements and in contextualizing them within the larger scope of our contemporary cultural production; on the other side are those readers who, having given themselves over to the vertigo of Blanchot's textual play, confess their inability to emerge from it unscathed as clear-sighted critics or theoreticians.[1]

For the members of the second group, there is an *experience* of reading Blanchot that remains primordial, even visceral in its intensity, beyond which it is impossible to venture into the realm of aesthetic disinterest or theoretical abstraction. Perhaps the most compelling, if somewhat theatrical, account of this peculiar experience came from the pen of Bernard Noël, who described the immediate act of reading Blanchot as a malaise and as a radical reversal of categories in which Writing and Death join together. While reading Blanchot on the train one day, Noël first became nauseated and then haunted by the bizarre, surrealistic thought that the writer of *L'Arrêt de mort* (*Death Sentence*) had "fallen into his own mouth" ("Il est tombé dans sa propre bouche"): "To fall into one's own mouth would be to place the outside inside. Is this not the process of language and of death which, literally, place us inside before emptying the inside outside?" (28). And later in the same passage, Noël prefigures the Derridean notion of *narrative invagination*:[2] "In the same way that the genitals of a woman are the inversion of a man's genitals, there are texts that carry death with them" (32–33).

The essential difficulty in writing *about* Blanchot, in wrapping up Blanchot within an interpretive discourse based on categorical distinctions, is that his fictions perform the anticipatory deconstruction of all analytical inclusiveness as such. This has been noted quite explicitly by Jeffrey Mehlman and Emmanuel Levinas, both of whom dwell on the images of inclusion and envelopment in their descriptions of the interpreter's plight when caught within the infolding of Blanchot's texts:

How could the critic then hope to supplant, exceed or even accompany [*accompagner*]—(Littré: "to follow, to honor, to admire ceremonially")—a text which so clearly includes his own? In despair, the commentary degenerates into an imitation, or worse, into a parody of its subject. (Mehlman, "Orphée scripteur," 458)

The significance of his world [that of Blanchot] concerns our own. But such a work resists (rejects) interpretation. Blanchot's work is perhaps in its entirety the rupturing of the envelopment with which noncontradictory statements attempt to surround all movement. Should one try to catch some of these scintillations without fear of extinguishing them? Everything must be expressed here in the hypothetical mode, as Blanchot does himself when he wishes to explain what his books have said. (Levinas, *Sur Maurice Blanchot*, 78, note 1)

Whether the critic emphasizes the resistance of Blanchot's fictions to analytic envelopment (Levinas) or grants these writings an anticipatory enveloping force over the act of reading as such (Mehlman), the issue is that of the apparently insuperable distance between original text and analytical commentary; and it is the honest recognition of this distance as necessary precondition to any attempt at interpreting Blanchot that distinguishes the rich, complex, problematical essays of Mehlman and Levinas from the schematized efforts of those critics whose hermeneutic grids pretend to encompass the author. Mehlman's remark on the seemingly inevitable "degeneration" of the analytical act into parody deserves some scrutiny, however, in that Blanchot himself has written cogently on the question of literary commentary, accentuating the ways in which critics repeat the original text, but without Mehlman's rhetoric of decline and loss.

Nowhere are Blanchot's views on commentary as literary activity more forceful and explicit than in his essay entitled "Le Pont de bois (la répétition, le neutre)" ("The Wooden Bridge: Repetition and Neutrality"), whose ostensible subject is Marthe Robert's remarkable comparative study of *Don Quixote* and Kafka's *Castle*.[3] As is often the case in Blanchot's critical writings, however, the apparent subject gives way rapidly to more general considerations. The smaller part of the article is devoted to Blanchot's disagreement with Robert concerning the relative importance of the Homeric and Judaic worlds for Kafka, whereas the greater portion of Blanchot's argument dwells on commentary as such. According to Blanchot, the act of criticism, in its repetitious *delirium*, is not a sign of the futility of the critic's task but rather the logical corollary of the inner structure of literary works. If my essay on Blanchot's narrative fictions does nothing more than repeat what these fictions have to say (or if Blanchot's or Robert's writings on Kafka have the same essential result), it is because, in writing *about* Blanchot, I mimic the inner repetition that founds or establishes all fiction. Indeed, for Blanchot there is within the literary work a lack, a void, or a distance around which the work as verbal expression constitutes itself; when the work is completed and finished in its outward appearance, it still attempts or tends to repeat itself, to hover incompletely around the void that is its source. Thus criticism, which is the insinuation of meaningfulness into the initial founding void of the written word, in fact repeats the repetition *within* the text without which there can *be* no text. In Blanchot's own terms (which I have just "repeated"):

> The act of commentary should not be confused with all criticism, in the multiple yet confused meanings that this word holds. Commentary (by a pretension that, perhaps, in fact, envelops all criticism) repeats the original work. But to repeat it is to seize—to "hear" within it—the repetition that founds it as unique work. Now this repetition—this original possibility of existing as a double form—cannot be reduced to the imitation of an inner or outer model. . . . Reduplication in this sense presupposes a different kind of duplicity—i.e., what a work expresses emerges through the silencing of something. . . . Moreover, the work expresses something in silencing itself. There is within the work a void of itself which constitutes it as work. This lack,

this distance, this utterance unexpressed because covered over by expression, though already expressed perfectly and incapable of being expressed again, nevertheless tends inevitably to reexpress itself, thereby calling forth the infinite act of commentary in which, separated from itself by the lovely cruelty of analysis (which, in truth, does not separate the work from itself arbitrarily, but rather in virtue of this separation which already is at work within it, a noncoincidence which could be called its slight heartbeat), the work waits for an end to the silence which is its own. (*L'Entretien infini*, 570–71)

What Blanchot formulates here—in terms that may seem formidably abstract to the reader uninitiated in the writer's involuted prose style—is, in fact, applicable to the concrete reading of literary texts such as Kafka's *Castle*—an enigmatic but uncannily engaging fiction in which Blanchot sees both the void of a primary open symbolism (the castle means anything and everything to critics of divergent methodological persuasions) and the potential for infinite commentary. Significantly, Blanchot is not innocent of the perennial gesture of interpretation as he defines it—the filling in or plugging of the text's founding emptiness—though his hermeneutical prudence does honor to Levinas's hypothetical mode. At the end of his article, he suggests that the Castle as symbol might be "la souveraineté du neutre et le lieu de cette étrange souveraineté" (580) ("the sovereignty of the neutral and the space of this strange sovereignty"). Now it happens that *le neutre* is one of the key terms in Blanchot's critical vocabulary, a term that continually surfaces throughout his analytical essays, from *L'Espace littéraire* (1955) (*The Space of Literature*) through *L'Ecriture du désastre* (1980) (*The Writing of the Disaster*) and beyond. In introducing this highly charged notion into the concluding moment of his argument as an apparent solution to *The Castle*, he seems to close off the openness of the text's void, but this closure is only apparent, as le neutre itself is not a descriptive term capable of enveloping the central emptiness of Kafka's universe but is rather a term curiously resembling (repeating) the text's resistance to interpretive description. If le neutre cannot account for the text for which it has been chosen by the critic, it is because

> le neutre cannot be represented or symbolized or signified; moreover if it is conveyed by the infinite indifference of the entire narrative, it is everywhere in the narrative (in the same way as everyone, according to Olga, belongs to the Castle, whence one should conclude that there is no Castle), as if it were the point of infinite regress through which the words of the narrative and, in it, all narrative and all commentary on all narratives gain and lose their perspective, the infinite distance of all relationships, their perpetual reversal, their abolition. (581)

At the end of "Le Pont de bois," the filling in of the *Castle's* void by the unrepresentable, atopical emptiness of Blanchot's le neutre as point of infinite regress does little to clarify or to illuminate in the classical exegetical sense the deeper meanings of Kafka's text.[4] Like Derrida's recurring "themes" of *différance, dissémination*, and *invagination*, which have a strategic deconstructive effect in the dismantling of metaphysically anchored binary oppositions without lending themselves to conceptual fixity or closure, Blanchot's continually repeated terms—*le neutre, le désoeuvrement, l'autre nuit*, and, in his later writings, *le fragment*—function as convenient reference points for the reader, but, in their twisting of logical relationships, their rhetorical reversals, and their undoing of all perspective, contain within themselves the radical questioning of the theoretical enterprise as such. It is especially important to keep in mind the complex, problematical status of these terms because, as a general rule, critics tend to approach Blanchot's "obscure" fictions through the relative "clarity" of the author's prolific critical writings.[5] One might wonder just how clear a critical opus is when its central theoretical concepts are (act as) the decentralization of theoretical conceptualization, and it would be intriguing to imagine an analytical essay on Blanchot written *from* the fictions in the direction of the criticism—a path never taken until now, but promising in its unsettling, bizarre potential.

For the reader who has had the courage to attempt the penetration of Blanchot's voluminous criticism, a feeling of monotonous repetition often sets in. The essays tend to say the same thing endlessly, and it is difficult, on a general thematic level, to discern a recognizable evolution in the author's critical views. Unlike some of our more visible literary and cultural commentators today, whose intellectual transitions through structuralism, semiotics, *psychocritique*, reception aesthetics, deconstruction, and new historicism can be dated and debated in journal articles, Blanchot seems to have remained faithful to a central core of critical insight that was expressed forcefully and somewhat programmatically in his early volumes *L'Espace littéraire* (1955) and *Le Livre à venir* (1959). If there is an evolution of any kind from the fifties to the eighties, it is not in methodological perspective or in the replacement of one theoretical (atheoretical) concept (conceptual impossibility) by another, but rather in a minute slippage of these terms from an initial adherence to a minimal degree of logical/rational stability toward a maximum of semantic displacement and ironical instability. Thus, whereas at the beginning of *L'Espace littéraire* Blanchot does not hesitate to direct his reader to the theoretical center of his book in an act of "methodological loyalty," in *L'Ecriture du désastre*, twenty-five years later, the very notion of centrality and of origins has taken on a distinctly Nietzschean, aphoristic, serene negativity:

> [From *L'Espace littéraire*]: Even a fragmentary book has a center that attracts it: not a stable center but a center that moves through the pressures of the book and of the circumstances that govern its composition. Stable also, nevertheless, in that, if it is a true center, while it moves it stays the same and becomes always more central, more hidden, more uncertain, and more imperious. He who writes the book writes it out of desire, out of ignorance of this center. The feeling of having touched it can well be

only the illusion of having reached it; when a book of illuminations [clarifications] is being written, there is a kind of methodological loyalty in saying toward which point it seems that the book is directed; here, toward the pages entitled *Le regard d'Orphée* [*Orpheus's Gaze*]. (5)

[From *L'Ecriture du désastre*]: There is no origin, if by origin one presupposes an original presence. Always past, past from the very beginning, something that has passed without being present, here is the time immemorial that forgetfulness gives us, saying: every beginning is reiteration. (180)

Blanchot's meditation on the quasi-magnetic attractiveness (*attirance*) of a center in movement at the beginning of *L'Espace littéraire* itself exhibits a complex double movement. Until the last phrase of the passage, he insists upon the elusive quality of the center, its lack of fixity, its distance from the writer, whose apparent grasp of the center's essence may be pure illusion; but in the final twist of his argument, in his evocation of methodological loyalty or honesty, he justifies the necessity of his readers' having a didactic or pedagogical orientation toward the true center of his set of essays—the article "Le Regard d'Orphée." At this early stage of his critical activity,[6] Blanchot uses his essays to express views on literature that, taken in their accumulated repetitions, amount to a literary theory exhibiting a distinct Romantic and occasionally Symbolist orientation.[7] If it is possible to classify the writings of *L'Espace littéraire* and *Le Livre à venir* in this way, it is because Blanchot, at this moment in his career, despite the circuitousness of his prose, nevertheless espouses an explanatory conception of literary criticism. The pointing toward the center of his own Literary Space is emblematic of the straightforward pointing-function of all pedagogically oriented literary criticism, whether traditional or modern in thrust. Yet it is significant that the article toward which the writer directs our gaze as readers is precisely about the deviance of Orpheus's gaze, about his impossible but necessary effort to seek out and, in turning around, to grasp the center of the night *within* the night, rather than merely bring back and reveal, via Eurydice, the significance of the night for (and within) our daytime understanding. Blanchot makes use of the Orpheus myth to elaborate an allegory of literary creation in which the literary act is removed from daytime experience and transported to the realm of l'autre nuit. This "other night" is unconnected to the natural cycle whereby night inevitably gives way to day, in which night is merely a temporary lack of light. The inner movement of Blanchot's allegory contains the logical and rhetorical convolutions we saw at work in "Le Pont de bois" (l'autre nuit is a concept as difficult to immobilize theoretically as le neutre in the later essay), but its insertion within the broader inclusiveness of the overt, directed theoretical purpose of *L'Espace littéraire* lends it a certain outer significant solidity, thereby tempting the reader to see in this central essay the "key" to Blanchot's conception of literature. Here, myth is reinterpreted in order to buttress a modern theory of artistic creativity.

In *L'Ecriture du désastre*, on the other hand, the notions of origin and centrality, rather than being the focus of critical definition, however subtle and problematized, become the target of absolute negation, of an assertive annihilation. There is no origin of a work, there can be no center, even if evanescent and meandering, because of the nature of time itself. Whatever point one might wish to choose as generational center has *already* passed beyond, and, in a strict sense, has never "been present"—this according to Blanchot's interpretation of Nietzsche's "Eternal Return of the Same" that informs large sections of *Le Pas au-delà* (1973) as well as *L'Ecriture du désastre*. The replacement of the spatial figure of the moving center and of the images of sight and light that traverse the Orpheus essay by the blank temporal abyss in which beginnings sink into inevitable repetition announces the radical impossibility of theoretical discourse (*theorein* being understood etymologically as discerning visual apprehension of relationships). Indeed, in one fragment of *L'Ecriture du désastre*, Blanchot states:

> Theoretical activity is necessary (for example, theories of language), necessary and useless. Reason works toward exhausting itself, organizing itself into systems, searching for a positive form of knowledge where it can alight and refresh itself and at the same time move onward toward an extremity that establishes stasis and closure. We should pass through this knowledge and forget it. . . . Theoretical combat, even directed against a form of violence, is always itself the violence of incomprehension; let us not be sidetracked by the partial, simplifying, reductive quality of comprehension as such. This partiality is the distinguishing trait of all theory: "the banging of the hammer," said Nietzsche. (122)

With the sweeping negation of origins and the ironization of theory as inevitable but incomprehending violence, Blanchot voids *L'Ecriture du désastre* of any positive point of reference that might convey a literary opinion or aesthetic judgment. In a moment of supreme irony toward the end of his reflexions (one is tempted to say "irony of irony" to paraphrase the German Early Romantics whose fragmented theories of language occasionally glimmer on the surface of Blanchot's fragmented text), Blanchot appears to parody himself, rewriting in negative form the structure of *L'Espace littéraire*, when he introduces another Greek myth[8]—that of Narcissus—as a coda to his preceding aphorisms. But here there can be no confusing of the myth with the higher purpose of a literary-theoretical framework. From the moment he introduces the Narcissus story, via its Greek origins and Ovidian transformations, Blanchot cautions that any reinterpretation of the myth, like the Nietzschean banging of the hammer, will be excessively heavy and, in its narrative coherence, far too packed with verbose clarity to adhere to its model—which remains wrapped in an "oracular" mystery:

> Greek myths in general say nothing, seducing us by a hidden oracular knowledge that calls forth the infinite play of guesswork. What we call sense (meaning), or even

sign, is foreign to them: they signal to us, without signifying, revealing, hiding, always limpid, stating transparent mystery, the mystery of transparence. So that all commentary is heavy, verbose, and especially so if it expresses itself in the narrative mode, the mysterious story evolving then intelligibly in explicative episodes which in their turn imply an elusive clarity. (194)

What differentiates *L'Ecriture du désastre* from *L'Espace littéraire* and *Le Livre à venir* is not only its nonexplanatory use of myth, but also, in a more general sense, its refusal to become a self-clarifying text. Blanchot's subtle remarks on the figure of Narcissus never reach the stage of exegetical centrality; they signal without signifying, they draw the reader into the movement of signification without offering hope of an end to this movement. In his later criticism, Blanchot no longer engages himself in the process of commentary—that process which, as we observed in "Le Pont de bois," consists of an inevitable repetition, a repetitious enveloping of the work of fiction by the critical text that mirrors the primordial, constitutive distance and displacement residing within the core of the fiction's void (vide, manque). If one wishes to remain within proximity of the transparent mystery that is literature, one must not join with the process of comentary—which is heavy and verbose (superficially "chatty," *bavard*),[9] especially if it takes on an explanatory, *narrative* form. There is an intriguing, implicit equation in *L'Ecriture du désastre* between commentary and narrative. If Blanchot moves away from or beyond commentary in the aphoristic, nonexegetical fragments of *Le Pas au-delà* and *L'Ecriture du désastre*, he also goes beyond a certain conception of narrative as sequence of "episodic explanation." When Blanchot steps outside the circle of repetitions he himself had defined as formative of all criticism, the tone with which he describes the act of commentary changes: no longer is commentary merely an objectively inevitable part of a process; it is now much closer to a masking or a betrayal of the enigmatic clarity of literary works that the critic situates below or on the near side of significance.

If my sole interest were Blanchot the critic, I might be satisfied to note the transformation of this idea of commentary and the evolution of Blanchot's essays toward an increasingly fragmentary playfulness and "uselessness." But there remains an unanswered question located somewhere between the lines of his essays that I would like to formulate explicitly and pursue at this point: Is the notion of narrative as explanatory betrayal only an aberration within the realm of criticism, or is the betrayal of commentary a movement at work within *all* narrative, whether critical or fictional? To examine this problem, I shall proceed in two stages: first, I shall discuss briefly Blanchot's analyses of three major modern novelists, with special emphasis on the moments at which he uncovers the inner contradictions that threaten to undermine the success of their aesthetic projects; and second, I shall attempt an interpretation of certain formal peculiarities of Blanchot's own fictions, in an effort to determine whether the issues raised in his critical writings find an echo within the strange, obscure clarity of his narrative fantasies.

Although Blanchot's duties as regular contributing critic to the *Nouvelle Revue Française* involved him in assessing a broad, heterogeneous group of writings, his preference has been for authors whose works exhibit a self-reflexive quality—poets who do not merely write beautiful or technically rigorous verse, but whose poetry constitutes a meditation on the possibilities and limits of their art form (Hölderlin, Mallarmé, Rilke, Char), and novelists whose fictions are part of an ambitious aesthetic project (Proust, Musil) or whose creations, by their combination of a deceptively transparent narrative organization and apparently opaque symbolic potential, provoke endless interpretation (Kafka).[10] The essays on Proust, Musil, and Kafka that I have chosen to highlight here contain two common properties: they exhibit Blanchot's obvious sympathy for the difficult, perhaps unrealizable goals the writers set for themselves; and they dwell on the crucial points at which the firmness of these goals begins to crumble under the internal pressure of the literary work against itself. At some moment, the novelist misunderstands his own precepts, writes "blindly" against the clarity of his own insight, in a movement Proust taught us to recognize in Ruskin, and Paul de Man in the most sophisticated modern critics.[11] In each of these essays, Blanchot's argument is tripartite:

(1) He delineates the author's project, his formal, theoretical, or philosophical intentions.

(2) He uncovers the precise point at which these intentions falter and run aground.

(3) He suggests, sometimes quite directly, sometimes with greater reserve, how the author might have remained faithful to his ideas—even providing, in some cases, his own illumination of the blind spot, his own rectification of the deviance that set the work off course.

For purposes of expository economy, I shall reduce my discussion of Blanchot's articles on Proust, Musil, and Kafka to a minimal, schematic presentation, in which I stress the tripartite organization rather than attempt to do justice to the rich variety of occasionally digressive comments that exceed the bounds of this tight structural dialectic.

PROUST

"L'Expérience de Proust"

In this very short early essay characterized by a Heideggerian vocabulary,[12] Blanchot emphasizes the theme of anguish (*angoisse*) in the *Recherche*, justifiably reminding Proust's readers of its importance as thematic counterpoint to the joyfulness that pervades the epiphanies of involuntary memory and artistic revelation in general.

(1) Sympathetic paraphrase of the alternations between anguish and felicity and exposition of Proust's desire to extend the psychological process of involuntary memory into the realm of knowledge (*connaissance*).

(2) Criticism of this effort at extension. Blanchot argues that there is absolute discontinuity between the moments of anguish experienced in their authenticity and the narrator's inauthentic efforts to resolve them through aesthetic transformation. Proust remains closest to the central core of his inspiration when he respects the mystery of the phenomena of memory and time in whose aura he writes; he betrays his own genius when he reduces these phenomena to a series of laws, to objects of positive knowledge.

(3) Indirectly and unexplicitly,[13] Blanchot suggests that the true work of art is located within anguish (understood in a rigorous existential sense) and that any move by the author or the critic to bypass or subdue it is a sign that he is blind to the hidden source of his art.

"L'Expérience de Proust," Second Version

Despite the title, this later essay is completely different from its predecessor both in content and in critical vocabulary.[14] Here Blanchot combines cogent remarks on the levels of time in Proust's work with his own explanation of the seemingly miraculous metamorphosis of Marcel Proust from immature and conventional third-person novelist in *Jean Santeuil* to innovator of first-person fiction in *A la recherche du temps perdu*.

(1) Description of Proust's theory of writing, including a section on the novelist's design to compose a "pure narration" (*récit pur*). In this connection, an interesting development on Proust's "transformation of time into imaginary space (that space inhabited by images" [23])[15] and a comparison of the *Recherche* to the formal perfection of a sphere.

(2) Criticism of *Jean Santeuil* as failed pure narration. Rather than render the timelessness of his aesthetic revelations palpable to the reader, the young Proust depicts these magical instants as *scenes*; and, rather than catch human beings in their hidden essence as momentary apparitions, he immobilizes them in *portraits* (32).

(3) The *Recherche* succeeds where *Jean Santeuil* fails—in representing the density of lived time and in restoring to the work of fiction what Blanchot calls "the immensity of the emptiness of space" (33). Blanchot implicitly suggests that, unlike *Jean Santeuil*, the *Recherche* approaches the essence of literature in its figuration of the central void from which narrative coherence derives. (In *Jean Santeuil*, Blanchot writes, "emptiness is not represented, but remains empty," whereas the final novel realizes the oxymoron of "emptiness as fullness" [33] ["le vide comme plénitude"].)

MUSIL

"Musil"

Blanchot's remarks on Musil's monumental and unclassifiable work of prose
The Man without Qualities (*Der Mann ohne Eigenschaften*) center on its impersonal narrative voice and on its mixed mode of discourse—half novel, half
treatise.[16] Blanchot deals briefly with the most controversial problem of the
work for Musil criticism—the apparently irreconcilable disparity, both formal
and thematic, between its two separately published parts—and includes a
personal judgment on the meaning of the concept *Eigenschaft* itself (which he
prefers to translate as *particularité* rather than *qualité*).

> (1) Description of Musil's ambitious project to write a novel that does not obey the
> laws of narrative chronology or succession, to forge a technique of fiction writing that
> abolishes Time as duration. Blanchot admires Musil's conception of literary language
> as equivalent in difficulty and abstraction to philosophical reasoning but as distinct
> from philosophy in expressing ideas that are "not *yet* thoughts" (204). The writer of
> fictions, in Blanchot's reading of Musil's intentions, is free to say anything and every-
> thing, except "la très habituelle parole qui prétend au sens et à la vérité" (ibid.) ("the
> most habitual word that pretends to express meaning and truth").
>
> (2) Although in the most beautiful parts of his work, Musil managed to distinguish
> carefully between the form-giving function of literary language and the truth telling
> of discursive thought, Blanchot finds that, in the end, Musil too often succumbs to
> the desire to explain, to theorize, to guide his reader through artificially contrived
> scenes whose didactic purpose is all too transparent.
>
> (3) In his negative final evaluation of Musil, we find an echo of Blanchot's own *ars
> poetica*, stated with uncharacteristic explicitness:
>
>> I see him [Musil], rather, as being unfaithful to himself for having consented to
>> divide his work into already specialized thoughts and concrete scenes, into theo-
>> retical statements and active characters, instead of moving back to the more
>> original point where, in the decision of a unique form, the word which is not yet
>> particularized, states the fullness and the void of the being without particulari-
>> ties [man without qualities]. (206)

KAFKA

"Kafka et l'exigence de l'oeuvre"

This is one of Blanchot's most penetrating analyses of Kafka, a study that
relies heavily on quoted material from the *Tagebücher* (*Diaries*) of 1910–1923
for illumination of Kafka's motivation to write.[17] At the center of Blanchot's
essay is the thesis that Kafka's deepest preoccupations were not exclusively

focused on the act of writing but also on the religious question of salvation (*le salut*).

(1) Description of the complex and murky confusion of writing and religion throughout Kafka's career, with emphasis on his fascination with the Zionist movement in the final years of his life. According to Blanchot, Zionism represented a temptation for Kafka in that it offered the hope of an end to exile, "the affirmation that the terrestrial sojourn is possible, that the Jewish people have as their dwelling place not only a book, the Bible, but earth itself and no longer dispersion in time" (80).

(2) Blanchot criticizes Kafka for subordinating the exacting demands of the literary work ("*l'exigence* de l'oeuvre") to his latter-day religious qualms, and he finds in the figure of the land surveyor (the protagonist of *The Castle*) the man of infinite wandering, the man of permanent exile, a more adequate representation of the truth of Kafka's work than the hopeful projections of the *Diaries* on the possibility of reaching the Promised Land.

(3) For Blanchot, there is an analogy between the land surveyor's perpetually deferred search and the movement by which the literary work tends toward its origin. In preferring exile to Zion, desert wandering to domestic sojourn, Blanchot allegorizes the act of literary creation as pure, never to be closed distance, or, in the words of his conclusion to this essay, as pure *exteriority*. For the poet (unlike the religious believer), there is no world in the sense of an extended space that can contain and ultimately overcome anguish through the harmony of a divinely guided human community; for him, there exists only the outside as uncontainable "flow": "le dehors, le *ruissellement* du dehors éternel" (98).

By juxtaposing Blanchot's essays on Proust, Musil, and Kafka in the abrupt form I have adopted for my own narrative purposes, it becomes possible, I hope, to see the outline of the movement of betrayal that runs through each individual article like a red thread. In his criticism of each author, Blanchot has corrective measures to propose: if Proust had remained faithful to his original insight on the temporal essence of the work of art, he would not have created the fixed scenes and portraits that mire *Jean Santeuil* (and some parts of the *Recherche* as well) in excessive immobility; if Musil had been true to his conception of the novel as the expression of the "not *yet* thought," he would not have become bogged down in explanatory commentary; and if Kafka had been able to distinguish between the impulse toward writing and the call of religion, his work would have expressed with greater clarity (with less rhetorical and symbolical confusion) the exiled condition of the writer, his state of permanent wanderer. In each case, the novelist under scrutiny is not far from the truth of the literary work—which Blanchot defines as the infinitely deferred and repeated hovering around an inexpressible original void; and the betrayal consists in the novelist's effort to free himself at some point and in some way from this circularity (the specific form this effort takes in an individual writer could be called his personal "style"; Proust, Musil, and Kafka have unique and incomparably interesting and beautiful ways of seeking escape from the labyrinth of their predicaments *as* writers).

In writing about Proust, Musil, and Kafka, Blanchot stands at a distance from their writings, and it would appear, at certain identifiable moments of his critical argumentation, that he knows something the novelist does not (that he has remembered the truth the novelist has forgotten or repressed). He suggests, throughout his essays, that the narrative fictions he is studying are not close enough to the inexpressible/unnamable source toward which they gravitate, and from which they ultimately recede. What remains at the level of suggestion in all these essays, however, is the notion of a narration (or narrative mode) that would be capable of adhering to the source, of translating its presence without betraying it through the excesses of theatrical representation (Proust), bavardage (Musil), or the confusion of categories (Kafka). If, for the creator of fictions, there is no other world beyond the domain of pure exteriority—as conveyed enigmatically in the image of the "ruissellement du dehors éternel"—then how does one *narrate* this exteriority? Is there a narration *of* exteriority that does not fall into the trap of attempting to trap (envelop) the ceaseless outward flow that it is destined (in Blanchot's critical scheme) to attain and transmit? Or, in the simplest terms, is narration condemned to be always a trap, an envelopment?

There is, within the devious circular ruminations of *L'Entretien infini*, one essay that addresses the problem of narrative in an explicitly theoretical mode—"La Voix narrative (le 'il,' le neutre)" and that appears to offer a way out of the envelopment impasse as I have described it. Blanchot begins his argument with a look backward toward *L'Espace littéraire* and the assertions therein concerning the impersonality of narrative, the passage from *je* (I) to *il* (*he*) that, in his view, constitutes the essence of the récit. He explains further that the adoption of third-person narration does not merely tend toward the kind of ironical distance characteristic of Flaubert (a distance that authorizes, in this author, a suspicious "jouissance contemplative," or narcissistic, contemplative pleasure or ecstasy), but that, beginning with Kafka, the separation between author and work *enters into* the work itself, in the form of an "irreducible strangeness" (562). No longer is it possible for the reader to keep his distance (preserve an attitude of aesthetic disinterest) from a text that, having swallowed up the constitutive distance-effect of narration, now becomes radically removed (*insituable*). Blanchot observes that because the reader no longer has a foothold in the unfolding of the narrative, because he is deprived of all interest, he is no longer in a position to observe at all: "Henceforth it is no longer a matter of vision. Narrative ceases to be that which makes things visible through the intermediary and within the point of view of a chosen actor/spectator" (563).

Understood in Blanchot's rigorous terms, narration is a movement of destitution or disappropriation of consciousness itself, a process of linguistic interruption that short-circuits the flow of understanding as conveyed by the priv-ileged image of light. Blanchot defines the narrative voice (*voix narrative*) as that which, being inaudible (*aphone*), having no existence of its own, lying in suspense throughout the récit, is radically exterior: "Elle vient de l'extériorité même, ce dehors qui est l'énigme propre du langage en l'écriture" (565) ("It comes from the very outside, that outside which is the proper mystery of language within writing"). Here, Blanchot brings back the notion of the "ruis-sellement du dehors éternel" and inserts it into a theoretical discourse that affirms the superiority of an exterior, spectral, phantomlike mode (the voix narrative can borrow the voice of a fictional character temporarily but can never "incarnate itself" permanently) over what he calls the narrating voice (*voix narratrice*). Blanchot never explains openly what he means by voix narra-trice (the term appears just once in the essay and is never defined), but it seems clear that it designates the "opposite" of the voix narrative—or, in the most general sense, that it is associated with the fullness of consciousness, of memory, of subjectivity. In his reading of Blanchot's elliptical récit of madness and light *La Folie du jour* (*The Madness of the Day*), during one of his own theoretical pauses, Jacques Derrida describes the terminological dichotomy in these terms:

> The narrative voice [voix narrative], says Blanchot, is "a neutral voice that expresses the work from that place without a place where the work is quiet": a silent voice, therefore, withdrawn in its voicelessness. This voicelessness [*aphonie*] distinguishes it from the "narrating voice" [voix narratrice], which literary criticism, poetics or narratology try to situate in the system of narration or of the novel. The narrating voice derives from a subject who tells something, remembering an event or a histor-ical sequence, knowing who he is, where he is, and of what he speaks. (*Parages*, 149–50)

If there were to be a narration of pure exteriority, therefore, it would be the expression of the voix narrative rather than of the voix narratrice; it would be inaccessible to poetics and to narratology; and it would not be traceable to a remembering and knowing subject. *La voix narrative, c'est l'insituable*: this, in its most concentrated formulation, is Blanchot's theory of a narration that can never be situated within a theory. At this point of theoretical impasse, I would like to turn to the analysis of Blanchot's method or manner of narration, using three of his prose fantasies—*Thomas l'obscur* (*Thomas the Obscure*), *Au Moment voulu* (*When the Time Comes*), and *L'Attente l'oubli*—to study the degree to which his fictional praxis fits, extends, or negates the insights of his critical readings and the speculative logic of his narrative theory.

To begin an analysis of Blanchot's fictions is particularly difficult not only because of their obscurity (the near-indescribable quality of their content, structure, and temporal progression) but also because of their inextricable interconnectedness. Each fiction implies or calls forth its neighbor, and the boundaries separating the individually dated and titled works often seem to recede in favor of an intertextual nexus of relations whose uncanny connotative capacity exceeds all limitations of narrative ordering and formal control. In his prefatory remarks to the 1950 version of *Thomas l'obscur*, Blanchot explains that all works of the imagination are indefinite in the forms they temporarily assume: they all contain within themselves as a constitutive feature the capacity to be rewritten. Because the act of writing is an infinite search for an absent origin, because all texts gravitate around this original point without ever reaching it, it is in the nature of texts to repeat themselves, to emerge in repeatedly new representational or figural guises. This general law applies to the specific fiction entitled *Thomas l'obscur*, whose 1950 version has a history:

> There is, for every work, an infinity of possible variations. To the pages entitled *Thomas l'obscur*, written beginning in 1932, submitted to the editor in May 1940, published in 1941, the present version adds nothing, but since it removes much from them, one can call it different and even entirely new, but also exactly the same, if, between the figure and what is or appears to be its center, one is correct in not distinguishing, each time that the completed figure itself expresses only the search for an imaginary center. (7)

Using the same rhetoric of centrality he will employ five years later in the preface to *L'Espace littéraire*, Blanchot emphasizes not only the importance of the major surgery he has performed on the text (the elimination of one of the two female characters and of much episodic material; the toning down of a rather precious Giralducian style)[18] but also the paradoxical idea that a seemingly "new" fiction, a fiction with changed narrative boundaries and altered stylistic qualities, is, on a deeper level, *the same* as its predecessor, in that it also is nothing but the movement toward the void of an imaginary center. Essential to Blanchot's argument is the collapsing of center and figuration into each other; the two become inseparable or indistinguishable because the superficial differences between *Thomas*-first version and *Thomas*-second version, for example, are mere scintillating traces that disappear once one has recognized the immutable inevitability of figuration *as* search for the center. What is at stake in *Thomas* and in all of Blanchot's fictions is the question of figuration as such—and the difference between what could be called surface figuration (the observable, codifiable semantic and formal features that are unique to a given work and that distinguish it from all others, those elements accessible to narratology and poetics) and deep figuration (the fundamental identity between what is represented and its movement toward representation, the return of figural displacement per se to its point of origin in the text's generational void). I shall keep this issue and this distinction in mind as I turn now to the cryptic illuminations of *Thomas l'obscur.*

Of all Blanchot's fictional experiments, *Thomas* is perhaps the clearest in its straightforward narrative presentation, its adherence to an evolution of temporal and spatial order. In its rewritten version, it stands at the crossroads between the Kafkaesque and fantastical allegories of *Aminadab* (1942) and *Le Très-Haut* (1948)[19] and the increasingly pure *récits* of the fifties and sixties that seem to dispense not only with the mythical/symbolical mode but also with the delineation of scenes whose concatenation results in the illusion of progression: *Au Moment voulu* (1951) (*When the Time Comes*), *Celui qui ne m'accompagnait pas* (1953) (*The One Who Was Standing Apart From Me*), *Le Dernier Homme* (1957) (*The Last Man*), *L'Attente l'oubli* (1962). If one were obliged to describe the subject of *Thomas l'obscur*, one might call it a novel of consciousness, a fictional representation of the movement of consciousness as negative dialectic, as experience of ultimate absence. The *récit* itself is divided into twelve numbered but untitled chapters each of which thrusts the protagonist Thomas or his female companion Anne into a new scene or situation; and each scene becomes the imaginary space of a mental testing—whether in the form of a game, *épreuve*, or hallucinatory encounter with the frightening forces of alterity.

The first five chapters center on Thomas, who moves progressively from the ocean to a cave to a restaurant to a room to a cellar; in these places, his consciousness undergoes radical transformations, and he struggles not only with death but also with the violence of the written word and with the dispossessing force of his thought divided against itself.[20] Thomas's descent into the cellar and his subsequent return in chapter V are represented as death followed by a kind of resurrection: the same form prevails later, in chapter VIII, when Anne's descent and return are described in mythological terms, as the path of Eurydice (97). The central chapters are devoted to the "union" of Thomas and Anne, where the question of Love merges with a discourse on Being. After Anne's sickness and death (chapter X), there is a complex meditation on existence—one could call the passage that occupies the second half of chapter XI Blanchot's cogito—and a final chapter in which the protagonist walks through a vernal countryside surrounded by a profusion of images that assault and seduce his senses.

As a whole, the *récit* is highly metaphorical. The text begins and ends with water imagery, and the other primary elements, especially earth and fire, constantly reappear in a variety of guises. Blanchot's "themes" are creation, life, love, and death; they are developed poetically as the *merging* of Thomas's consciousness with the elements of nature, as the smooth interchange of properties between Thomas as cognizing subject and the world from which he derives and into which he projects his imaginative freedom. From the very beginning of the story, when Thomas plunges into the ocean, Blanchot emphasizes the disappearance of the boundaries separating the human subject from its natural environment:

. . . whether because of fatigue or for some unknown reason, his limbs gave him the same sensation of strangeness as the water in which they floated. This sensation seemed pleasurable to him at first. He pursued, in swimming, a kind of dream in which he merged with the water. The ecstasy of leaving one's own body, of slipping into the void, of releasing oneself into the water's thought [*la pensée de l'eau*], caused him to forget all malaise. (11)

Thomas is enveloped in the ocean, which appears itself to be wrapped up within a dream. The water may be, in its poetic truth, the thought *of* water ("la pensée de l'eau"); and, in general, it is difficult to localize where the phenomenal world ends and the consciousness *of* things begins. Throughout *Thomas*, the two protagonists experience the world as a prodigious mass of images, as a hallucinatory space whose metamorphosing elements result in a kaleidoscope of hybrid, supranatural, monstrous forms. We are in a universe reminiscent both of Flaubert's *La Tentation de Saint Antoine* and of Rimbaud's *Illuminations*, in which levels and categories and species collapse, then come together to create impossible, violent, and seductive visions:

It seemed to him [Thomas] that the waves were invading the abyss that he had become. Yet this worried him little. He focused his attention uniquely on his hands, which were busy recognizing the beings mingled with him whose character they could discern partially—a dog represented by one ear, a bird replacing the tree on which it used to sing. Thanks to these beings that had given themselves over to acts escaping all interpretation, edifices and entire cities built themselves up, real cities of nothingness and of thousands of piled on rocks, creatures rolling amid the blood and sometimes tearing the arteries, who now assumed the role of what Thomas once called ideas and passions. (18–19)

Once Thomas's consciousness has become a permeable abyss, not only is it impossible to distinguish between the "inside" of human mental activity and the "outside" of objective reality, but the representatives and representations of the real themselves lose unity and wholeness. The imaginary world into which we penetrate here, and which will appear in increasingly expanded descriptive frenzy as the protagonist's psychodrama unfolds, is that of the *fragment*. As in the paintings of Hieronymus Bosch, parts of the human being and of animals and of artifacts of civilization cohabitate in grotesque juxtaposition. In Blanchot's visionary mode of creation, there is no transcendent subjectivity to encompass the scene and give it order: Thomas, as "invaded abyss," as space of neutral openness, is reduced to a bare optical attentiveness; separated from his own body, he can only observe its manifestations and transformations. Into this essentially visual configuration Blanchot injects a linguistic—or, more precisely, rhetorical—dimension when he describes the "beings" attached to Thomas's hands as "a dog represented by one ear, a bird replacing the tree in which it used to sing." The emphasis here and in the subsequent lines of the description is on the difficulty, or even the impossibility, of interpreting these figures *in* their fragmentary presentation. Through the synecdochic relation of the ear to the dog, we might, with some luck, recompose the whole from the evidence of the part; but in the case of the purely haphazard spatial link between bird and tree, it is only the narrator's assertion (his "word") that allows the reader to pass through the given image of the bird to the tree it supposedly replaces. It is precisely *because* these figures are entirely arbitrary and thereby escape all interpretation that cities made from rock *and* nothingness can rise up on the horizon of the imagination, blocking out and replacing the manifestations of consciousness (the "ideas and passions" from Thomas's past life, from his life before the plunge into the abyss of images).

In the movement of its self-negation, consciousness recedes into nothingness; its disappearance brings on the emergence of images, their profusion, their dynamic progression. At the center of the figural narration of *Thomas l'obscur* is a void, a spot that has no existence itself but that remains as both the evidence of a vanishing and as the organizing principle of the récit. The narrator calls our attention to this principle as his text slips into a theoretical reflection on its own constitution:

> It was a story empty of events, empty to the point that all memory and all perspective had been eliminated from it, and yet drawing from this absence its inflexible course which seemed to carry all things away in an irresistible movement toward an imminent catastrophe. (55)

In *Thomas*, the inflexible course of narration carries us from an original absence toward an imminent "catastrophe"—which we might best understand, in the etymological sense, as an *overturning* or a *sudden turn*. Narration is the progression from the void of a self-negating consciousness to the proliferation of figures, to the twisting and turning of tropes. And this passage from nothingness to figuration produces, in Blanchot's text, the power of *vision*— the apotheosis of light as focal point and mirror for the infinite engendering of fantastic metamorphoses. We see the origin of light and of figural play in the negative cogito as pronounced by Thomas in the text's eleventh chapter, from which I excerpt a short but representative passage:

> "I think, therefore I am not" [*Je pense, donc je ne suis pas*]. These words brought toward me a delicious vision. In the middle of an immense field, a flaming magnifying glass received the dispersed rays of the sun, and, by these rays, became conscious of itself as a monstrous self, not in the points at which it received them, but at the point toward which it projected them and unified them in a unique cluster. At this focal point, center of a terrible burning, the glass was marvelously active, it illuminated, it burned, it devoured; the entire universe became flame where it was touched by the devastation of the glass. And yet I saw that this mirror was like a living animal

consumed by its own fire. The earth it engulfed in flame was its entire body reduced
to powder and, from this ceaseless fire it drew, in a torrent of sulphur and gold, the
consequence of its incessant annihilation. (114–15)

From the initial anti-Cartesian declaration,[21] we move toward the appearance of a vision, which itself depends upon the principle of metamorphosis:
the magnifying glass becomes a mirror, which changes into an animal con-
suming itself in fire. In representing visually and allegorically the theme of
centrality and of origins that we have seen at work in his critical writings,
Blanchot here imagines the conflation of unification and destruction in the
image of a glass whose projective focal energy results in universal annihilation.
It could be argued that *Thomas* as text never truly exceeds the problematic of
consciousness, as the transformations of the vision from magnifying glass to
mirror to animal conclude in a curiously concrete and apocalyptic figuration
of the "drawing of consequences"—itself a privileged act of the human consciousness. The allegory of figuration as derivation from an initial void, as
narrative of images emanating from the endless reversals of negation, does not,
finally, attain a level at which language emancipates itself from the imagining
subject. In *Thomas l'obscur*, Blanchot opens up the domain of figural play from
the origin of an absent source, but that source, in remaining present even in
its "presque disparition vibratoire," is never itself open to question, and there
is no liberation of the signifier in the absolute Barthesian sense. What remains,
when Blanchot's text has consumed itself in the fire of its metaphorical richness, is the *question* of the origin of figuration, of tropic displacement as such,
and this question is inseparable from the problem of *narrative* origins, as we
shall see in his later fictions, toward which we now turn our gaze.

Published in 1951, just one year after the second version of *Thomas l'obscur*,
Au Moment voulu (*When the Time Comes*) inaugurates a series of récits, written
by Blanchot in the fifties and early sixties, whose universe shrinks to that of an
impersonal room or series of rooms connected by a hallway, in which a narrator-protagonist shares his life with a woman or women. Although it is quite
difficult to affirm with any degree of certainty what these narratives are about
(there is no plot or action in the traditional sense), and because the issues with
which the disembodied "characters" wrestle are often at a very high level of
abstraction, the most that can be said is that there seem to be two themes that
predominate: (1) the nature of the relations (rapports) that link together the
characters—the brusque fluctuations between erotic intimacy, indifference,
and violent repulsion that punctuate the movement of the text; and (2) the
problem of time as it is lived by the characters, as it is reflected on by them in
dialogue, and as it embodies narrative progression per se. In *Au Moment voulu*,
both themes assume a fundamental role in the construction and resolution of
the récit. The nameless narrator-protagonist begins his story by a description
of his encounter with a woman named Judith, whom he had known at an

undefined moment in the past, and who, to his great surprise, opens the door to the dwelling in which the remainder of the fiction will take place *instead of* the woman he expected to find in this situation, whose name is Claudia. Blanchot establishes immediately that the significance of his story will hinge on the evolving rapports of the triangle composed by the protagonist and the two women and that the degree of closeness of each figure to the other will depend upon the complex temporal movement of the text. Thus, we read in the opening paragraph:

> In the absence of the friend who lived with her, the door was opened by Judith. My surprise was extreme, inextricable, much greater, assuredly, than if I had met her by chance. The surprise was such that it expressed itself in me through these words: "My God! another acquaintance!" [literally: "My God! another figure of my knowledge!"—*Mon Dieu! encore une figure de connaissance!*]. (Perhaps my decision to walk straight toward this figure had been so strong as to render it [the figure itself] impossible). But there was also the discomfort at having come to verify on the scene the continuity of things. Time had passed, and yet was not past; that was the truth that I should not have had the desire to put into my presence. (7–8)

In this introductory passage, Blanchot sets forth in somewhat enigmatic terms the essential questions that will be developed, in the style of theme and variations, throughout the remainder of *Au Moment voulu*. As will be the case later in the text, language is engendered through chance meeting and violent confrontation, through a situation in which an uncanny substitution takes place (here, Judith appears instead of Claudia). The phrase "Mon Dieu! encore une *figure de connaissance!*" is both innocuous in its literal sense (the protagonist has met, or seems to have met, Judith before and to have much in common with her, as we discover further on in the narrative) and full of connotative potential for this context and for the entirety of the récit: Judith *as* character can be interpreted as a figure of knowledge, as a figuration of the process of understanding as such. The word *figure* and the problematic of figuration emerge so often in the text, in dozens of scenes, in innumerable concatenations, that it would not be an exaggeration to affirm that the principal problem of *Au Moment voulu*, what makes it function as text, is the figure. But we know, from the start, not only the not-so-comforting fact that the word *figure* can function both literally and figuratively but also that its association with knowledge does not preclude its own destruction or "impossibility"; the narrator's purposeful steps toward Judith, his straightforward walk, seem to figure the impossibility of figuration, to block out the figural in the precipitation of an overly directed pace. At the same time, we learn that the process of verification employed by the narrator to ascertain what he calls the "continuity of things" founders against the negative truth of time—the paradox of a temporal process that has run its course but that *also* has not passed, is not *of* the past. The revolutionary nature of *Au Moment voulu* as fiction consists of its simultaneous coupling of figuration and temporality to questions of truth and knowledge and of its presentation of impossibility and paradox as the *états-limite* of the figural and temporal dimensions of the récit. As the reader moves through the text, his twin interpretive concerns become (1) how is the figure created, from what point does it originate, what level of presence/absence does it occupy? and (2) what is the narrative organization of a récit constructed on temporal paradox; are there articulations within the structural design of the fiction that point to a narrative order of some kind; and if so, is this order describable, knowable within the framework of critical/theoretical understanding?

When confronting the matter of figuration in *Au Moment voulu*, it is necessary to keep in mind that it does not emerge immediately in theoretical abstraction or as an obvious subject for literary meditation; it is associated, rather, with the changing levels of intimacy of the three major characters in the story and with the theme of *passion* as such. As in Bataille's scheme of love, erotic moments in Blanchot are violent and absolute—they participate in the movements of démesure and subjective dispossession. One senses that the strong impulses motivating the protagonist of *Au Moment voulu* to join with Claudia in a physical union are less those of "possession" in the usual sense than of annihilation. Yet when, after emitting a "prodigious cry"[22] and throwing himself upon Claudia in an act of powerful disregard for her person, the narrator pauses to reflect upon the nature of his contact with her and Judith, he begins to see himself as existing *outside* the constricted physical universe of the story, outside the rooms and the hallway, away from the objects of his desire. It is as if the momentary achievement of close physical contact had as its principal effect (*contre-coup*) the projection of the protagonist not only away from Claudia and Judith but also away from himself; and it is in the very moment of this projection that the word *figure* invades the text, as expression of the protagonist's status as outsider and unreal, phantom like observer of the inaccessible inside. After the scene of erotic violence, when Claudia returns to the room, the narrator writes: "Je compris que je me trouvais là-bas, dans le froid léger, calme, nullement désagréable du dehors" (92) ("I understood that I was now over there, in the light, calm and not unpleasant cold of the outside"). He then proceeds at greater length:

> Certainly it would have been simpler for me at that moment to be a figure of the outside [*une figure du dehors*] plunging into the inside of the room and questioning with my gaze those who were living there, and no doubt I did really have this feeling, but perhaps such a figure was all I could comprehend then and all the others could stand of the truth. . . . And what was I then if I was not the reflection of a figure without speech and to whom no one spoke, only capable, with the support of the endless tranquillity of the outside, of questioning the world in silence, from the other side of the window? (93–94)

The effort of the protagonist to enfold and negate the woman in the violence of his grasp results in his expulsion from the center of the love drama, in his new location on the tranquil outside, at the periphery of things. It is the impossibility of seizing or destroying the other (*l'autre*) that transforms the human, living self into a figure—or even a reflection of a figure. To be a figure, according to the figurations of *Au Moment voulu*, is to be *merely* a reflection—that is, a secondary, insubstantial image hovering at some distance from the truth. This is not just the case for the protagonist but also for Judith, who, at one point in her life (if we believe the narrator's suppositions) departed the domain of substance and entered the realm of the image:

> Something happened to her [Judith] which resembled the story of Abraham. When the latter came back from Moriah, he was not accompanied by his child, but by the image of a ram, and it is with the ram that he had to live henceforth. The others saw the son in Isaac, because they were ignorant of what had taken place on the mountaintop, but he saw the ram in the son, because he had made of his son a ram. Overwhelming story [*Histoire accablante*]. I think that Judith had gone up to the mountain, but freely. (147)

In the biblical story (Genesis 22:1–14), God asks Abraham to sacrifice his son Isaac, and Abraham's anguished willingness to do so stands as dramatic testimony to the overcoming of self and family that is a necessary step toward the understanding of Divine Will in its challenging and paradoxical manifestations. God's reward to Abraham—his last-minute substitution of a ram for Isaac—is also a transformational ruse with linguistic implications as, to the believer, the ram comes to *symbolize* the son, to carry the significance of the son in its image (in Christian typology, the "lamb of God" of the Genesis story will be seen as one in a series of foreshadowings of God's ultimate sacrifice of Christ for the redemption of humankind). In Blanchot's reading of the story as *histoire accablante*, Abraham returns from the mountain unable to see his son in his physical reality, now seeing only the image of the ram—the insubstantial figure that, from God's standpoint, was intended only as a temporary and expendable substitute for the son and his significance. Judith is like this Abraham, except that her descent into images was an act of freedom and not the final consequence of an initial constraint. It is tempting to read in this free-fall into the space of image or figure, this living with the insubstantiality of reflections, an allegory of the writer's fate as phantom exiled to the margins of existence, as pure optical presence on the *other* side of human drama. The possibility of such an interpretation, indeed its inevitability, emerges from the central scene of the récit, the moment at which the temporal progress of the narration inscribes its origin.

Despite the meandering movement of the story through much of its length, toward the end of its development the narrator seems to trace for us the central action from which the entirety of the fiction derives. While the observing eye of the protagonist looks on from its place of privileged distance, Claudia contemplates the sleeping Judith; then, in an attempt to wake her, she begins to open Judith's closed fist. At this moment, "Judith, with prodigious vitality, sat up and screemed two words,—then sank back into bed" (132). Several pages later, we learn that these words were "*Nescio vos*, 'Je ne sais qui vous êtes'" (137) ("*Nescio vos*, 'I do not know who you are'"). Judith's violent assertion of the impossibility of knowing her two interlocutors stands as/at the origin of the récit; whatever temporal movement the fiction possesses moves outward from this center. Yet the narrator warns us cryptically that the moment itself, although it seems to have occurred once and once only, although it seems to bring in its wake the necessity of "meditation," may not have caused or engendered any definable subsequent action:

> Of such a scene, no one could ever say that it had already taken place; it had happened a first and unique time, and its exuberance had all the vigor of the origin, from which nothing derives [*et son exubérance était la vigueur de l'origine, d'où rien ne découle*]. Even when I came back to the scene to think about it—and it necessitated that: a powerful meditation—, it led me nowhere. (133–34)

At first, the scene's "original vigor" blocks out all relations with past and future time; the very uniqueness of the scene is such that the protagonist becomes lost in his search for coherence. Yet we learn shortly after this passage that when Claudia returns toward the protagonist (immediately after Judith's Latin cry of *Nescio vos*), looking at him from the hallway through the open door, her physical attitude—the geometry of her body—reminds him of a moment from his past when another woman in a similar setting looked at him in the same way. This instant was so perfect in its ideal tranquillity, so devoid of all anguish and threats of intimate violence, that the narrator calls it *le moment voulu* (139)—the wished-for or willed moment—which is, of course, the title of the récit. Thus the possibility arises that the central or original moment of the story—the moment willed by the author and wished for by the reader—is *not* the absolute vigor and void from which nothing derives but rather an event that can be contextualized, that evokes, via memory, the unity of a man's life, its essential continuity, its sameness. In fact, Blanchot does not decide between these two interpetations of the origin of his story, but insists upon the ambiguity of temporal occurrences as such. What remains from the vigor of the original scene is not its substance but its *figure*, and this figure entertains with time "the strangest of relations." I now quote one final pasage from *Au Moment voulu*, whose rhetoric of paradox prepares us for the complexities of *L'Attente l'oubli* and for Blanchot's turn away from the form of the récit:

> But this figure [i.e., the figure of the scene] was not concerned with memory, it was fixed but unstable. Had it taken place once? One first time and yet not the first. It

entertained with time the strangest of relations, and that also was cause for exalta-
tion: it did not belong to the past, a figure and the promise of this figure. It had, in
a sense, looked at and seized itself in a unique instant, after which had taken place
this terrifying contact, this mad catastrophe, which could be considered its fall into
time, but this fall had also passed through time in burrowing within it an empty
immensity, and this abyss appeared as the jubilant festivity of the future: a future
that would never be again, just as the past refused to have taken place at one unique
time. (135)

In the end, the figure emerges as that paradoxical "event"that cannot belong
to the past and as that reverberation of human space which cannot be located
within a temporal frame. The figure participates in what Blanchot calls the
"movement of catastrophe," a fall through time that digs within time an immense void; and this fall, this descent within the atopic dimension of a "jubilant future," is narration—or, more precisely, is the figuration of Blanchot's
voix narrative in all its unlocalizable, disruptive power. At the conclusion of
Au Moment voulu, the multifaceted problematic of the figure merges with,
melts into, the abyss of time. The récit turns into itself and becomes the
reflected image of its own narrative emergence from the empty center of the
human unknowable.

L'Attente l'oubli, Blanchot's last sustained fiction before the concentrated
and elliptical *La Folie du jour* (1973), repeats and finalizes the series of works
from 1951 until 1962 whose universe had been the limited space of the impersonal room and its meandering hallway. As in *Au Moment voulu*, the action or
"plot" of *L'Attente l'oubli* is reduced to the story of the relations (rapports)
between an unnamed protagonist and a female figure (in this case there is
only one woman, but she has no name and no identifiable characteristics); but
in the latter work, the nature of the relation is less erotic than purely linguistic,
and the theme of time, which had been essential but not alone in importance
within the totality of *Au Moment voulu*, becomes so overwhelming in its omni-
presence as to overshadow all other themes in the récit. *L'Attente l'oubli* is one
lengthy dialogue; or, more precisely, it stages the possibilities and limits of
verbal exchange against the backdrop of a constantly shifting temporal flux.
From the very beginning of the narration, the female character begins to utter
what will become the leitmotiv of the text: "Fais en sorte que je puisse te
parler" (14, 24–25, 57, and *passim*) ("Make it possible for me to speak to you").
Yet in uttering her request or prayer (*prière*), she is already speaking; and
Blanchot plays, throughout the fiction, with the following temporal paradox:
that the two characters, who do not seem to know where or whether they have
met before, who may have nothing in common—no shared experience, no
shared past—nevertheless are engaged in the very process about whose possibility they are anxiously inquiring. This circularity of the *toujours déjà* (always
already) scheme that characterizes the dispossessed position of the human

being within language (and that became, in structuralist and poststructuralist critical discourse, a leitmotiv in its own right) is not sufficient in itself to explain Blanchot's preoccupation with the way in which speech, especially dialogue, originates. We are always already *in language*, but the word for which we search may not be of the same essence as the words we are already uttering while searching for that word. We are carried along in time, in dialogue, and in human relations, but what we seek is behind or beyond or beside all this, for we seek an *other* word (*une autre parole*):

> She gave the impression, when she spoke, of not knowing how to link [relate] her words to the richness of a previously existing language. They were without history, without relation to the past of all people, even without relation to her own life, or to the life of anyone. . . .
>
> He began to hear next to what she said, and as if behind her voice, but in an expanse without depth, without high nor low, and yet with a material location, an other word [une autre parole] with which his own had almost nothing in common.
>
> *Make it possible for me to speak to you.* (24–25; Blanchot's emphasis)

One can understand, from passages such as these, why Blanchot has been labelled a hermetic or esoteric writer. The mysterious "other word" not only exists in an expanse without dimensions, but it is "without relation" to human life as such. The purified form of expression that has its peculiar mode of being alongside the language of received human significance never touches or intersects with the existential sphere, yet we are invited to believe that this language beyond language, this speech in its possibility as speech, stands at the very center of the récit's significance and of its narrative origination. *L'Attente l'oubli* is the story of the temporal alternations between waiting and forgetfulness that characterize the dialogic situation; but it is also the properly narrative movement that derives from, reproduces, or figures the search for the pure language of otherness that repeats itself compulsively throughout the text.

In a crucial sense, *L'Attente l'oubli* is the logical final stage in the process that passes from the metamorphoses of consciousness (*Thomas l'obscur*) through the problematic of figuration within a temporal framework (*Au Moment voulu*) to a meditation on the pure or empty form of temporality as it exists beyond human relations and historical determination. In this process, we move increasingly away from concreteness and from that which lends itself to representation, and we arrive at that conception of literature as self-referential and "irresponsible" exteriority which has become especially suspect in recent times. It may be that the immediate and anguished task of the next generation of literary scholars and philosophers, given the documented pasts of figures such as Heidegger, Blanchot, and Paul de Man, must become the examination of the temptation that a purified notion of temporality represents for human beings who have reasons to deny time in its concrete historical reality.[23]

If *L'Attente l'oubli* possesses a narrative order of some type, this order must convey the temporal frame of the rapports between the protagonist and the woman with whom he pursues his dialogue. The man and the woman are (or find themselves [*se trouvent*]) in a small hotel room with a long, winding corridor—but how did the woman arrive at this place, and what, if any, is the evolution of the relations linking the two characters from their first encounter until the end of the story? If we can answer these simple questions (even if the answers prove complex), we can say something about the narrative mode of the récit. If such questions are unanswerable or irrelevant to the textual structure, the very possibility of speaking *about* narrative becomes problematic, suspect.

Despite the high level of abstraction of the ideas exchanged in the dialogue, and despite the fiction's apparent organization as a series of disconnected atemporal fragments, Blanchot is obviously and explicitly concerned with the concrete question of the origin of the encounter between the man and his female companion. The author's multiple presentation of the encounter in separate passages of *L'Attente l'oubli* gives evidence of his interest in the temporal predicament of the couple. Thus, one-third of the way through the text (after there has already been substantial verbal exchange between the two participants), the narrator writes:

> She was seated, immobile, at the table; stretched out against him on his bed; sometimes standing near the door and then coming from very far away. It is thus that he had seen her first [*C'est ainsi qu'il l'avait vue d'abord*]. Standing, having entered without saying anything and not even looking around her, as if she had gathered together within herself all the presence of the place. (59)

In this particular presentation, the narrator affirms unequivocally that there was an original moment, an original moment of encounter ("C'est ainsi qu'il l'avait vue *d'abord*"). But the way in which the woman appears to the protagonist is discontinuous, fragmented: she is sometimes seated and immobile, sometimes stretched out in bed, sometimes near the door. She appears in isolated, frozen postures that tend to negate temporal flow in the evolutionary or developmental sense. As in the prose of Claude Simon, the accumulation of participial forms (*étendue* [stretched out], *venant* [coming], *étant entrée* [having entered]) produces the impression of separate photographic images rather than the continuity of film. At the end of the passage we are left with the mystery of a female presence who, we are told, did once appear in the room for the first time, but who seems to have gathered within herself, from the very beginning (*depuis toujours* [from the beginning before all particular beginnings]), the "presence" of the place: the woman becomes a curious modern incarnation of the classical genius loci.

As one progressively penetrates the pages of *L'Attente l'oubli*, one begins to surmise that the characters as actants within the dialogic structure of the text are less important in their specificity or particularity than is the verbal/temporal drama in which they are engaged and which far surpasses their limits. What matters most in the récit may not be the humanized figuration of one's waiting and forgetting, but rather the pure structures of waiting and forgetting precisely insofar as they exceed all particular figures for whom one might wait and whom one might forget. Within Blanchot's paradoxically formulated definitions of l'attente and l'oubli, we recognize clearly that the objects of waiting and forgetting are secondary to the empty movement that encompasses them:

> Since when had he begun to wait? Since he had made himself free for waiting by losing the desire for particular things and even the desire for the end of things. Waiting begins when there is nothing else for which to wait, not even the end of waiting. Waiting ignores and destroys that for which it waits. Waiting waits for nothing.
>
> However important the object of one's waiting, it is always infinitely surpassed by the movement of waiting. Waiting makes all things equally important, equally vain. (51)

> We do not go toward forgetfulness, no more than forgetfulness comes to us, but suddenly forgetfulness has always already been there, and when we forget, we have always already forgotten everything: we are, in the movement toward forgetfulness, linked to the presence of the immobility of forgetfulness.
>
> Forgetfulness relates to that which forgets itself. And this relation, which renders secret that to which it relates, holds the power and the meaning of the secret. (87)

The structures of waiting and forgetfulness are such as to deny and destroy the significance of particular things and specific moments, of the punctual nature of phenomena and illuminated instants. From the unlocatable (insituable) "moment" at which the protagonist liberated himself from the desire for particular things, he also freed himself from the desire for finality—which is the principal law of narrative progression: the "sense of an ending" without which there can be no definable or analyzable narrative order. To define waiting as waiting for nothing, to call it a leveling force that renders all things equally important and equally vain, is to evoke a movement that exceeds the scheme of cause and effect, before and after, without which narratologists cannot spin their hierarchies and classifications. To say that forgelfulness is not forgetfulness of something but an infinite, always already annihilation of everything from the memory is to affirm that this movement as well has thrown time out of joint, to such an extent that the very notion of temporal succession (or projection, or retrospection along a determined chronological axis) is evacuated from the pure, self-enclosed, paradoxical logic of the récit. When, toward the end of L'Attente l'oubli, the narrator includes a four-page passage (117–20) that returns to the "first" meeting of the man and woman and that seems to establish its margins in the moment of an original sign and its reception (the protagonist has made an undecipherable gesture toward the woman, who is on her balcony, and it is presumably for an interpretation of this gesture that she comes across to the protagonist's room), the only way for the reader to take this scenic representation of origins seriously is to *forget* what the narrator has already told him about forgetfulness and waiting, to repress his negative foreknowledge of the empty, pure, relationless nature of the text and its inaudible (aphone) call for meaning.

There is within *L'Attente l'oubli* a double rhythm. On the one hand, through repetition and an apparently conclusive recapitulation, the récit stages the drama of narrative origination and inscribes the seductive possibility of anchoring itself *in* time within its own pages, en abyme. In Blanchot's own theoretical terms, this effort to localize and to define within time and space would be the task of the voix narratrice, which would be at work here as re-membering subject, as historicizing, temporalizing consciousness. On the other hand, however, in the recurring ironical undercurrent of the narrator's atemporal meditations on the significant potential of the terms *attente* and *oubli*, we recognize the neutrality, the exteriority, and the limitless atopicality of the voix narrative.

Like the novelists whom he criticized for introducing excessive explanatory commentary into the pure design of their aesthetic projects, Blanchot does not avoid falling away from the voix narrative as pure voice of the *insituable* into the particularizing determinations of the voix narratrice. But this fall, which, for reasons of our own theoretical coherence, we should call a *betrayal*, is a necessary, entirely unavoidable element in the constitution of the récit. Despite the increasing purity of Blanchot's narrative fictions—as conveyed in the passage away from consciousness through the problematic of figuration and toward a logic of absolute paradox beyond all definable representational norms—the end point of a narrative completely free of things and of history is never reached. One can summon, in and through language, an image of writing as empty exteriority and call it the "ruissellement du dehors éternel," but in narrating this exteriority, one falls into the constant betrayals of excessive meaningfulness, referential saturation, time as impure process. If Blanchot never achieved the pure narrative of which he dreamed, it is not because of some technical failure nor because of an insufficiency in his theoretical apparatus, but rather because of the impurities of the narrative flow itself—those foreign objects, those erring, hard-to-assimilate, jagged and scintillating edges, whose function is to keep alive subjective memory, even as the mind projects itself, inevitably and precariously, into the places beyond time of its self-made fictional fantasies.

Chapter Six

BECKETT AND THE ETHICS OF FABULATION

> "La fin est dans le commencement et cependant on continue."
> —*Fin de partie*
> "The end is in the beginning and yet you go on."
> —*Endgame*

> "Se créant des chimères pour tempérer son néant."
> —*Compagnie*
> "Devising figments to temper his nothingness."
> —*Company*

IN NEARLY ALL of Samuel Beckett's works—both drama and prose fiction—the question of an impending finality looms large on the horizon of the reader's interpretive expectations. We sense, as readers or spectators, that something is moving ineluctably toward an end point, even though, in a number of Beckett's writings, it would seem that the end of human life has already been reached and that we find ourselves at a purgatorial threshold, waiting for the door to open outward—but unsure that there is an outside beyond the confines of our limited physical world and reduced mental capacities. Hamm's cryptic statement in *Fin de partie* (1957)[1] quoted above—"La fin est dans le commencement et cependant on continue"—is emblematic not only of what has been called, perhaps reductively, Beckett's "pessimism" (i.e., what is the point of continuing if the end is already included within the beginning?), but also, perhaps more crucially, of the inevitability of what I shall call *narrative fabulation*: the unrolling of a fiction as end-oriented process from within an initial static situation that appears to preclude imaginative flight. One continues *nevertheless*, whether to live, in the usual sense of that word (to subsist within a physical or natural environment), or to tell stories, in order to pass the time. Or, to borrow from the narrator's ruminations in *Compagnie* (1980), a text far removed from *Fin de partie* both in its generic constitution and in the chronology of Beckett's oeuvre, the remembering human figure lying on his back in the dark, "se créant des chimères pour tempérer son néant," is also, like Hamm, a deviser of fictions, a creator of imaginative fables whose essential power is the illusion they convey of a possible escape from existential bondage toward some elsewhere, some place beyond the muck and the mess.

For the purposes of this chapter, *Fin de partie* and *Compagnie* will stand both as individual and irreducible texts (i.e., I shall attempt to interpret some of their stylistic and semantic peculiarities as they relate to the overall meaning-fulness of each work) and also as illustrations of the complex movement of intersection between narrative and significance that characterizes Beckett's writings as a unit. My contention is that the question of meaning in Beckett is inseparable from that of narration, and that both questions tend toward or flow into a critical examination of the nature and limits of what it is (what it means) to be human. Beckett has his own literary-allusive and theatrical meth-ods of placing the human figure within a space (we are not very far from Heidegger's *worldliness*, but with less abstraction and a greater wealth of ob-jects for the hand to grasp) wherein his solipsistic reflectiveness must play against the appeal toward others that is generated, incessantly and necessarily, in his fictional discourse. It is in and through this fundamental conflict be-tween the sometimes enveloped and sometimes exposed self that Beckett situates the dramatic alternations of his fluctuating literary creations in their apparent *and* less-apparent formal evolution.

COMPAGNIE AND THE LATE BECKETT

For literary historians of the postmodern period, the short novel *Compagnie* stands both as a rich thematic recapitulation of the author's earlier fiction and as the first stage toward a mode of experimental writing that continues with *Mal vu mal dit* (1981) and *Worstward Ho* (1983).[2] In each of these three texts, Beckett's prose is terse, elliptical, and, to a large extent, devoid of syntactical complication. Seemingly disjointed paragraphs follow one after the other in a cumulative series of repetitions and variations, so that, in the end (via the temporal meanderings of the text), the reader has experienced the progressive deepening of images and of imagined actions. As Brian Finney has argued in a recent assessment of this new "Trilogy," the formal significance of such works within the whole of Beckett's prose writings is a certain overcoming of the minimalism that had characterized his fiction since the slow and muddy impenetrability of *Comment c'est* (1961) (Finney, 65). One should add, espe-cially in the case of *Compagnie*, that the repeated use of sense associations and of the remembrances of the narrator's central consciousness brings back to Beckett's fictional universe an undeniable appeal to the outside world as refer-ential sphere that had been largely absent in the short "fizzles," "remnants," and "residual writings" of the sixties and seventies.[3]

Although it is too early to pass judgment on the critical reception of *Com-pagnie*, a text that, in its autobiographical (or ironical-autobiographical)[4] and self-reflexive nature, seems destined to attract a multiplicity of readings, it is nevertheless possible to focus on two of its key elements: (1) the importance of narrative *voice*, and, specifically, of the split of that voice into two or more parts—a split that has caused critics to label the work in its totality a schizo-text;[5] and (2) the presence, throughout the novel, of a highly cogent and coherent metadiscourse *on* narrative, such that the book as a whole becomes a rhythmical alternation between the protagonist's memories and physical sensations on the one hand, and a narrating voice's reflections concerning the nature of fictionality on the other. How one brings together lived experience, the palimpsest of memory, and a theoretical metalanguage is the ostensible task not only of the text's narrator but of its challenged reader as well.

"Une voix parvient à quelqu'un dans le noir. Imaginer" (*Compagnie*, 7) ("A voice comes to one in the dark. Imagine"[*Company*, 7]). With these words begins the narration of *Compagnie*, which will become the gradual expansion of the first paragraph's four essential elements:

(1) voice (its nature and its origins, its *provenance*);
(2) the "someone" to whom the voice speaks (its past, its origins in time and human experience, its memories);
(3) the darkness (the hellish atmosphere in which the "someone" lives and its poetic opposition to the image of light); and
(4) the act of imagination (as related to fiction and fabulation).

It should be noted at the outset that the infinitive form of the verb *imaginer* in fact carries the force of the imperative, and that throughout the text the sporadic moments at which the imagination illuminates the darkness of the reclining figure come as the result of a strong will or desire: what propels the narration onward is a compulsion to imagine or to relate, and this compulsion is what overcomes the solitude of the figure by temporarily negating the physical limits of his imprisoning immobility. We learn from the beginning that the variations on a theme we are about to read are polyphonic in the strict sense:[6] there is a voice, which addresses the reclining figure in the second person (the *tu* form in the French version of the text); there is a third-person narrative alternating with this direct address; and one finds, only very seldom, the eruption of a first-person form,[7] which, however, is undercut by the initial reflections of the narrative metadiscourse:

L'emploi de la deuxième personne est le fait de la voix. Celui de la troisième celui de l'autre. Si lui pouvait parler à qui et de qui parle la voix il y aurait une troisième. Mais il ne le peut pas. Il ne le fera pas. Tu ne le peux pas. Tu ne le feras pas. (8–9)

Use of the second person marks the voice. That of the third that cantankerous other. Could he speak to and of whom the voice speaks there would be a first. But he cannot. He shall not. You cannot. You shall not. (9)

In unequivocal terms we are told that the *je* cannot speak for himself but that his life and his consciousness will become accessible to us through the alternations of the *tu* and *il* forms. But what (or who) are these two separate voices, the one personal and direct, the other removed (and "cantankerous" in the English version)? Where are they, and how exactly can their position be defined in relation to the passive *je*? In general, *tu* takes over whenever the figure's familial and formative past is evoked, and *il* is used either in the theoretical metadiscourse or when the movements of the figure before his ultimate fall into the reclining state take on the form of an objective, factual pattern. If we remain at this level, the book can be read as an interesting experiment in the combination of confessional autobiographical discourse with abstract, textually self-referential commentary, and one can then classify it as a latter-day, technically innovative extension of the problems posed by Gide's *Les Faux-Monnayeurs*, for example. However, the question of the location or position of the two major voices is not easily solved nor easily reduced to a static duality in which the confessional/autobiographical and the theoretical/textually self-reflexive remain at a safe distance from each other and from the *je* about whom they meditate. On the one hand, the familiar *tu*-voice that "comes to" the figure can come either from inside or outside his consciousness. Whether someone is speaking to the *je* from above or whether the *je* is speaking to himself is not clear (here, we are much closer to the Butor of *La Modification* than to Gide): it is the ambiguous strain of the undecidability between inside and outside that characterizes, for the reader, the particular interpretive tensions of the work. On the other hand, the distance at which the *il* operates, once examined and excavated, yields uncannily confused and *abysmal* results. The *il*-voice that stands "above" its inventions is not itself free from inner splits and from the infinite regress of fictional mirroring:

> Inventeur de la voix et de l'entendeur et de soi-même. Inventeur de soi-même pour se tenir compagnie. En rester là. Il parle de soi comme d'un autre. Il dit en parlant de soi, Il parle de soi comme d'un autre. Il s'imagine soi-même pour se tenir compagnie. En rester là. La confusion elle aussi tient compagnie. (33)

> Deviser of the voice and of its hearer and of himself. Deviser of himself for company. Leave it at that. He speaks of himself as of another. He says speaking for himself, He speaks of himself as of another. Himself he devises too for company. Leave it at that. Confusion too is company. (34)

Just as the narrative shifts from *tu* to *il* without ever coming to a point of rest or resolution, in the same way, on the most fundamental thematic level—that of the source or origin of the voice, its history or genealogy—the text seems to hesitate between the clarity of chronological coherence and what the narrator slyly calls the "confusion" of the vocal proximity and interchange designated by the term *company*. In a first interpretive moment, the reader can reconstruct the story of the arrival of the figure in his dark and silent refuge, and in doing so can establish with some degree of assurance the boundary line between a *before* (the days of the figure's childhood, as reflected in numerous memory sequences in the *tu* form) and a *now* (the present moment of the text). As was the case in Beckett's earliest fiction and in many of his plays, the distinction between before and now translates physically, as a progressive loss of locomotion: once, in an earlier day, the protagonist of *Compagnie* could walk, run, play; later he could only crawl; now he lies on his back in the dark. The company the figure keeps now is with the devisings of voices rather than with the community of humans he once knew. As the third-person narrator puts it in laconic form:

> Il gagna peu à peu le noir et le silence et s'y étendit. Au bout d'un temps très long ainsi avec ce qu'il lui restait de jugement il les jugea sans retour. Et puis un jour la voix. Un jour! Enfin. Et puis la voix disant, Tu est sur le dos dans le noir. Tels ses premiers mots. (22)

> Slowly he entered dark and silence and lay then for so long that with what judgment remained he judged them to be final. Till one day the voice. One day! Till in the end the voice saying, You are on your back in the dark. Those its first words. (22)

The movement inward, from the macrocosm of lived human relations to the microcosm of the mind imagining its own figments, is perhaps the archetypal Beckettian itinerary—a journey whose metaphysical or symbolical potential has been the target of Beckett critics since the 1950s. Crucial to all readings, independent of any particular methodological stance, is the clarity of the distinction between *before* and *now*: these two poles must be kept apart, at a distance, so that interpretive schemes can be created and justified. It may be that the final resting place of Beckett's disembodied, devising minds is open to interpretation as symbolical topography, but the place itself must be defined against the expanse within which the figure's earlier peregrinations were represented, and it is its relational or positional link to that broader space that allows for interpretive oppositions and for aesthetic judgment as such. One could say, in punning French: *point de repaire sans point de repère* (no hiding-place without reference-mark).[8] One escapes *from* something, one hides *from* something, one retreats *from* some (other) place. The rather considerable problem, however, is that the narrator of *Compagnie* himself questions whether such oppositional logic can define the complex spatial and temporal dimensions of the strange gray universe in which the protagonist exists:

> Que ressent-il avec ce qu'il lui reste de sentiment à propos de maintenant par rapport à avant? Lorsque avec ce qu'il lui restait de jugement il jugea son état sans retour. Autant demander ce qu'alors par rapport à avant il ressentait à propos d'alors. Comme alors il n'y avait pas d'avant de même il n'y en a pas maintenant. (28)[9]

> What with what feeling remains does he feel about now as compared to then? When with what judgement remained he judged his condition final. As well inquire what he felt then about then as compared to before. When he still moved or tarried in remains of light. As then there was no then so there is none now. (29)

The third-person narrator suggests here that the act of judgment becomes impossible once comparative relations (rapports) are revealed to be undecidable. The coherent story (relation) of a passage from the macrocosm to the microcosm, in which each sphere has its own definable characteristics, becomes a fictional convenience or contrivance that masks the essential nonrelatedness of the elements subjected to the totalizing flow of the narrative. It may be significant, in this regard, that Beckett removed the sentence "When he still moved or tarried in remains of light" from the French version, as that sentence provides precisely the kind of *repères*, both symbolical and temporal (light *versus* its opposite, darkness; *still versus* the implicit *now*), that his narrator subjects to ironical scrutiny in the remainder of the paragraph.

The twin activities of imagining and interpreting remain unimaginable and uninterpretable in a universe from which all relations among the *this* and the *that*, the *now* and the *before*, are absent. Yet it is precisely the presence of such a gray universe that is evoked, sporadically and explosively, alongside the subjective memories of childhood that enliven the text with a nostalgic, Proustian dimension, anchoring it in the familiarity of family romance.[10] The schizoid nature of *Compagnie* exceeds the technical level of the *il-tu* alternation and can be expressed as the simultaneous positing of a story (the establishing of distinct links among poetic elements) and the impossibility of telling that story (the de-construction of the edifice erected on the false stability of rapports). The story flows, nevertheless, and it is the task of the reader both to acknowledge its illusory continuity and to dwell, like the figure of the fiction, within the illusion itself, within its relational impasse.

Compagnie is a fictional text—within its pages, as we have noted, is the relation of what occurs to a figure with a certain past now lying in the dark—but it is also, simultaneously, a text about fiction, its possibilities, its impossibilities, its paradoxes, its limits. As the story progresses, the third-person narrator of the metadiscourse attempts to humanize the protagonist and his surroundings, to add what is called, in modern journalistic jargon, "human interest" to a situation whose immobility and drabness otherwise might repel the reader. Thus, in one of the narrator's earliest interventions, we read:

> N'y aurait-il pas moyen de bonifier l'entendeur? De le rendre d'un commerce plus agréable sinon franchement humain. Côté mental peut-être place pour un peu plus d'animation. Un effort de réflexion tout au moins. De remémoration. Voire d'articulation. Des traces d'émotion. Quelques signes de détresse. Un sentiment de faillite. Sans sortir du personnage. (36)

> Might not the hearer be improved? Made more companionable if not downright human. Mentally perhaps there is room for enlivenment. An attempt at reflexion at least. At recall. At speech even. Conation of some kind however feeble. A trace of emotion. Signs of distress. A sense of failure. Without loss of character. (36–37)

If these reflections strike one as ironical in the extreme, it is perhaps because the kinds of "improvement" suggested remind one inevitably of the criticisms habitually leveled at Beckett since the *succès de scandale* of *En attendant Godot*. If only there were more of emotion, of memory, of articulated thought, or even of distress and failure in recognizable form, the reader might identify with, and thereby understand, the author's fictive projections. The narrator reminds us here that what many readers want is a character (*personnage*) who seems to resemble a person—i.e., a figure with distinctive, individuating and identifying marks; and, in later interventions, the narrator seems to accede to the desires of these hypothetical readers by granting his protagonist a temporary "name"—first "H" then "M" (42, 58). But in the end no name can stick to the reclining figure, who recedes into the grayness of unidentifiable unnamability. As the text evolves toward its conclusion, the voice of the metadiscourse increasingly emphasizes the pure imaginary nature of the fictional as such, in opposition to the fullness of existential experience which, although it is accessible through memory as image, nevertheless cannot negate the "chimerical" quality of both the protagonist and his third-person creator (who, for part of the text, calls himself "W" before also giving up his "identity"):

> Puisqu'il ne sait pas penser qu'il y renonce. Reste-t-il à ajouter à ce croquis. Son innommabilité. Même M doit sauter. Ainsi W se remémore sa créature telle que créée jusqu'ici. W? Mais lui aussi est créature. Chimère. (62)

> Since he cannot think he will give up trying. Is there anything to add to this esquisse? His unnamability. Even M must go. So W reminds himself of his creature as so far created. W? But W too is creature. Figment. (63)

In the end, the voice of the metadiscourse asserts the absolute, irreducible fictionality of his "creature," who can be called nothing but "figment" (from the Latin *fingere*: to fashion, to feign; the product of fictitious invention) or *chimère*—vain illusion. Viewed from the perspective of modern literary history, Beckett's *Compagnie* contributes to the radical undermining of the substantiality of "believable" characters, whose status as mere or vain fictions constantly reemerges from under all efforts to humanize them. The despair of Beckett's narrators consists of the foreknowledge that, although narration as process is an inevitable and integral part of our cultural activity (there will always be some beginning to our stories, however staged and forced, and some ending, however artificial and contrived), its relation (rapport) to that which is specifically human is problematic. It is, significantly, in the writings of an author whose allusive images and symbolic diction seem to point most clearly to a beyond, to an extratextual referent, to a specifically human predicament, that the warnings against the humanization of the fictional are at their strongest and most challenging.

Unlike some of the most recent experimental works of the nouveaux romanciers, however, in which the self-reflexivity of texts seems to have progressed so far as to exclude all reference to the human community as definable or recognizable totality, *Compagnie* remains tethered to the problem of what it is to be human. At the midpoint of the text the narrator asks, then answers: "Quelle est cette espèce d'imagination si entachée de raison? Une espèce à part" (45) ("What kind of imagination is this so reason-ridden? A kind of its own" [45]); and, near the conclusion of the story, he evokes, in the second person, the "maux de ton espèce" (82) ("woes of your kind" [83]). At the center of Beckett's preoccupations is the human being in its difference from the nonreasoning animal world, in the woes that are specific to its "kind." Although its fictional status, its chimerical nature, cannot be passed over and ignored in an interpretive reading, the figure reclining in the dark must nevertheless also stand for or represent that which is human: it is a human figure and a figuration of the human as such. And what characterizes our kind, *notre espèce*, is the fundamental incapacity to give up and to finish, as well as the forever recurring need for company. The impossibility of acceding to passivity and renunciation in the existential realm corresponds to the impossibility of ending the story—even if this story reduces itself, from work to work in Beckett, to the most elliptical of formal constructions:

> Pourquoi ne pas simplement gésir les yeux fermés dans le noir et renoncer à tout. Et finir avec tout. Avec dérisoire rampade et chimère vaines. Mais s'il lui arrive de perdre courage de la sorte ce n'est jamais pour longtemps. Car peu à peu dans son coeur d'écroulé le besoin de compagnie renaît. (76)

> Why not just lie in the dark with closed eyes and give up? Give up all. Have done with all. With bootless crawl and figments comfortless. But if on occasion so disheartened it is seldom for long. For little by little as he lies the craving for company revives. (77)

Although the physical situation in which one finds Beckett's characters is that of solitude, even abandonment, the fundamental *condition* of these figures, what defines their specificity, is their craving (*besoin*) for company, for the presence, however illusory, of the other *as* other. To conjure up the presence of the companionable other, the figure, himself a mere figment, creates a web of figmentation: he will always be alone but will always have the need for company, and this need expresses itself as a story that can never end. In an important sense, *Compagnie* is the amplification, the working out, of the paradoxes, the apparent logical contradictions, the ambivalences, that inhabit the opening pages of *L'Innommable* (1953) (*The Unnamable*):

> Je ne serai pas seul, les premiers temps. Je le suis bien sûr. Seul. C'est vite dit. Il faut dire vite. Et sait-on jamais, dans une obscurité pareille? *Je vais avoir de la compagnie.* Pour commencer. Quelques pantins. Je les supprimerai par la suite. Si je peux. . . . Le plus simple serait de ne pas commencer. Mais je suis obligé de commencer. C'est-à-dire que je suis obligé de continuer. Je finirai peut-être par être très entouré, dans un capharnaüm. Allées et venues incessantes, atmosphère de bazar. Je suis tranquille, allez. (8–9; my emphasis)

I shall not be alone, in the beginning. I am of course alone. Alone. That is soon said. Things have to be soon said. And how can one be sure, in such darkness? *I shall have company*. In the beginning. A few puppets. Then I'll scatter them, to the winds, if I can. . . . The best would be not to begin. But I have to begin. That is to say I have to go on. Perhaps in the end I shall smother in a throng. Incessant comings and goings, the crush and bustle of a bargain sale. No, no danger. Of that. (294)

Alone in silence and obscurity, the Beckettian narrator begins to fabulate, and he begins, or rather continues, because he must. This obligation to create from nothing, from out of a darkness that is absolute, to project phantoms or puppets (*pantins*) onto the reader's consciousness, lends Beckett's works an ethical as well as an aesthetic dimension. The serious playfulness that characterizes the mood of his writings is a major source of hermeneutic embarrassment to his critics, who have tended to interpret his diverse texts either symbolically, as coded messages that refer to the fate of humankind in a threatened, late phase of civilization, or formally, as experiments in self-contained, self-representational writing. The problem here—that of the relation or nonrelation between the inside of a Beckettian text and an outside to which it may or may not refer—affects the meaning of the essential themes and the very vocabulary with which the author expresses himself, and also subtends the entirety of Beckett's literary production, from the earliest writings until *Compagnie* and the "New Trilogy." Thus, for example, *to begin, to continue*, and *to end* can take on radically differing meanings according to their frame of reference: when applied to the backdrop of human destiny, they resonate with portentous, possibly tragic overtones; when limited to the space of the white page, they appear to designate uniquely the problem of narrativity in theoretical abstraction.

In the second part of this chapter, I shall develop some of the issues I have raised in reading *Compagnie*—notably those of voice and of narrative metadiscourse—but shall be addressing them in a discussion of the well-known and much-commented work that thematizes the problematic of beginning, continuing, and ending in the clearest, most dramatic form: *Fin de partie*. We turn now from prose fiction to the theater, but we keep at the center of our reflections the peculiar coupling of narrative order to intra- and extratextual significance that inheres in the specificity of Beckett's literary style.

FIN DE PARTIE AND THE EARLIER BECKETT

Between 1946 and 1949, Beckett composed the novels *Mercier et Camier* (first published in 1970), *Molloy, Malone meurt*, and *L'Innommable*, and then ended this period of intense productivity with the thirteen short fictions entitled *Textes pour rien* (1950). By critical consensus, the latter evanescent texts represent an impasse in the evolution of Beckett's prose—an impasse that required a detour through the theater in the 1950s before the new (albeit quite disconcerting) beginning of his fiction with *Comment c'est* in 1961. Throughout the 1960s, 1970s, and 1980s, once the prose had moved beyond the threat of stagnation and silence, the theater experienced its own distinctive variations of theme and structure, and the two genres preferred by the author continued to follow their own laws of evolution, in parallel for the most part, but with interesting moments of intersection and mutual influence. Thus, to mention only one case that concerns us here, Beckett himself was actively involved in creating and overseeing the stage adaptation of *Compagnie*, directed by Pierre Chabert and performed in 1984 at the Théâtre du Rond-Point Parisien. If *Compagnie* was adaptable to the theater, if its generic qualities were hybrid enough to permit this kind of crossover, it is no doubt a result of the translatability of the text's narrative voices into a dialogue of audible human voices on the stage—which could be represented either directly (in the present moment of the actor's utterances) or indirectly (in some ghostly "past," as conveyed by the uncanny absence of a taped speech).[11]

Before such a crossover was to become possible, however, Beckett had to experience firsthand the possibilities and limitations specific to the theater medium—which he did, rapidly and with great success, in his writing and subsequent cooperative directing of the modern classics *En attendant Godot* (1953) and *Fin de partie* (1957). What was it in the physical context of the theater that allowed Beckett's wrestling with words to emerge in a highly idiosyncratic but also highly communicative expressivity? What was it, in the theater medium, that seemed to allow Beckett's difficult, uncompromising thought to pass unimpeded into the consciousness of the spectator? Ludovic Janvier has offered the best explanation, in a modestly phrased but elegant hypothesis that invites reflection:

> The turn toward the theater will be explained, with the faith necessary for such an explanation—credo quia absurdum—by reference to a definite space, a minimal level of identity, a permanence of the Same strong enough not to undo itself word by word, in brief by all those methods capable of stemming the hemorrhage of the verbal flow. One must be silent, or else be able to continue speaking. To continue speaking, here are visible limits, "guardrails" [*garde-fous*]. Such is Beckettian theater, from immutable space to prudent discourse, even if that discourse proves destructive: such is the antepurgatory where the writer, as if exhausted, rests his word and defines his creatures. He no longer aims or strains toward his identity, but sees and hears himself. He no longer chases after himself in the meanderings of unfaithful talk, but with the help of faithful discourse and of others in flesh and words, he waits, endures, and inhabits time. (200–201)

What Janvier has done here, with admirable subtlety, is to engage himself in a double writing, in a double judgment. On the one hand, he recognizes the danger of simplification (or even of "absurdity" [*credo quia absurdum*]) inherent in the critical gesture of finding a coherent explanation for an aesthetic evolution that may be unconscious in nature and fundamentally arbitrary, without cause (in fact, *who knows* why Beckett shifted to the theater? One would not have been surprised to hear Beckett himself deny any relevant knowledge). Yet, on the other hand, Janvier presents us with an account of the change in genre that seems convincing on several levels and that appears to describe, in a few eloquent phrases, the recognizable, essential elements in Beckettian drama. Central to the logic of Janvier's hypothesis is a series of oppositions between the characteristics of the prose writings that had resulted in the impasse after *L'Innommable* and those qualities of the theater as medium that allowed for a new expressive beginning in the continuum of Beckett's literary production. These oppositions can be represented, schmatically, as a grid in which the horizontal axis—divided between Prose and Theater—crosses with the vertical axis—divided among what might be considered the three constantly recurring dimensions of Beckett's imaginary universe—Space, Time, and Voice. Such a crossing yields the following tableau:

	PROSE	*THEATER*
SPACE	(its status before the impasse) Indefinite, Changing Locations Invisibility of Reference Marks (*Repères*) Abstract Space	(its power to unblock the impasse) Immutable Space Visibility of Reference Marks Concrete Space as "Guardrail" (*Garde-fou*)
TIME	Mutability of Self and Surroundings Separation of Self from Temporal Process	"Minimal" Permanence of Self and Surroundings Involvement of Self in Temporal Process
VOICE	Voice as Meandering Search for Identity Voice as "Unfaithful Talk"	Voice as "Hearing and Seeing Oneself" Voice as "Faithful Discourse"

Although it would be possible to challenge Janvier's system of polarities at certain specific points of the grid (one wonders, for example, just how "faithful" the discourse of theatrical voice is in Beckett's plays, how the notion of "faithfulness" itself can function within works that thrive on a combination of accumulated clichés and constantly shifting irony), he insists on one major difference between the two genres that appears unequivocal: the greater degree of concreteness in the theater of those reference marks (repères) that had been of primary importance in the complex semantic structure of *Compagnie*.

On the stage, especially in the early plays *En attendant Godot, Fin de partie,* and *Happy Days (Oh les beaux jours),* the playwright creates a scenic representation replete with objects in space to be manipulated by the characters, while simultaneously alluding to the equally significant space outside which, in *Godot* and *Fin de partie,* seems to resonate with an unmistakable symbolic potential. In each of the early plays the spectator is also aware of the varying levels of temporal process, as they affect both the evolution of the drama itself and the underlying theme of finitude that permeates their significance. And finally, each play stages the pathos of the human voice—its attempts to tell coherent stories that usually end in chaotic fragmentation. Because the dimensions of space, time, and voice carry with them a physical weight they do not possess in the prose works, because their embodiment in the characters and objective correlatives of the stage creates the illusion not only of precision but of fixity, the spectator is tempted to believe that the degree of resistance of the plays to interpretive understanding is not as great as that of the prose, that the garde-fous Beckett supposedly set up for himself against the increasing "folly" of his prose fiction can protect the spectator as much as the author from the indefiniteness of polysemic proliferation. In the section that follows, I shall examine the matter of the interpretability of *Fin de partie,* keeping in mind the three dimensions of space, time, and voice, with a final development on the specific relation of voice to narration.

As was the case already in *Godot,* the stage setting of *Fin de partie* is stark and nearly empty: what objects do exist carry heavy significant potential, and the scene itself is almost endlessly evocative. The spectator sees a bare interior with, front right, two garbage cans (containing Hamm's parents, the characters Nagg and Nell); in the center, initially covered by a sheet, the protagonist Hamm in his wheelchair; and front right, next to the door, the fourth character, Clov. The door leads to Clov's kitchen, a place we never see but into which Clov occasionally goes; and on the walls at the back of the stage we find two small windows placed very high, initially covered by curtains (*Fin de partie,* 13–15; *Endgame,* 92–93). At the beginning of the play's action, Clov opens the curtains on the windows, lifts then replaces the lids of the garbage cans, and removes the sheet covering Hamm—each action accompanied by brief laughter. This combination of burlesque activity and silence leads to Hamm's first words: "Fini, c'est fini, ça va finir, ça va peut-être finir" (15) ("Finished, it's finished, it must be nearly finished" [93]).

The meaning of this intriguing space has haunted critics from the beginning. Given the end-of-the-world atmosphere that pervades the play, some have surmised that the stage setting represents a bomb shelter; others have likened the entirety of the darkly illumined area with its highly perched windows to a skull (with two "eyes") in which the actors are "thoughts" and, in particular, the raising of the garbage can lids resembles, in comic form, Proustian *souvenirs involontaires* (involuntary remembrances).[12] The various interpretations of the stage's significance are far too numerous to catalogue here, but whether critics choose to see in the setting the depiction of an outer space (bomb shelter, hospital, or asylum) or an inner space (cerebral), what matters most in the elaboration of the interpretation is the establishing of boundary lines between what we see on the stage and what lies beyond.[13] Inside, there is a certain rhythm to the daily routine, a certain order among the objects that circulate from hand to hand. Outside, there is grayness, water that appears to be rising mysteriously, and virtually nothing on the horizon except, toward the end of the play, the immobile profile of a boy (who is described at some length in the original French text, but who almost disappears from the English version—a matter I shall address later in this chapter).

In the early moments of the action, Hamm exclaims: "Hors d'ici c'est la mort" (23) ("Outside of here it's death" [96])—which would seem to imply that the inside space we observe, the space of visible manifestation is, in some minimal sense, a continuation of life. And what allows such life as this to endure is the protective wall that separates inside from outside, the remaining traces of human sentiment and intellection from the inhuman or no-longer-human desert landscape. When, in a prophetic moment, Hamm evokes the end of the world (in a religious tone suggestive of the Last Judgment), he imagines Clov looking at the wall and addresses him thus:

> Tu regarderas le mur un peu, puis tu te diras, Je vais fermer les yeux, peut-être dormir un peu, après ça ira mieux, et tu les fermeras. Et quand tu les rouvriras il n'y aura plus de mur. (*Un temps.*) L'infini du vide sera autour de toi, tous les morts de tous les temps ressuscités ne le combleraient pas, tu y seras comme un petit gravier au milieu de la steppe. (53–54)

> You'll look at the wall a while, then you'll say, I'll close my eyes, perhaps have a little sleep, after that I'll feel better, and then you'll close them. And when you open them again there'll be no wall any more. [*Pause.*] Infinite emptiness will be all around you, all the resurrected dead of all the ages wouldn't fill it, and then you'll be like a little bit of grit in the middle of the steppe. (109–10)

The existence of the wall—its concrete presence for both the play's characters and spectators—is what holds in abeyance the threat of absolute dissolution, undifferentiation, solitude. Its consistent functioning as repère, as garde-fou (including its reassuring tactile reality for Hamm when he takes his "stroll" with Clov), make of it the envelope or atmosphere that encloses the characters in a world of their own that, whatever its bizarre and repugnant qualities, possesses its own lawfulness and orderliness.

An examination of the spatial dimension in *Fin de partie*, and of the inside/outside polarity in particular, inevitably entails consideration of the temporal sphere as well. What Clov sees when he looks out the high windows now (at the moment of the dramatic action) does not resemble the world as it existed before, and this world, invisible to the spectator of Beckett's play, is accessible only through the occasional and fragmented memories of the characters. Thus, we learn that Nagg and Nell lost their legs in a tandem bicycle accident in the Ardennes (at Sedan, significantly, the point at which the Germans penetrated France on the west in May 1940)[14] and that, in a less painful moment, they spent a romantic April afternoon at Lake Como (*FP*, 36; *EG*, 102). Clov remembers a time in which there still were bicycles and horses (*FP*, 22; *EG*, 96), and Hamm recollects the day of Clov's arrival, the day his servant passed from the outside world to the inside (*FP*, 55; *EG*, 110). Most often, however, references to temporal process and change occur in enigmatic short statements and in comical one-liners that emphasize not only the destructiveness of time but also the impossibility of our understanding it.[15] Time is not merely the dimension that renders Nagg's dreams of lovemaking grotesque in his "present circumstances" but is also, most crucially, the element closest to our human reality and simultaneously farthest from our intellectual grasp.

In a general sense, one can say that there are three essential levels of time at work in *Fin de partie*:

(1) The temporal movement of the play itself, its own self-sustaining and highly self-reflexive development (the entirety of the dramatic process—the problem of ending—is contained within Hamm's first words, and the characters punctuate the play throughout its length with both inquiries and assertions concerning the imminence of this end: their sense of time as characters resembles that of actors or musicians who have already played (in) the same piece and who easily intuit the approach of the work's conclusion because they have lived with it for some time)

(2) The *now/before* opposition, as related to the spatial polarity of *inside/outside*; the problematic of temporal mutability (the world outside is now a desert; we are now immobile and aged. How and why did these changes take place?).

(3) An imagined future—expressed, in the earlier stages of the play, by Hamm's quasi-biblical prophecies and, at the conclusion, by Clov's preparation for departure.

If we combine the three levels, we obtain, schematically: the end is contained within the beginning, we know it is coming and we live the time of its imminence in rhythmical anticipation; the world outside has changed while we continue to fabricate a life inside; we pause at the threshold of the beyond, to die (Hamm) or perhaps to leave (Clov). What remains both central and incomprehensible in this scheme is the notion of mutability itself. Although there has been a change, discernible in retrospect, it has been/is invisible and absolutely resistant to the human consciousness. As Clov says in the moment before his presumed departure:

Bon, ça ne finira donc jamais, je ne partirai donc jamais. (*Un temps.*) Puis un jour, soudain, ça finit, ça change, je ne comprends pas, ça meurt, ou c'est moi, je ne comprends pas, ça non plus. Je le demande aux mots qui restent—sommeil, réveil, soir, matin. Ils ne savent rien dire. (*Un temps.*) J'ouvre la porte du cabanon et je m'en vais. Je suis si voûté que je ne vois que mes pieds, si j'ouvre les yeux, et entre mes jambes un peu de poussière noirâtre. Je me dis que la terre s'est éteinte, quoique je ne l'aie jamais vue allumée. (*Un temps.*) Ça va tout seul. (*Un temps.*) Quand je tomberai je pleurerai de bonheur. (108–9)

Good, it'll never end, I'll never go. [*Pause.*] Then one day, suddenly, it ends, it changes, I don't understand, it dies, or it's me, I don't understand that either. I ask the words that remain—sleeping, waking, morning, evening. They have nothing to say. [*Pause.*] I open the door of the cell and go. I am so bowed I only see my feet, if I open my eyes, and between my legs a little trail of black dust. I say to myself that the earth is extinguished, though I never saw it lit. [*Pause.*] It's easy going. [*Pause.*] When I fall I'll weep for happiness. (132)

When the moment of the end arrives, when Clov projects himself forward into an imaginary present tense, into a final walk that culminates in a fall and ultimate "happiness," all reference marks, all *repères*, have disappeared. Not only can he not understand the origin of the sudden changes—whether in the world or in himself—but the words that used to signify reality in oppositional relations (sleeping *versus* waking; morning *versus* evening) have lost all meaning. What Beckett offers as a final vision exceeds any category of existential despair, any attitude of pessimism: he evokes here a *relationless* universe, a space and time within which, in the absolute and forever, oppositional logic will have been useless ("I say to myself that the earth is extinguished, though I never saw it lit"). One wonders in retrospect, looking over one's shoulders from the stance of the exiting Clov, how human speech in its relational and oppositional essence ever did function in such a place, how verbal communication could draw together the floating, monadic entities called Hamm and Clov, Nagg and Nell.

To pose this question is to raise the issue of voice in *Fin de partie*—that third dimension of the theatrical text that Janvier defined as "hearing and seeing oneself" and as "faithful discourse" in contradistinction to the less reliable meanderings of the subject's search for identity in the prose work via the complexities of a properly narrative voice. Although one can understand the commonsense idea subtending Janvier's contrast of the two genres—Hamm's voice *is* Hamm in a way and to a degree not comparable to the tenuous and fluctuating link between the reclining figure in *Compagnie* and the voice that comes to him in the dark—his remarks are nevertheless suspect on two counts: (1) As I remarked earlier in passing, the notion of "faithfulness" is not relevant to the ironical and cliché-ridden discourse of characters whose "thoughts" may not be accessible to representation in the usual sense; and (2) *Fin de partie* is so full of stories of various kinds, from Nagg's joking tale of the tailor (*FP*, 36–38; *EG*, 102–3) to Hamm's elaborate fiction on the Christmas Eve visit of the stranger and his abandoned child (*FP*, 70–75; *EG*, 116–18), that the very distinction between prose narrative on the one hand and theater on the other tends to disappear. *Fin de partie* is a play, but its essential form alternates between dialogue and narrative, and the narrative sequences themselves are as effective in bringing together the characters in a community of speech as are the exchanges in the dialogue. In a universe that tends toward an absolutely relationless state, it is, ironically, the need (the craving, *le besoin*) to relate stories that predominates. I would add that if one were to search for the single simple element that could not be discarded, negated, subdivided, or superseded in Beckett's world, that one element that defines at the minimal level, that without which one cannot be human, it would be the need to narrate: *fabulari humanum est*.

The importance of narrative voice and of the story-telling act for the meaning of *Fin de partie* as an aesthetic whole is nowhere more evident than in Hamm's long monologue on the Christmas Eve visit of the stranger who has abandoned his child. In reading this rich and complex passage, the interpreter faces two primordial questions: (1) is the story true (i.e., did the events described happen to Hamm himself) or fictional (is the character who arrives at the threshold of his home a creature of Hamm's invention)?; (2) is there a semantic relation between the microcosm of the story and the macrocosm of *Fin de partie* as enveloping unit of significance? I shall begin with the second question in order to gain access to the first.

The five-page passage (*FP*, 70–75; *EG*, 116–18) is itself framed by a contextual setting or "situation"[16] that requires some elucidation. We are at the midpoint of the play, and we have heard from all four characters; their present circumstances and certain fragments of their past lives have become known to us; and, perhaps most important, we as spectators have become immersed in Hamm's routine—his physical and emotional needs as attended to by Clov in an orderly, temporal succession. As is often the case for the elderly infirm in our own world, the day is subdivided into segments designated specifically for certain activities or the giving of certain medicines: the morning check of the catheter, the noonday meal, the afternoon stroll, the evening sleeping-pill. For Hamm, the rather mad succession of stimulants and depressants is interrupted not only by his wheelchair "walk around the world" but also by periodic moments of narrative intervention: just as there is a time for a pill, there is also a time for a story. Story telling as such, viewed within the particular context of *Fin de partie*, is on the same level as the body, and it functions as a relieving of the body's pains and as an alleviation of the oppressive weight of time.

When, in the frame segment preceding the story, Hamm asserts "C'est l'heure de mon histoire" (67) ("It's time for my story" [115]), his immediate problem is finding an audience. Clov is not interested in hearing an anecdote he may have heard many times before ("my story," like a child's game of marbles, is both a proudly held personal possession and a means of repeatedly luring others into one's circle), so Hamm enlists his father as hearer by offering him (more precisely, by bargaining with him over) a *dragée* (a sugared almond one eats in France especially at holiday time, translated in the English version as "sugar-plum"). When the story is complete and Nagg demands payment for his services as listener, Hamm gives him nothing, for "Il n'y a plus de dragées" (76) ("There are no more sugar-plums" [119]). Thus the frame that surrounds the story of a father's abandonment of his child is that of a child's abandonment of his father—in the form of a broken promise.[17] One senses, from the outset, that Hamm's story, whether it happened to him as an event in his life or occurred to him as an imaginative idea, includes within its allusive folds concentrated reflections of the larger drama to which it refers.

Although Hamm's story itself merits detailed stylistic analysis (especially its consistent use of ironical metadiscourse in the form of Hamm's commentary on the narration as it begins to assume a coherent form), for our limited purposes here I shall emphasize two essential elements: (1) its dramatic movement from beginning to end; and (2) its strong biblical and literary resonance—both of which contribute to its contextual or "situational" significance within the play. There are three characters in the story: the first-person narrator, Hamm, who either experienced or created the events he relates and who exists *in* the narration as protagonist, as the busy man of some means to whom a second personage addresses supplications; and a third, absent figure, the male child of the suppliant who remains in the outer darkness, "plongé dans le sommeil" (74) ("deep in sleep" [118]) at a walking distance of three days from Hamm's (the protagonist's) residence. As told in the past tense (the literary and formal *passé simple* in the French version), the narrative proceeds in the following stages: (1) the suppliant approaches, dragging himself slowly on his stomach; (2) the suppliant turns his tearful gaze toward Hamm, who orders him to avert his eyes, saying: "Je suis assez occupé, vous savez, les préparatifs de fête" (71) ("I'm a busy man, you know, the final touches, before the festivities, you know what it is" [117]);[18] (3) the suppliant, after revealing that only he and his child still live in the nearby outer world, asks Hamm for bread to feed his boy; (4) Hamm refuses his request, with the violent outburst: "Mais réfléchissez, réfléchissez, vous êtes sur terre, c'est sans remède!" (73) ("Use your head, can't you, use your head, you're on earth, there's no cure for that!" [118]); (5) Hamm invites the suppliant to enter into his service, but he refuses to take in the child as well. The passage ends with the protagonist's description of the suppliant as he reacts to the firm resolve of the gentleman who, in offering him a new life, would simultaneously condemn his child to death: "Je le revois, à genoux, les mains appuyées au sol, me fixant de ses yeux déments, malgré ce que je venais de lui signifier à ce propos" (74) ("I can see him still down on his knees, his hands flat on the ground, glaring at me with his mad eyes, in defiance of my wishes" [118]).

The significance of the fable, like that of the play surrounding it, depends upon our interpretation of the inside/outside polarity on which it is constructed. Here, a man is able to penetrate the interior of Hamm's domain, to pass from outside to inside and to be taken in as servant by an authoritarian master; should he choose to remain, however, he cannot also be with his child, and his choice of comfort and a fresh beginning for himself implies the impossibility of returning to the exterior world where his son waits in enigmatic sleep. If the supplicant stays, therefore, he is obliged to embrace Hamm's assertion "Hors d'ici c'est la mort" as a statement of truth and to accept the limitations of his new dwelling's walls as being, henceforth, those of his existence. If the supplicant decides to remain in the comfortable inside, he will be like Clov—or perhaps, he will *be* Clov. The possibility arises that the story Hamm tells within the larger context of the play does not merely reflect, as fictional addendum, the general theme of abandonment as found throughout *Fin de partie* but that it describes the origin of the situation in which the characters now find themselves. Hamm's fable becomes the actual or real story of Clov's arrival, the relation of his original (rite of) passage from exterior to interior space. In this reading, the story (*histoire* as fable) is disguised as fictional *divertissement* but becomes, through our interpretation of the elements within it that relate to its frame, the inner pocket, the abyme in which the drama as a whole announces its generation (*histoire* as historical account).

Although the reading I have proposed here—an allegory of origins—cannot be verified in a definitive sense (the question of the fictionality or degree of fictionality of Hamm's story will be a matter of conjecture always and for all critics), there is nevertheless one passage, near the end of the play, that tends to substantiate it: the moment in which Clov, having climbed his ladder for the last time, looks out the small windows and discovers someone in the distance, apparently a small boy (*FP*, 103–5; *EG*, 130–31). Here one is tempted to see, in the macrocosm of the play, confirmation of the historical dimension of the microcosm that is Hamm's story: the young boy whom Clov observes just before preparing himself for ultimate departure from his master's universe is the boy he once abandoned, the boy to whom he now returns in a final act of paternal love. The dynamics of the drama, the *grandes lignes* of its development, become clear: the protective shelter created by Hamm is one in which one son has abandoned his father and mother to animal existence in garbage cans; it is also the place in which Clov has sought refuge and found a new father—Hamm[19]—while concurrently abandoning his own son in the outer darkness—that gray, formidable outside that can only be viewed at a distance in the play but which represents the crepuscular origin *and* finality of Clov's obscure quest.[20]

In interpreting Hamm's narration as the historical account of Clov's origins, and in viewing Clov as the figure who, unlike Hamm, may be able to overcome, cancel, or negate his initial neglect of his familial obligations by a second, compensatory act, we obtain a contrast not only between two characters but between two modes of being-in-the-world: the one based uniquely upon power relations (Hamm as master in an unending master—slave dialectic), and the other upon an ethical stance—a stance not adopted by Hamm (who could have shared, but did not, his goods and comfort with others), yet perhaps to be adopted by Clov in his voyage into outer darkness toward his son. Beckett underlines the ethical dimension in an ironical way by placing in the mouth of Hamm certain biblical phrases that contrast with his egocentric actions. After exclaiming that there is no "cure" (remède) for our suffering in this world, Hamm asks his supplicant, with considerable malice: "Mais enfin quel est votre espoir? Que la terre renaisse au printemps? Que la mer et les rivières redeviennent poissonneuses? Qu'il y ait de la manne au ciel pour des imbéciles comme vous?" (73–74) ("But what in God's name do you imagine? That the earth will awake in the spring? That the rivers and seas will run with fish again? That there's manna in heaven still for imbeciles like you?" [118]). The manna referred to here is the bread from heaven that fed the Israelites during their arduous exile and exodus from Egypt to the Promised Land (symbolized here by the awakening of the earth and the rivers running with fish), and it represents the gift of life from God, the very sustenance that Hamm refuses his supplicant. A second biblical allusion in the same passage has a similar resonance: in the earliest part of his admonitions to the supplicant, Hamm refers to the wheat (or, in the King's English, "corn") he has in his storerooms—"Du blé, j'en ai, il est vrai, dans mes greniers" (73) ("Corn, yes, I have corn, it's true, in my granaries" [118]). This is a shorthand reference to the story of Joseph in Egypt (once again, the theme of exile), and notably to the episode in which Joseph's brothers, who had previously abandoned him and sold him into slavery, go to Egypt for grain and encounter, in the person of the Pharaoh's second-in-command, the man who is their brother but whom they do not at first recognize (Genesis 42–45). The story of Joseph is complex, full of the kind of rebondissements, "underplots," (FP, 103; EG, 130) that Hamm fears so much, but its central point is clear: in the end, after toying briefly with the power that he possesses over his brothers as supplicants, Joseph takes them in, offers them hospitality, and reveals his true identity; his temporarily assumed power as Pharaoh's second man is eclipsed by the ethical obligation he has to his brothers as family and as fellow humans. Thus Hamm, in refusing his supplicant's entreaty, is an anti-Joseph, an antihost hoarding his wheat and his affection; the story of his actions (the play Fin de partie) is the negative image of its biblical model.

RECUEILLEMENT

If I have insisted at such length on Hamm's story-within-a-play, it is not only because of its intrinsic semantic density and its significance as historical underpinning to Clov's own story, but also because one of its moments recurs, in concentrated form, in Hamm's soliloquy at the very end of the drama. Shortly after the protagonist, in mock lyrical abandon, cites a verse from Baudelaire's poem "Recueillement," he returns to his story, as follows:

> (*Un temps. Ton de narrateur.*) S'il pouvait avoir son petit avec lui . . . (*Un temps.*) C'était l'instant que j'attendais. (*Un temps.*) Vous ne voulez pas l'abandonner? Vous voulez qu'il grandisse pendant que vous, vous rapetissez? (*Un temps.*) Qu'il vous adoucisse les cent mille derniers quarts d'heure? (*Un temps.*) Lui ne se rend pas compte, il ne connaît que la faim, le froid, et la mort au bout. Mais vous! Vous devez savoir ce que c'est, la terre, à présent. (*Un temps.*) Oh! je l'ai mis devant ses responsa-bilités. (111)

> [*Pause. Narrative tone.*] If he could have his child with him . . . [*Pause.*] It was the moment I was waiting for. [*Pause.*] You don't want to abandon him? You want him to bloom while you are withering? Be there to solace your last million lost moments? [*Pause.*] He doesn't realize, all he knows is hunger, and cold, and death to crown it all. But you! You ought to know what the earth is like, nowadays. Oh, I put him before his responsibilities. (133)

As the play draws toward ultimate silence, Hamm concludes his discontinu-ous ruminations with one final, perversely ironical act—the twisting of the meaning of the word *responsibility*, which he turns on its head and forces to signify its opposite. The supplicant, if he were responsible in the usual sense, would return to his child; instead, if he chooses to remain in Hamm's protec-tive kingdom, he is placed before the "responsibility" of abandoning his son in darkness.

Because the play ends with Hamm's soliloquy, and because this soliloquy emphasizes the hopelessness of the human condition ("what the earth is like, nowadays"), critics have too often equated the protagonist's voice and his mood with the supposed message of the work as a whole—hence the disserta-tions on Beckett's pessimism that have been in circulation for some time and that will be with us for the foreseeable future. In the midst of the play's bleak atmospherics, however, lies its central dramatic (conflictual) *issue*: the alterna-tive between the abandonment and the taking in of one's fellow humans, be-tween the erection of containing walls on the one hand and their abolition on the other (i.e., their overcoming in an *issuing forth* toward the outer world [Clov's imminent departure] or in an act of hosting and *welcoming in* [the pity of Joseph for his brothers as *not* enacted by Hamm]). The essence of this fun-damental dramatic conflict is contained within one word—the verb *recueillir*: *recueillir*, in its transitive sense, can mean "to take in" (as in "to take in an abandoned person"); while its reflexive sense, *se recueillir*, signifies "to reflect, to meditate, to withdraw into oneself." Hamm uses the first, transitive form of the verb in his microcosmic narration ("Il finit par me demander si je consen-tirais à recueillir l'enfant aussi" [74]); "In the end he asked me would I consent to take in the child as well" [118]); and, in his final soliloquy, in which he uses poetry as a means of withdrawal from the world and its responsibilities, he alludes to the second verse of Baudelaire's "Recueillement"—which nominative title carries with it the second, reflexive sense of the verb. At the end of his time, Hamm opts for some Romantic poetry; specifically, for a sonnet that represents, in allegorical form, the melancholy distance of the narrating voice from the world, its distance and difference from the "multitude vile" (v. 5) of humanity searching for crude pleasure far below, far beyond, far outside the voice's privileged sphere of mastery. The poet addresses a part of himself as "ma Douleur," and it is the dialogue between the two sides of his split consciousness—the narrating voice and the personified Douleur who "accompanies" him on his walk away from human cares and concerns—that constitutes the narrative and dramatic center of the poem:

RECUEILLEMENT

Sois sage, ô ma Douleur, et tiens-toi plus tranquille.
Tu réclamais le Soir; il descend; le voici:
Une atmosphère obscure enveloppe la ville,
Aux uns portant la paix, aux autres le souci.

Pendant que des mortels la multitude vile,
Sous le fouet du Plaisir, ce bourreau sans merci,
Va cueillir des remords dans la fête servile,
Ma Douleur, donne-moi la main; viens par ici

Loin d'eux. Vois se pencher les défuntes Années,
Sur les balcons du ciel, en robes surannées;
Surgir du fond des eaux le Regret souriant;

Le Soleil moribond s'endormir sous une arche,
Et, comme un long linceul traînant à l'Orient,
Entends, ma chère, entends la douce nuit qui marche.

MEDITATION
(*Translation by Richard Howard*)

Behave, my Sorrow! let's have no more scenes.
Evening's what you wanted—Evening's here:
a gradual darkness overtakes the town,
bringing peace to some, to others pain.

Now, while humanity racks up remorse
in low distractions under Pleasure's lash,
grovelling for a ruthless master—come
away, my Sorrow, leave them! Give me your hand . . .

See how the dear departed dowdy years
crowd the balconies of heaven, leaning down,
while smiling out of the sea appears Regret;

the Sun will die in its sleep beneath a bridge,
and trailing westward like a winding-sheet—
listen, my dear—how softly Night arrives.

Like *Fin de partie*, "Recueillement" evokes the ending of a day, which could
represent the end of a life. The crepuscular moment, a privileged one for
Romantic poetry and for Baudelaire in particular, is that transitory and transi-
tional point at which the human consciousness, having called for the repose
of the Evening, must face its regular, inevitable, deathlike march. The considerable power of "Recueillement" resides in its capacity to transform what the
Bible calls the "sting" of death into a series of soothing poetical images; and
this transformation is achieved by a double split: (1) within the self or subject
who narrates the poem; and (2) between that self and others. In a first move,
the self divides into two opposing parts or figures: the narrating voice as such
and the personified and feminized "Douleur" whom the voice both addresses
and leads/controls. In a second move, the self sets itself apart from the world
of Pleasure, from the domain in which the multitude of mortals "va *cueillir* des
remords dans la fête servile" (l. 7). The contrast here is between the spiritual
attitude of *recueillement* achieved by the narrating voice as he leads his feminine companion beyond despair to a realm of pure contemplation (in this
regard, it is significant that, after the dramatic enjambement from line 8 to line
9—"viens par ici/Loin d'eux"—the two imperative verb forms used are "Vois"
(l. 9) and "Entends" (l. 14), both verbs of perception) and the very direct,
physical thrust of the metaphorical expression "*cueillir* des remords"—to pick
or pluck remorse from degrading activity, in the way one would pluck fruit
from a tree.

The initial split within the narrating voice allows the subjective consciousness to control its anxiety. The personification/allegorization of "ma Douleur,"
the transformation of a depressed mental state into a character (figment,
chimère) to accompany the *je* on his vesperal walk, constitutes a metamorphosis of the concrete presence of human mortality "below" into a spectacle, a
pure visual tableau in which even the most threatening of images—the Night
compared to "un long *linceul* traînant à l'Orient" (l. 13)—is enveloped in an
otherworldly tranquillity and sweetness ("la *douce* Nuit qui marche" [l. 14]).
The second division—between the self and others—establishes the dominion
of the narrating voice over the exterior world as such, a world reduced to the
cruel stage on which mastery and servitude, sadism and masochism, alternate
endlessly.

For "Recueillement" to achieve its particular effect of tranquil distance and meditative mastery, it is essential that the narrating voice, by means of its double split, not participate in, not be a part of, the world above or against which it creates its web of images. One can understand why Hamm cites this poem at the close of his day (life), as his own creation of a separate inner universe and his own insistence on the inviolability of protective walls mimics or repeats the rhetorical strategies of Baudelaire's melancholy poet. In the Baudelairian schizo-text, the division of consciousness within itself and against the outside world produces a self-contained system of images; an internalized allegorical vision replaces and supersedes all activities and relations outside or beyond its purview. When taken to its extreme in Beckett's late fiction, this enveloping of the world within literary discourse leads to the figments of a self-representational, self-referential sphere in which, ultimately, the very existence of those reference marks by which we live (day *versus* night, light *versus* dark, here *versus* there, now *versus* before) is undercut, ironized, negated.

The crepuscular grayness that characterizes the melancholy moments in Baudelaire's poetry also defines the purgatorial threshold situations in Beckett's works in which the human being, no longer either separate from or participating in his world, subsists in a relationless topography. At the same time, however, in his forceful play on the word *recueillement*, in his association of narrative not merely with self-reflexivity but also, simultaneously, with the ethical dimension of *taking in* one's fellow human, Beckett questions his Romantic heritage and the strategies of envelopment and containment whereby Romantic poetry neutralizes, via stylization, the concrete "situations" in which narrator *relates to* narratee. In the end, Beckett's works—both late prose and early theater—are poised between the extremes of radical fictional self-containment (the relationless mode of the figment) and the conception of literature as an openness toward the human community and the "woes of its kind." The shifting middle ground occupied by his creations is far from a compromise, however; it is the field of a constant semantic and stylistic explosion, the sphere in which primal words such as *recueillement* split, then transmute into the narrative polyphony that lies dormant within their significant potential.

CONCLUSION

MY GOAL in this study has been twofold: first, to provide readings of individual works of contemporary experimental fiction with close attention to their formal specificity; second, to analyze these works within the general thematic of literary referentiality. Thus, an account of the significance of the texts I have undertaken to read (an examination of the identifiable techniques, structures, and rhetorical strategies that combine to produce *what* these writings mean) merges with the constant preoccupation with uncovering their varied modes of reference (i.e., *how* they denote, *how* they gesture beyond the confines of their formal limits toward some imagined or real world).

In spatial terms, therefore, what underlies each chapter of my book is a certain play between inside and outside, between a fiction's apparent self-referential self-sufficiency and its appeal (*appel, Ruf*) to a topography beyond itself, a topography that has its being in the concrete particularizations of community or history. In the case of Camus's *La Chute*, a dramatic monologue based on the vocabulary of humanistic existentialism masks a strong self-referential turn, whereas both Robbe-Grillet's *Topologie d'une cité fantôme* and Simon's *Les Géorgiques*, highly constructed writings based on an abstract design and containing unmistakable traces of theoretical self-reflection, become readable only when their narrative constraints explode and become subsumed within the expansiveness of the referential turn, the movement from the word to the world. Similarly, what I have called the *prepositional rhetoric* of Marguerite Duras's *L'Amant* and of Nathalie Sarraute's *Enfance* is to be understood as an outward facing dynamic in which the forces of desire (Duras) and of linguistic truth-testing (Sarraute) take the reader beyond the absorption of the self in its own constitution and toward its integration into a complex cultural continuum.

If Part 1 of this study can be characterized essentially by the productive tension between self-referential formalism and the power of referential extensiveness and worldliness, Part 2 renders explicit what had been only implicit in the first four chapters: namely, that there is an important link between the literary question of referentiality and the ethical dimension of human being-in-the-world. This is already apparent in the rhetoric of responsibility of the young Nathalie in *Enfance*, whose amusing literalizing of the commands given her by adult voices is based on an adherence to magical "laws of the mouth"—to a presumed accord between proffered directives and their realization. In the cases of Blanchot and Beckett, the impossibility of a pure fiction and the uncovering of the solipsism underlying a Romantically conceived, distanced poetic meditation lead to a postulation of the ethical as *that domain to which the aesthetic, in its referential function, points, and on which the aesthetic as such finds its ultimate ground.* This statement, which is the conclusion toward which my own readings point, needs some clarification and justification.

The first point I should underline is that my conclusion is not tantamount to assigning a *specific moral function* to literature. The aesthetic domain as such (its specific lawfulness and playfulness) does not exist in order to fulfill or enact some practical or ethical imperative. As I stated in the introduction to Part 1, I take seriously George Steiner's admonitions in his essay "Real Presences" concerning the moral power of art, but I find the logic of his argument to be flawed. In an attempt to counter what he considers to be the destructive nihilism of deconstructionism (which would appear to consist of a dangerous undermining of the priority of the original work over critical and theoretical commentary and of a noxious, irresponsible freeplay of the critical imagination in its interpretive activities), Steiner borrows from Kant's philosophical system, but improperly. He states that the only way to fight the deconstructionist enemy and to preserve the integrity of the aesthetic realm from annihilation is to read *as if* the text incarnated "a real presence of significant being," *as if* our encounter with a work of art involved "the commonplace mystery of a real presence" (86–87). Steiner arrives at the *as if* not through the internal logic of his argument against the deconstructionists, but rather through a categorical imperative: *we must read "as if."* If we are to avoid polysemic chaos, we *must* read in a certain way (in a way that preserves what Steiner, significantly, calls our feeling of being *at home* in our cultural pleasures [77]). What Steiner has done is to transfer one of the founding powers of Kant's *Critique of Practical Reason*—the categorical imperative—from the domain of the moral to the realm of the aesthetic. In so doing, he subordinates the aesthetic to the practical or moral, thereby restricting it to a certain kind of text (the type that speaks of the "presence or absence of the god" [89]) and to a certain configuration of meanings (which he calls "sacramental"). The (categorical) misuse of the categorical imperative here has as its principal effect the enslavement of the aesthetic under the boot of the moral: this enslavement is what allows us, as readers, to be at home in our cultural pleasures (and one assumes that, for Steiner, reading is one such pleasure).

What separates Steiner from experimental contemporary writers like Camus, Blanchot, and Beckett is that the latter, in the wake of Franz Kafka, discovered, in their stylistically diverse ways, that the essence of literature is not home (or even the seductive promise of the return home), but exile,—permanent, irremediable exile. Exile is to be understood here not just as an existential theme (the lostness of the individual in an alienating environment) but as a constitutive factor in the construction of the aesthetic as such. The aesthetic as delimited topography of significant play exists, first and foremost, on its own, at a distance from the practical world, exiled from that world. The difficult and complex link between the aesthetic and the world as real, historically determined referent cannot be forged by an a posteriori, artificial imposition of moral values on the aesthetic. Rather, to remain faithful to Kant's vocabulary and to the subtleties of his system, we should say that, if the aesthetic does indeed have something in common with, something "to do with," the ethical, it is via *artistic indirection*. To repeat Kant's formulation in the *Critique of Judgment*: "The beautiful is symbol of the good."[1] This does not mean that the work of art *should* express a given moral message, but rather that an intimate link *of an analogical sort* exists between the two separate domains, such that they can, and on occasion do, communicate. It is significant that when Kant explicates the symbol as "indirect representation of a concept," he speaks of the "*transfer* [*Übertragung*] of the reflexion on an object of one's perception to an entirely different concept" (*Kritik der Urteilskraft*, 213; my translation). *Übertragung* is the Germanization of the Greek word *metaphor* (transport, transfer). If the realm of the aesthetic relates to, refers to, the moral, it is not by the arbitrary imposition of a categorical imperative from the moral onto the aesthetic, but by metaphorical transfer from the aesthetic toward the moral—that transport of words into the world that has constituted the topic of the present study.

It is perhaps no coincidence that Jean-François Lyotard, one of the most articulate proponents of postmodern artistic experimentation, locates "the impetus and the logic of avant-gardes" ("What is Postmodernism? " 77) in Kant's notion of the sublime as developed in the *Critique of Judgment*. Re-placing himself in the Kantian context and using Kantian terminology, Lyotard reminds us of the crucial difference between the beautiful and the sublime, emphasizing the way in which the experience of the sublime blocks the "formation and the stabilization of taste" (78). The explanation that follows illustrates clearly that whereas Steiner's proposed aesthetic is that of the beautiful and of a stabilized shared taste, Lyotard's model of postmodern art, based on the Kantian sublime, rests on the fundamental, apparently paradoxical notion of the "presentation of the unpresentable":

> [The sublime occurs] when the imagination fails to present an object which might, if only in principle, come to match a concept. We have the Idea of the world (the totality of what is), but we do not have the capacity to show an example of it. We have the Idea of the simple (that which cannot be broken down, decomposed), but we cannot illustrate it with a sensible object which would be a 'case' of it. We can conceive the infinitely great, the infinitely powerful, but every presentation of an object destined to 'make visible' this absolute greatness or power appears to us painfully inadequate. Those are Ideas of which no presentation is possible. Therefore, they impart no knowledge about reality (experience), they also prevent the free union of the faculties which gives rise to the sentiment of the beautiful; and they prevent the formation and the stabilization of taste. They can be said to be unpresentable. (78)

Lyotard goes on to define as postmodern (and as challenging, worthy of study) that art which devotes its technical expertise "to present the fact that the unpresentable exists" (ibid.). And the only way to do so, precisely because the artist wishes to express Ideas for which there are no logically or conceptually available examples or "cases," is to *invent a metaphorical language.* This language is aesthetic in its construction and therefore available to us an an oject of study *in its aesthetic form*—which is why I have emphasized, in the present book, the importance of close reading. At the same time, however, the very movement of *Übertragung* or metaphorical transfer involves the reader in passing from the word to the world, in "lifting his/her eye from the page" (Bonnefoy) toward the human space of ethical modalities in which we live. In this sense and only in this sense does the aesthetic find its ground and ultimate horizon in the ethical.

In the final paragraph of "What is Postmodernism?" Lyotard heightens the polemical tone of his essay by shifting his mode of address from the first-person singular to the first-person plural. In his own way, and with a purpose entirely opposite to that of Steiner, he introduces a categorical imperative. After reminding us that "it is not *our* business to supply reality but to invent allusions to the conceivable which cannot be presented" (81; my emphasis), he concludes thus: "Let us wage a war on totality, let us be witnesses to the unpresentable; let us activate the differences and save the honor of the name" (82). What Lyotard calls for in his volitive statements is not only the creation of a certain kind of art (which would be truly postmodern in his terms, and not "nostalgically modern" like the examples chosen by Steiner) but, equally important, the establishing of a community of readers. Indeed, although it is the writer who "invents allusions," it is the reader who joins the writer in being "witness to the unpresentable" and in "activating the differences."

Referential anxiety manifests itself most strongly when texts constructed on a monologic self-sufficiency pass beyond their theoretically determined formalism to become enacted in the dialogic structure of the reading situation, the reader being situated simultaneously inside and outside of the text, as that entity which enacts the meanings of the words while referring them to the world. The only categorical imperative that *applies to literature* is the volition: "Let us interpret; we must read."

NOTES

INTRODUCTION

1. Whereas in *Blindness and Insight* (1971) de Man asserts that "readers degrade the fiction by confusing it with a reality from which it has forever taken leave," in *Allegories of Reading* (1979) he argues that the real as referential outside is an "aberrant" yet necessary element in the narrative process of reading, an element from which one never "takes leave" and from which no fiction can pretend to separate itself. Most crucial to de Man's conception of the notion of referentiality as it evolves in and beyond *Allegories of Reading* is its inscription as a "moment" within the movement of interpretation, its textual immanence. In his subtle and cogent study *The Ethics of Reading* (1987), J. Hillis Miller argues that the referential is bound up with the category of the *ethical* in de Man's writings. He demonstrates convincingly that the referential and the ethical in de Man's precise and idiosyncratic sense do not exist beyond language but within it: "Whenever we think we have pushed beyond the borders of language we find that the region we have reached magically reforms itself as still or already contained within the borders of language. Though language contains within itself the evidence of its own limitation, the knowledge of that limitation can never be formulated in a way that is wholly reasonable or clear, since any formulation contains the limitation again" (57–58).

In the Introduction to Part 2 of the present study, I shall address the issue of the relation of the referential to the ethical by introducing an alternative to the linguistically immanent de Manian conception as formulated in *Allegories of Reading* and as explicated in *The Ethics of Reading*. I will allude to an important text by the distinguished contemporary poet Yves Bonnefoy that clearly sets apart the textual as tissue of signs from the referential as world toward which texts point and around which they err. Where one *situates* the ethical is of primary concern to me in the final two chapters of this book.

2. For further analysis of the "imaginary" or textually immanent referent in *On Referring in Literature*, see Ross Chambers, "Are Baudelaire's 'Tableaux Parisiens' about Paris?" (95–110) and the two essays by Anna Whiteside, "The Double Bind: Self-Referring Poetry" (14–32) and "Theories of Reference" (175–204). In the latter, Whiteside argues that even the use of names and the act of referring to concrete conditions within a given society should not be confused with real reference: "When Stendhal refers to Napoleon, Baudelaire to Paris, Chekhov to Moscow, and Dickens, Mark Twain, Balzac, and Steinbeck to particular social conditions, however realist or naturalist their art, . . . they refer not so much to the extratextual primary referent mentioned as to their own highly connoted intertextual and intratextual literary artifact" (179).

3. The word *postmodern* is both infelicitous as a term (one wonders what will happen "after postmodernism"—just how innovative can our contemporary period be?) and much debated in its meaning or meanings. One of the most complete theoretical articulations of the postmodern in its differentiation from the modern is to be found in Jean-François Lyotard's *Postmodern Condition: A Report on Knowledge*. In the Appendix to this volume ("Answering the Question: What is Postmodernism?"), Lyotard states:

The postmodern would be that which, in the modern, puts forward the unpresent-able in presentation itself; that which denies itself the solace of good forms, the consensus of a taste which would make it possible to share collectively the nostalgia for the unattainable; that which searches for new presentations, not in order to enjoy them but in order to impart a stronger sense of the unpresentable. A postmodern artist or writer is in the position of a philosopher: the text he writes, the work he produces, are not in principle governed by preestablished rules, and they cannot be judged according to a determining judgment, by applying familiar categories to the text or to the work. Those rules and categories are what the work of art itself is looking for. (Lyotard, 81)

For a reading of the controversy between Lyotard and the German philosopher Jürgen Habermas that underlies the argument of *The Postmodern Condition*, and for a critical assessment of the term *postmodernism* in both architecture and literature, see the Fall 1984 issue of *New German Critique*, notably the essays by Andreas Huyssen ("Mapping the Postmodern"), Fredric Jameson ("The Politics of Theory"), and Jürgen Habermas ("The French Path to Postmodernity"). For a provocative "theme and variations" series of essays on postmodernism (not only in literature, but also in art and architecture), including a programmatic distinction between the modern as aesthetic of "depth" and the postmodern as aesthetic of "surface," see Fredric Jameson's recent *Postmodernism, or, the Cultural Logic of Late Capitalism*.

In the present study, I shall use the term *postmodern* in a descriptive and nonpolem-ical sense to indicate the experimental literature that follows the tradition of high modernism (Proust, Joyce, Kafka) and that seems both to build upon that tradition and to search ever more radically for the "rules and categories" by which it can read itself.

4. Such colloquia were held in various locations, but the most important and most notorious took place in successive years at Cerisy-la-Salle. The proceedings were published by Union Générale d'Editions in the paperback *10/18* edition, and include the following:

1. *Nouveau roman: hier, aujourd'hui*, vols. 1 and 2, 1972.
2. *Butor: Colloque de Cerisy*, 1974.
3. *Claude Simon: Colloque de Cerisy*, 1975.
4. *Robbe-Grillet: Colloque de Cerisy*, 1976.

From year to year, as the Cerisy encounters became increasingly important in defining not only the accomplishments of the *nouveaux romanciers* but also the goals to be reached in the near future, Jean Ricardou, the most theoretically minded of the experimental novelists, began to take over the generalship of the proceedings. This is most notable in the colloquium devoted to the writings of Claude Simon, in which Ricardou's opinions seem to displace those of the future Nobel prize-winner. At the risk of over-generalization, I would say that the years 1956 until 1971 were characterized by fictional experimentation accompanied by theoretical reflection, whereas the period from 1971 until approximately 1980 saw an interesting inversion of what George Steiner would call the "natural order of things": a primary focus on theory, with the fictions being the concrete "laboratory results" of that theory. In Ricardou's case especially, novels became the working out of theoretical propositions. For an excellent discussion of Ricardou's influence on Simon, and for a cogent analysis of the predictability of fictions that are reduced to the elaboration of theoretical tenets, see chapter 7 of David Carroll's book *The Subject in Question: The Languages of Theory and the Strategies of Fiction* (1982).

5. Gide's original reference to the *mise en abyme* technique occurs in an 1893 entry to his celebrated *Journal*: "I like to see in a work of art, transposed to the scale of its characters, the very subject of this work. Nothing illuminates the work better, nothing establishes with greater sureness all the proportions of its totality. Thus, in certain paintings of Memling or of Quentin Metsys, a small, somber and convex mirror reflects, in its turn, the interior of the room in which the represented scene takes place. Thus, in the painting *Las Meninas* by Velazquez (but somewhat differently). Finally, in literature, in *Hamlet*, the scene of the comedy; and elsewhere in many other plays. In *Wilhelm Meister*, the puppet scenes or the castle festivity. In *The Fall of the House of Usher*, the reading to Roderick, etc. None of these examples is absolutely correct. What would be more adequate to the subject, what would express more precisely what I wanted to say in my *Cahiers*, in my *Narcisse* and in *la Tentative*, is the comparison with the procedure in the art of heraldry which consists of placing, in the first shield, a second '*en abyme*' " (quoted in Dällenbach, *Le Récit spéculaire*, 15).

6. This emphasis on the close reading of individual texts separates my study somewhat from that of Dina Sherzer, who, rather than engage in textual interpretation in the classical hermeneutic sense, prefers the mode of "thick description" (on this point, see chapter 1 of *Representation in Contemporary French Fiction*). The rhythmical interweaving of theoretical considerations with the detailed reading of literary works that characterizes the present study is a distinguishing feature, as well, in David Carroll's *Subject in Question* (1982) and Ora Avni's recent *Resistance of Reference: Linguistics, Philosophy and the Literary Text* (1990). Avni's book provides an excellent overview of the intersections between linguistic and philosophical theories and literary works. Her central thesis is that, despite the efforts of certain forms (and theories) of art to bypass or "negate" the world as referential outside, this world *resists* such efforts: the referential outside inevitably remains as the very basis of all art:

> A certain conception of art (or language, or comprehensive theories) may well wish to negate the world of objects and bodies and to reign alone (thus keeping company with Kant's naive bird that thinks it would soar to unlimited heights were it not for the stubborn resistance of the air). But there comes a time when the existential weight of "things" (or bodies) and the raw material of each art form or discipline (language itself in literature and, as Frege noted, in philosophy) will thwart its simplistic albeit essential wishful thinking and expose the extent to which these objects, bodies, and raw materials are the very foundation without which art (or language, or comprehensive theories) would not exist. (168–69)

7. It is perhaps no coincidence that the turn toward the referent on the part of the writers of fiction in the early 1980s is accompanied by a parallel or analogical move in the field of literary criticism, especially narratology. The important works of Peter Brooks (*Reading for the Plot: Design and Intention in Narrative*) and Ross Chambers (*Story and Situation: Narrative Seduction and the Power of Fiction*) appeared in 1984, when Robbe-Grillet, Duras, and Sarraute were publishing their autobiographies. Both Brooks and Chambers acknowledge that the emphasis in their analyses on human emotion ("desire" for Brooks, "seduction" for Chambers) is in part a reaction against the exces-

sive formalism of narratological theory (just as, in Dällenbach's terms, the autobiographical impulse of former new novelists could be taken as a reaction against the excessive self-reflexivity of their earlier fictions).

CHAPTER ONE
VERTIGINOUS STORYTELLING: CAMUS'S *LA CHUTE*, 1956

1. It has been surmised that *La Chute* is, in part, a belated intellectual reaction to Francis Jeanson's unfavorable review of *L'Homme révolté* [*The Rebel*] in the May 1952 issue of *Les Temps Modernes*. For a concise summary of the events leading up to the break between Camus and Sartre's group, and an assessment of the psychological damage done to Camus by this violent controversy, see Herbert R. Lottman, "Sartre vs. Camus," 495–507.

2. The principal reason for the feelings of frustration shared by most readers of *La Chute* is the polysemous nature of the work's symbolic references. The remarks of F. W. Locke in 1967 and those of Carl Viggiani in 1980 sound strikingly similar: despite undeniable advances of critical insight into *La Chute*, it seems as if no real progress has been made in deciphering the text's central enigmas.

"*La Chute* still remains, after the passing of almost a decade, the most enigmatic of Camus's works. There seems to be no significant accord among those who have confronted the *récit* as to what is going on there, even at the most literal level. Jean-Baptiste Clamence has been characterized by one critic as the 'modern Adam.' Another critic informs us that 'Clamence . . . falls from that state of terrestrial paradise as the result of a single event.' Such statements of course are implicit interpretations of the title of the work. To conceive of 'la chute' as involving Adam's fall from a terrestrial paradise is to accept the title as referring to the Fall of mankind from grace as recounted in the *mythos* of Genesis. That *The Fall* is a descent into Hell is also inescapable and was easily recognized. That Clamence is, too, an image of Satan rather than of Adam has been faced. But it would seem that no very precise literary conclusions have been drawn from these insights" (Locke, 306).

"*La Chute* is an enigma. As from antiquity, it is used to reach into the deepest mysteries of being. It asks and provokes a certain number of questions, then pretends to give answers: the answers turn out to be lies. Where are we? Amsterdam? Jerusalem? Hell? The Last Circle? The Vestibule? The Labyrinth? Who am I? Jean-Baptiste Clamence? John the Baptist? Adam? Jesus Christ? Satan? The Minotaur? And so on. Lies, or conjecture. The enigmatic cannot be circumscribed by words" (Viggiani, 274).

3. I refer here to the concluding argumentation of Clamence, who, after exulting in a minute recollection of his "crimes," turns the tables on his readers: "When the portrait is finished, as is the case this evening, I show it, full of desolation: 'Here, unfortunately, am I.' The indictment is completed. But at the same time, the portrait I hand to my fellow-man becomes a mirror" (1545). For an excellent reading of this passage in terms of literary self-representation, see Brian T. Fitch, "Le paradigme herméneutique chez Camus." Other articles by Fitch on *La Chute* include "*La Chute* et ses lecteurs," "Clamence en chute libre," and "Une voix qui se parle, qui nous parle, que nous parlons ou l'espace théâtral de *La Chute*."

4. In his analysis of the unpublished Cahier 7 (1951–1954), Carl Viggiani notes that *démesure* is the implicit theme of the theatrical works Camus was projecting in the early 1950s: "La Bacchante," *Les Possédés*, and "Don Juan-Faust" (271). *Démesure* is the polar opposite of Nemesis and the *pensée de midi* (literally, "Mediterranean thought" or "moderate thought") extolled at the end of *L'Homme révolté*. For a critical reading of Camus's *pensée de midi* and its ironization in *La Chute*, see David R. Ellison, *Understanding Albert Camus*, 133–43.

5. In so doing, I also establish the thematic importance of Blanchot's mode of interpretive reading for my book as a whole. Blanchot will reappear in Chapter 5 of this study.

6. There are many useful articles of exegetical or explanatory criticism dealing with the allusive tenor of *La Chute*. On the question of the biblical intertext and religious iconographical representation, see Ralph Berets, Jeffrey Meyers, and, more recently, the psychocritical interpretation of Jean Gassin. On Dante, Baudelaire, and Dostoevsky, see, among others, F. W. Locke, W. D. Redfern, and Gerald Stourzh.

7. On the importance of the neuter or the neutral (*le neutre*) in Blanchot, see Chapter 5 of this book.

8. See Warren Tucker and André Abbou.

9. On the question of reference points (*points de repère*) in contemporary experimental fiction, see my analysis of Beckett's *Compagnie* in Chapter 6.

10. The section of interest is 2:1: "Spiel als Leitfaden der ontologischen Explikation" ("Game as Guide/Clue to Ontological Explication"), 97–127.

11. See W. D. Redfern's conclusion in "Camus and Confusion": "Despite appearances, there is no joy for the critic in spotting the numerous literary borrowings and conversions in *La Chute*, and in the prolific name-dropping. It is saddening to see Camus so dependent" (340).

12. Baudelaire's prose poem can be summarized as follows: After reading moralizing pamphlets on the virtues of altruistic behavior, the narrator leaves his room in a state of exasperation. Upon reaching a cabaret in which he wishes to refresh himself, he sees a beggar and suddenly decides to *apply* to the poor wretch certain thoughts that an inner voice whispers to him: "Only he who proves himself is the equal of another man, and only he who conquers freedom is worthy of freedom." The application or proof of the poet's theory is a beating in which both combatants are disfigured. The end of the poem is a didactic *quid erat demonstrandum*, a discourse on equality pronounced by the narrating voice: "My good man, you are my equal! Won't you honor me by sharing my purse with me; and remember, if you are truly philanthropic, that when your comrades ask you for alms, you must apply to them the theory I have had the *pain* of testing on your back" (Baudelaire's emphasis; all quoted passages taken from the Pléiade edition of Baudelaire's *Oeuvres complètes*, 304–6).

13. W. D. Redfern quotes once from "De l'Essence du rire" in his essay "Camus and Confusion" (339), but confines himself to general remarks and does not analyze the intertextual games Camus's récit plays with Baudelaire's aesthetic treatise. Literary hearsay has it that Roger Martin du Gard proposed the definitive title of *La Chute* (Lottman, 563–64); if so, we are indebted to his (perhaps unconscious) clarification of Camus's indebtedness to Baudelaire.

14. See Blanchot's comments on p. 142 of *L'Amitié* and Steven Ungar's incisive article "Rules of the Game: First-Person Singular in des Forêts' *Le Bavard*."

15. Quoted by Germaine Brée in *Camus*, 128.

CHAPTER TWO
REAPPEARING MAN IN ROBBE-GRILLET'S *TOPOLOGIE D'UNE CITÉ FANTÔME*, 1976

1. I have chosen to study *Topologie d'une cité fantôme* (1976) as a single text in order to reveal its inner tensions and intrinsic structural organization. Another way to proceed would involve combining *Topologie* with *La Belle Captive* (1975) as interrelated texts (Robbe-Grillet repeats the first chapter of the latter, with minor variations, in the conclusion of the former). The major difference between the two works resides in their respective relationships to pictorial art. *La Belle Captive* is a "picto-novel" containing numerous reproductions of Magritte's paintings, so that the act of reading necessarily implies an active, creative passage from representation to words, through which one discovers how a fiction can be motivated by a visual framework. *Topologie*, on the other hand, is a novel that, by alluding to paintings and etchings without explicitly revealing them to the eye, both hides and suggests its origins: in this case, the reader has more freedom to create his or her own phantom-visions.

2. Bruce Morrissette, *The Novels of Robbe-Grillet*, 12–13. Barthes's essay represents an interesting rebuttal of Morrissette's "humanist" position, which is evident throughout the latter's work on Robbe-Grillet.

3. Alain Robbe-Grillet, *Pour un nouveau roman*, 23–24. Hereafter abbreviated as *PNR*.

4. See Françoise Meltzer, "Preliminary Excavations of Robbe-Grillet's Phantom City." Morrissette is the first to have used the term *topology* in connection with novel studies, but the use of narrative *generativity* goes back at least as far as Roussel and has been associated with the work of Jean Ricardou since the mid-sixties. For a theoretical discussion of generativity, see Ricardou's *Pour une théorie du nouveau roman*, 204–10. Ricardou has actively used the generative method in many of his novels, beginning with *La Prise de Constantinople*.

5. Examples: "Construction d'un temple en ruines à la déesse Vanadé" (15) ("Construction of a temple in ruins to the goddess Vanadé") and "Répétitions à mouvement ascendant pour une demeure immobile" (75) ("Repetitions in ascending order toward an immobile dwelling-place").

6. "Basically, his [Robbe-Grillet's] theory is this: to choose popular, ignoble, even worn-out fictional situations and themes from pornographic novels, detective stories, exotic action films, and Epinal engravings of sado-erotic tortures"("Generative Fiction," 260).

7. See Susan Suleiman, "Reading Robbe-Grillet: Sadism and Text in *Projet pour une révolution à New York*."

8. See the statements made by Robbe-Grillet in an interview with Jean-Jacques Brochier in *Magazine Littéraire* (September 1975), 103–4.

9. Magritte's "L'Echelle du feu" (1939) shows a tabletop with three objects burning: a wad of paper, an egg, and a key. Each object is obtrusively present in *Topologie*, as is the image of fire in the context of Vanadium's destruction. Even more evident is the reference to "L'Assassin menacé" (1926), which, as we shall see, could serve as the

visual representation of the novel's conclusion. Readers of Robbe-Grillet will recognize the oft-repeated theme of the murderer caught in the act, which begins with Wallace's actions in *Les Gommes* and returns, in its most sophisticated form, in *Glissements progressifs du plaisir*. Both "L'Echelle du feu" and "L'Assassin menacé" are reproduced in *La Belle Captive* and serve there as points of departure for the generation of the narrative.

10. Louis Scutenaire, *Magritte*, 15. Magritte's "problems" are reminiscent of the chance meeting on a dissection table of a sewing machine and an umbrella proposed by Lautréamont in his *Chants de Maldoror*. Toward the beginning of *Topologie*, Robbe-Grillet alludes to a "table d'opération" on which lies a sheet of paper containing "la règle du jeu"—rules of surrealistic object combination, perhaps.

11. This connection was originally made by Françoise Meltzer, in "Preliminary Excavations," 47–49.

12. It is possible that the origin of the red rose is Magritte's painting "Les Fleurs du mal" (1946), in which an orange-colored nude woman holds a rose in her hand. The reproduction of this work immediately follows "L'Assassin menacé" in *La Belle Captive*, so the substitution of the woman for the background men in bowler hats takes on the eminently structuralist form of *contagion métonymique*. A further, more humorous example of the intellectual game that consists of a playful substitution of pictorial elements within a literary text is the prophetic message in *Topologie*, which is nothing more than a combination of objects, themes, and titles of Magritte's work: "Après les vendanges, l'assassin menacé prendra garde aux oeufs de l'oiseau qui brûle" (180) ("After the grape harvest, the threatened assassin will watch out for the eggs of the burning bird"). A key and a wadded sheet of paper also appear in this passage.

13. Jacques Derrida, "Les Fins de l'homme," 144–46. Derrida gives as an example of this synecdochic circularity Kant's attempts to formulate moral laws, which must be universal and valid for all "reasonable beings in general": but the only "reasonable being," in the classical philosophical sense, is man.

14. Martin Heidegger, *Sein und Zeit*, 7 (English translation by Macquarrie and Robinson, *Being and Time*, 27). See Derrida's commentary on this passage in "Les Fins de l'homme," 149–52.

CHAPTER THREE
NARRATIVE LEVELING AND PERFORMATIVE PATHOS IN CLAUDE SIMON'S
LES GÉORGIQUES, 1981

1. For an amusing journalistic account of the disparity between cautious but solid scholarly enthusiasm for Simon and the public's near-total ignorance of his works, see the articles by Steve Lohr and Maureen Dowd that appeared in the *New York Times* the day after the awarding of the Nobel on 17 October 1985.

2. For a scathing account of the "unreadability" of *Les Géorgiques* in particular, see Philippe Dulac's review in *La Nouvelle Revue Française*. Dulac's thesis is that Simon has undeniable potential as a novelist but that his slavish adherence to the "geometric" theoretical dogmatism propounded by Jean Ricardou has vitiated his style and rendered it unnecessarily and artificially obscure.

3. One of the most lucid and controlled critical accounts of *Les Géorgiques* to date, Lucien Dällenbach's "*Les Géorgiques* ou la totalisation accomplie," deals with the way in which Simon's experimental fiction illustrates or replicates Bakhtin's theory of the novel

as "polyphonic orchestration of languages, texts, styles, and discursive formations," as "totalizing ambition," "cosmos," and "replica of the Great All" (1236–37). Dällenbach has also written the best overall interpretation of Claude Simon's oeuvre (in his *Claude Simon*, published by Minuit in 1988): in this study, Dällenbach rescues the Simonian aesthetic from its complex "appropriation" by Jean Ricardou.

4. For a sampling of methodologically and theoretically sophisticated analyses of *Les Géorgiques*, see Celia Britton ("histoire/discours"; "diversity of discourse"); Cora Reitsma-La Brujeere ("récit/métarécit/intertexte"); and Jean Dufy ("linguistic play/textual overdetermination").

5. For many critics, the novel *Histoire* (1967) is the turning point in the supposed evolution toward literary self-reflexivity and textual inwardness (mise en abyme) in Simon's novelistic production. Following are some examples of this idea, expressed with different degrees of emphasis and in different critical "languages":

> (1) According to Simon's own definition, the significance of a novelist must be measured in proportion to the degree by which he has transformed the genre. It is therefore comprehensible that he should attach more importance to the experimental works written since *Histoire* than to the previous and more traditional novels. In his latest works Simon has dispensed with the questing narrator and diminished pathos in favor of pure, self-generating description. The novels are constructed according to the principle of analogy, and the novelist explores whatever mental associations come to mind, however farfetched they appear. (Randi Birn, 290–91)

> (2) But it is true that even in the most *'romanesque'* of Claude Simon's novels, those which fascinate us most, it is impossible to ignore the *process of writing* and ultimately its fundamental importance to the reading. The reader is at the same time involved in what has also been called 'the adventure of writing.' One might therefore ask if what has been taken for a dialectic of order and disorder interpreted from a psychological point of view is not more simply the expression of a scriptorial tension between representational' and 'textual'. (Gérard Roubichou, 174)

> (3) Just as *Histoire* brings to an end the thematization of referential anguish that had tormented all of Simon's narrators until that time, in the same way the text of 1967 brings to a conclusion a certain kind of *mise en abyme*. Henceforth, the major emphasis will no longer be on the themes of restitution or transformation, but on the adventure of the writer in the act of writing. (Ralph Sarkonak, 63)

6. "Climates, seasons, sounds, colors, obscurity, light, elements, aliments, noise, silence, movement, repose, all things act on our organism and on our soul in consequence." The quotation from Rousseau serves to illuminate proleptically three major aspects of Simon's novel: (1) the profound emotional, quasi-visceral effects of Nature on the individual; (2) the confessional/autobiographical resonance of *Les Géorgiques*; (3) the subtle presence of a Virgilian intertext (*The Georgics*) subtending Rousseau and also underlying Simon's recurrent meditations on the harmonious relation between man as laborer and his natural surroundings.

7. Celia Britton and Jean Dufy have written on the complex intertextual relation between the fourth chapter of *Les Géorgiques* and George Orwell's *Homage to Catalonia*. The Englishman, called "O" in the narration of chapter 4, is thus a fictional construct to the second degree, and the section as a whole is a linguistically convoluted (and somewhat perverse) rewriting of Orwell's text (Britton 433–36; Dufy 171).

8. See *Oxford Latin Dictionary* (*OLD*), 1:1022–23.

9. I allude here to the philosophical and linguistic theory of J. L. Austin, as expressed in his rigorous and witty volume *How To Do Things With Words*. In his preliminary "isolation" of the performative utterance, Austin contrasts it with the ordinary mode of declarative statement, or constative. Performatives can be defined by what they do and do not do:

> "A. they do not 'describe' or 'report' or constate anything at all, are not 'true' or 'false'; and
>
> B. the uttering of the sentence is, or is a part of, the doing of an action, which again would not *normally* be described as saying something" (5; Austin's emphasis).

The first examples of performative utterances given by Austin are quite straight-forward:

> "E.*a*) 'I do (sc. take this woman to be my lawful wedded wife)'—as uttered in the course of the marriage ceremony.
>
> E.*b*) 'I name this ship the *Queen Elizabeth*'—as uttered when smashing the bottle against the stem.
>
> E.*c*) 'I give and bequeath my watch to my brother'—as occurring in a will.
>
> E.*d*) 'I bet you sixpence it will rain tomorrow'" (ibid.).

Austin goes on to say: "In these examples it seems clear that to utter the sentence (in, of course, the appropriate circumstances) is not to *describe* my doing of what I should be said in so uttering to be doing or to state that I am doing it; it is to do it" (6; Austin's emphasis).

What is perhaps most intriguing linguistically in the performative thus defined is its apparent abolition of all distance between speech and act, its jumping of the differential space between sign and referent. For the complex philosophical ramifications of this problematic jumping, as well as a deconstructive reading of Austin's unproblematized notion of context ("appropriate circumstances"), see Jacques Derrida's article "Signature Event Context"; John Searle's response to Derrida, "Reiterating the Differences: A Reply to Derrida;" and Derrida's lengthy and playful reply to Searle's reply, "Limited Inc abc. . . ."

The use of speech-act theory (whether problematized or unproblematized, deconstructive or "straight") by literary critics is on the rise. For three especially powerful and imaginative readings that rely heavily on speech-act theory and specifically on the play of the performative, see Paul de Man, chapters 11 and 12 of *Allegories of Reading*; Shoshana Felman, *The Literary Speech Act*; and Ora Avni, *The Resistance of Reference*.

10. Simon's phrase echoes Proust's peroration at the conclusion of the "madeleine episode" in *Du Côté de chez Swann*, in which the entire novelistic universe of *A la recherche du temps perdu* unfolds from the apparently trivial and insignificant sense impression of the little cake dipped in tea: "And just as in that game in which the Japanese enjoy dipping in a porcelain bowl filled with water small pieces of paper until then indistinct which, as soon as they are immersed, stretch out, gain contour, color, and differentiation, become flowers, houses, consistent and recognizable people, in the same way now all the flowers of our garden and those of Monsieur Swann's park, and the water-lilies of the Vivonne, and the good people of the village and their small houses

and the church and all Combray and its environs, all that which takes on form and solidity, town and gardens, emerged from my teacup" (1:47–48).

11. Near the end of *How To Do Things With Words*, after an elaboration of the constative/performative distinction, Austin decides "to make a fresh start on the problem" and "to reconsider more generally the senses in which to say something may be to do something, or in saying something we do something" (91). At this point, he moves from the dyad constative/performative to the triad locutionary/illocutionary/perlocutionary, where locutionary is the baseline or general level of speech use ("roughly equivalent to uttering a certain sentence with a certain sense and reference"[108]); illocutionary is "the performance of an act *in* saying something as opposed to performance of an act *of* saying something" (99); and perlocutionary is "what we bring about or achieve *by* saying something" (108).

According to these definitions, it is evident that the illocutionary mode of speech use corresponds, on a higher level of abstraction, to what was called the performative in the first section: "The doctrine of the performative/constative distinction stands to the doctrine of locutionary and illocutionary acts in the total speech act as the *special* theory to the *general* theory" (147; Austin's emphasis).

In the final chapter of the book (Lecture XII), Austin delineates several categories of explicit performatives, according to their degree of illocutionary force. The exercitive category is defined as follows: "An exercitive is the giving of a decision in favour of or against a certain course of action, or advocacy of it. It is a decision that something is to be so, as distinct from a judgement that it is so: it is advocacy that it should be so, as opposed to an estimate that it is so; it is an award as opposed to an assessment; it is a sentence as opposed to a verdict" (154).

12. Two of Simon's statements described in the *Actes* of the 1974 Cerisy colloquium devoted to his work are typical of his attitude: (1) "I absolutely refuse to be dragged into areas that I do not know well, for example, linguistics, semiology, or philosophy" (406); and (2) "As I said, I am not a philosopher and I have not read Derrida—or the little I have read of him I certainly read badly" (412).

13. Even when it is argued that the world is "always already" a text to decipher, the critic often presupposes the hierarchical superiority of the text's meaningful complexity over the semiological opacity (the resistance to interpretation) of the world, which is tantamount to the bracketing of the world as such and to the maintaining of a conceptual/categorical barrier between the two essentially heterogeneous spheres. This point of view has been questioned recently by critics who have devoted themselves to careful scrutiny of literary reference. See, for example, Linda Hutcheon, who contends that the deciphering of the world that is, in fact, our daily activity, is not to be differentiated from a properly textual hermeneutics: "The reader can read (or actualize or bring to life) the 'heterocosm' of fictive referents only through an act that is the *same* as . . . the decoding process s/he engages in constantly in coming to terms with experience of all kinds" (11).

14. At the 1974 Cerisy colloquium, Simon began his final remarks by emphasizing the notion of labor (*travail*) central to his own conception of writing and by deflating the elevated status reserved for the literary genius since Antiquity and through Romanticism (in this sense, it can hardly be said that Simon and Virgil converge on the *triumphant* nature of human work and art—"labor omnia *vicit*" is a statement that promises more than it can deliver according to Simon):

"First, I should express my satisfaction upon noting that many of those who have spoken [at this conference] were agreed in insisting on the notion of labor [travail] and its value—which was given its proper place: that which precedes all others.

I consider this fact extremely important, and even of capital importance in the context of a colloquium organized around the work of a novelist—personage to whom one normally grants a rather fabulous (fraudulent) status, both mystifying and farcical, of a man 'unlike all others' whose task supposedly consists simply of writing under the dictation of what one calls 'inspiration.' " (403)

Claude Simon's consistently modest demeanor in the most difficult of question-and-answer periods at colloquiums and conferences is not the sign of defensive distance or excessive *politesse*, but rather the logical expression of his dogged refusal to deny the concreteness of the writing experience in favor of seductive theoretical generalizing.

CHAPTER FOUR
THE SELF AS REFERENT: POSTMODERN AUTOBIOGRAPHIES, 1983–1984

1. Nathalie Sarraute's *Tropismes* (*Tropisms*) appeared in 1939, but it was during the fifties and sixties, with the publication of such works as Sarraute's *Martereau* (1953) and *Les Fruits d'or* (1963) (*The Golden Fruits*), Duras's *Moderato cantabile* (1958) and *Le Ravissement de Lol V. Stein* (1964) (*The Ravishing of Lol Stein*), and Robbe-Grillet's *Les Gommes* (1953) (*The Erasers*), *La Jalousie* (1957) (*Jealousy*), and *Pour un nouveau roman* (1963) (*For a New Novel*), that the so-called new novelists began to be studied as a group of revolutionary authors whose technical reworking of traditional narrative forms gained critical attention, if not the immediate support of the public.

2. See, for example, the difference in perspective between Pierre de Boisdeffre and Jeanyves Guérin on Robbe-Grillet's *Le Miroir qui revient*:

(1) de Boisdeffre: "*Le Miroir* brings—twenty years late and after much silliness—a categorical denial of the pretensions of yesterday's new novelists. . . . This tranquil return to traditional writing, only recently repudiated, and from what ironical heights!, this flaunted breeziness towards his own theories [those of Robbe-Grillet] . . . could only upset the light horsemen of the old 'new novel'" (428).

(2) Guérin: "Was he [Robbe-Grillet] finally going to make amends and, like Ionesco, return to the humanist fold? Much would then be forgiven him. However, although regression is in vogue, he persists with his usual signature. . . . Naturally enough, [*Le Miroir qui revient*] is an ambiguous, discontinuous, perforated narrative, a montage of heterogeneous fragments, an ironical juxtaposition of irreconcilable versions and hypotheses. The false [fictitious], the possible, the plausible, and the true are interwoven" (119).

3. Jean Montalbetti sees in Henri de Corinthe "the key character of *La Belle Captive* who already haunted, under other identities, *La Maison de rendez-vous* and *L'Homme qui ment* and whose historical model might be somewhere between Henri de Kérillis, the author of *De Gaulle dictateur*, and François de La Rocque, confederate of the Croix-de-Feu" (90). (The Croix-de-Feu was an association of right-wing veterans founded in 1927 and presided over by de La Rocque beginning in 1931). Georges Raillard also finds in Corinthe the figuration of Robbe-Grillet's family's far-right political inclinations, and he supports the identification of Corinthe with de La Rocque.

Le Miroir qui revient (1984) is the first volume of a projected autobiographical trilogy by Robbe-Grillet, which includes *Angélique ou l'enchantement* (1988) and the announced and soon to be published *La Mort de Corinthe*. In each of the three volumes, passages of significant length are devoted to Henri de Corinthe. On the role of Corinthe, and on the complex narrative techniques exhibited in both *Le Miroir* and *Angélique*, see Pierre van den Heuvel.

4. "The mirror which returns, however, is hardly Stendhal's, to be borne along the roadway reflecting life's accidents, but an opaque instrument reflecting the thoughts of its bearer" ("At a Steady Temperature," 412).

5. On the dialoguing narrative voices in *Enfance* and their simulation of the psychoanalytic process, see Elissa Gelfand and Françoise van Roey-Roux.

6. For a clarification of these terms, see Elissa Gelfand, Frank Kermode, and the analytical discussion of *Enfance* in the final section of this chapter.

7. On the various appearances of the Chinese gentleman as well as the intertextual richness of *L'Amant* in general, see Francine de Martinoir's excellent article.

8. On the theme of desire in Duras's oeuvre and its intimate link to the related themes of madness, alienation, and absence, see Carol J. Murphy.

9. The theoretical statements of Sarraute and Robbe-Grillet as expressed in colloquiums, interviews, and their own essays on the state of the modern novel are quite emphatic on this point. For them, the nineteenth-century novel, with its specific narrative conventions of linear causality and its "bourgeois" ideological underpinnings, is no longer possible as an art form. The creation of new forms is a precondition for the very existence of modern works of fiction that lay claim to originality. Underlying this argument is a rather straightforward conception of literary history as progress (as progressive negation and overcoming of formal stagnation) which is less revolutionary than the concrete fictional experiments of both authors.

10. Of the three works to be examined here, only Robbe-Grillet's *Miroir* in its dreamlike passages and evocations of sadomasochistic violence can be linked in the remotest thematic way to the texts of Leiris, autobiographical or otherwise. As Robbe-Grillet says in his interview with Jean-Pierre Salgas: "As far as Leiris is concerned, whom I like very much, in the end he exhausts my patience because his text disintegrates completely, which is his project. In my case, I have always held to an old Flaubertian project, at the opposite end from all disintegration. To constitute a work that, once again, will be like bronze. But bronze that moves. . . . A mobile book not to be confused with its author, but in any case an image of myself that would correspond somewhat to my work" (6).

11. On the complex intertextual relations linking *Roland Barthes par Roland Barthes* (*Roland Barthes by Roland Barthes*; hereafter abbreviated as *RB*), *Fragments d'un discours amoureux* (*A Lover's Discourse: Fragments*), and the failed project of a "Proustian" novel that occupied Barthes beginning in the year 1977, see Steven Ungar, especially "Circular Memories: Via Proust" (135–51).

12. *RB*'s originality resides, to a large degree, in its method of composition. The book consists not of chapters nor even of narrative blocks; it is a series of short to very short aphoristic paragraphs devoted to explicitly titled topics whose often violently juxtaposed diversity runs the gamut from the intellectually serious discussion of literary and political issues to the humorous and consciously frivolous expression of arbitrary personal tastes. The vertiginous shifts of perspective represented by a lineup of topics such as "Quand je jouais aux barres," "Noms propres," "De la bêtise, je n'ai le droit . . . ,"

"L'amour d'une idée," "La jeune fille bourgeoise," "L'amateur," and "Réponse de Brecht à R. B."remind the reader of similar jumps in *Mythologies*.

13. On *le neutre*, see also *Le Plaisir du texte*, 102: "Never accentuate enough the force of *suspension* in pleasure: it is a true *époché*, a halt that freezes in the distance all received [accepted] values (accepted by myself). Pleasure is a *neuter* (the most perverse form of the demoniac)." Le neutre used in a different sense from that of Barthes informs large sections of Maurice Blanchot's theoretical writings. On this question, see Chapter 5 of this book.

14. The term *jouissance* is amply developed in *Le Plaisir du texte* (*The Pleasure of the Text*), often in contradistinction to *plaisir*: "Text of *plaisir* [pleasure]: one that satisfies, fills up, produces euphoria; one that comes from culture, does not break with culture, and is linked to a *comfortable* practice of reading. Text of *jouissance* [bliss; ecstasy]: one that places its reader in a state of peril, that upsets him (perhaps even bores him), that causes his historical, cultural, and psychological foundations to vacillate, as well as the consistency of his tastes, his values, his memories, that undermines his relation to language" (25–26). But the two terms also overlap in *Le Plaisir du texte*, as Barthes explains in a moment of methodological reflection: "*Pleasure of the text, text of pleasure*: these expressions are ambiguous because there is no French word to cover both pleasure (contentment) and *jouissance* (fainting, loss of control). Thus, 'pleasure' here (and without warning) sometimes extends to *jouissance*, and sometimes is opposed to it" (33; Barthes's italics).

15. See Jean-Pierre Salgas, 6.

16. See the author's explanatory footnote on p. 10 of *Le Miroir qui revient*: "This volume was originally forecast to appear in the collection of the *Ecrivains de Toujours*, in the Editions du Seuil . . . . I had even signed a contract, still valid, with Paul Flamand. It is only the unsuspected turn taken by the text, in the course of its composition, that rendered it inappropriate for inclusion in this series of small books with imposed dimensions, with numerous illustrations, for which I am undertaking a very different project, in parallel."

17. In his interview with Salgas, Robbe-Grillet criticizes Barthes for having written an autobiography that is only apparently discontinuous and incomplete (whose concrete appearance does not correspond to its author's forcefully formulated "anti-Sartrian" (meaning here *anti closure*) theoretical/methodological assertions: "I continue to feel that in choosing the fragment, Barthes, who throughout his life was one of the great anti-Sartres, indulged in another type of fraud: he has created a kind of painting nevertheless, pointillist of course, but that ceaselessly borders on the formal limits of the *maxime* and of moralism" (6).

18. On Robbe-Grillet's use of ideologically charged but formally reinscribed *opérateurs de passage*, see Georges Raillard, 6.

19. Contrast, for example, John Sturrock's judgment: "[Robbe-Grillet] makes entertainingly free of the conventions of autobiography. But the greatest pleasures of a delightful book are conventional ones, to be got from the exactness and honesty of his recollections: especially those of his father and mother, who receive much cool yet kindly attention and are, it has to be said, shamelessly rounded characters" ("At a Steady Temperature," 412), with the detailed critical readings of François George and Georges Raillard, both of whom focus on the problems of formal fictional construction and antimimetic, ironical "open symbolism" in *Le Miroir*.

20. On the question of textual generativity, see Bruce Morrissette, Jean Ricardou (204–10), and my interpretation of Robbe-Grillet's *Topologie d'une cité fantôme* in Chapter 2 of this book.

21. The episode of the returning mirror, *because* of its symbolic complexity and indetermination, has given rise to varying critical readings, from the bemused nonattempt at interpretation of John Sturrock, to the precise erudition of Georges Raillard, to the allegorical version of François George:

> (1) *Sturrock*: "[The mirror] makes an intriguing piece of flotsam in the book, being hauled from the Bay of Biscay by one Henri de Corinthe, a pleasantly impossible guest in these mainly truthful pages whose several appearances are as delphic as his name (a throwback to *Les Gommes*, and its play on the Oedipus story)" (412).
>
> (2) *Raillard*: "Born of the sea, and returning there to seek the returning mirror, Corinthe is also the figure of a less personal folklore. He is the one who, in the legend (taken up by Michelet in *La Sorcière* and especially by Goethe, in the vampire version that Robbe-Grillet keeps), comes back after seven years to Corinth to look for his fiancée. Dead, she sucks his blood. In *Le Miroir*, the mysterious Henri de Corinthe returns seven times, mounted on his stallion" (6).
>
> (3) *George*: "We will never know [the significance of the 'returning mirror'].... But through it is suggested the fate of the writer, living-dead for having thought to see the unsayable, Orpheus who returns from the underworld without Eurydice but with a casket of spiritual jewels" (290–91).

22. In the section on his Nuremberg experiences, in which he unveils the sordid realities of Nazism badly hidden by the veneer of a clean "storefront" propaganda, Robbe-Grillet's warnings on the political and moral dangers of order pushed to an extreme remind one of Camus's *Homme révolté*. Some examples: "When one likes order, one classifies. And when one has classified, one pastes on labels. What could be more normal?" "When one tries to regulate the life of people, one must also busy oneself with regulating their death." "It is absolute order that engenders horror" (125–27). At this moment in his autobiography, Robbe-Grillet is in a sphere far removed from the Barthesian ideal of Neutrality.

23. On the reception of *L'Amant* among the general public, see Madeleine Borgomano: "The insolent success of *L'Amant* radically transforms the reception of Marguerite Duras's work.... A work that had remained largely confidential, generally considered to be boring, even unreadable, seems to become brutally accessible to the public at large and almost too easy.... Duras's narratives [during the last few years] were becoming purified to a vertiginous degree .... On the contrary, *L'Amant* returns to verbal splendor, to the seduction of less disincarnate characters, to the attractions of story-telling, and even to the charms of exoticism" (40). For Borgomano, one of the strongest attractions of the autobiography resides in its mimetic power, its referential anchoring: "*L'Amant*, in effect, adopts the 'autobiographical pact' that confuses author, narrator, and character in giving them a 'real' referent .... Events are henceforth defined, hooked on to a past declared authentic from which they began their drifting [dérive]" (47).

For the retroactively illuminating quality of *L'Amant*, see Marcelle Marini: "Then all the previous works become both clearly autobiographical or mendacious: or at least distinguished by the sin of fiction or of omission, the omission of the unavowable. Now they are no more than stepping-stones—Way of the Cross or of Glory—toward the

Royal Text that illuminates them all, explains them, and even reverses their temporal order: the 'fictions' henceforth 'derive' from this book of Truth. . . . We have arrived at 'the heart of Durasia,' at 'the source,' 'the fundamental scene': now we can read without anxiety Duras's works in reverse order, because now we possess their key" (9).

24. On the role of the brothers and mother in *L'Amant*, see Germaine Brée, who finds that the family drama per se is even more central to the autobiography than the crossing of the river: "But the real story, retrieved fragment by fragment, is in fact the desperate, stubborn, and blind will of the adolescent girl to wreak upon herself the inner havoc which will free her from the monstrous, claustrophobic bondage to unrecognized, quasi-incestuous family relations, worthy of Greek tragedy" (118).

25. The unlimited spatial extension of Marguerite, who cannot be captured or imprisoned within the gaze of her lover, reminds one of Proust's meditations on the "impossibility" of love in the relationship between Marcel and Albertine: "And I understood the impossibility against which love collides. We imagine that love has as its object a being that can be lying in front of us, enclosed within a body. Alas! it is the extension of this being to all the points of space and time that this being has occupied and will occupy. If we do not possess its [this being's] contact with a given place, with a given hour, we do not possess it" (*A la recherche du temps perdu*, 3:100).

26. For a sensitive and original reading of *L'Amant* in the context of postmodern French autobiography, see Leah D. Hewitt, chapter 3. In her analysis of *L'Amant*, Hewitt emphasizes Duras's "deconstruction" of traditional gender roles and refers to the limitless topography of desire in these terms: "[Duras's depiction of] romantic love stresses unselfishness, generosity, and interdependencies that exceed the narrow, demanding 'I' of the individual. It is not so much a sacrifice of the self (a frequent negative interpretation for the female victim who then becomes a slave or a martyr) as a joyful, outrageous expenditure (dispossession) of the self (selves), in love, drink, death, writing. . . . Duras thus manages to intertwine a certain seductive romanticism with her deconstructive assault on (masculine) individualism" (126).

27. For a highly complex "theme and variation" coupling of Music and Necessity, see *Moderato cantabile*.

28. On the question of authenticity in Sarraute's fiction, see Jean-Paul Sartre's preface to *Portrait d'un inconnu*. Thirty years after its publication, Sartre's essay remains one of the best short introductions to Sarraute's work: his equation of her world of *conversation* and the *lieu commun* (commonplace utterance) with Heidegger's "parlerie" ("das Gerede"; "idle talk") is especially probing and relevant, even if the term *authenticity* itself is pronounced today with decreasing frequency.

29. On the continuity between the fictions and the autobiography, see Françoise van Roey-Roux, Jacqueline Lévi-Valensi, and Frank Kermode.

30. Following is the passage in question: "I run down the slope, turning over and over in the close-cut and thick grass sprinkled with small mountain flowers, to the Isère [river] that glistens below the meadows between the tall trees. . . . I kneel down on the river bank, I dip my hands in its transparent water, I moisten my face with it, I stretch out on my back and I listen to it flowing, I breathe in the smell of wet wood from the enormous trunks of firs carried along in its current and that have run aground near me in the high grass. . . . I press my back, my crossed arms as hard as I can against the earth covered with moss so that all its sap can penetrate me, so that it can spread throughout my body, I look at the sky as I have never done before. . . . I melt into it, I have no limits, no end" (255).

In the second chapter of her *Autobiographical Tightropes*, Leah Hewitt asserts that Sarraute's *Enfance* contains traces of "the repressed, forbidden feminine" (72)—signs of strong sexual projections and identifications that lie underneath the controlled rationality of the text. Notably, according to Hewitt, Sarraute's relation to her mother is underplayed on the discursive surface of the autobiography but can be illuminated by a close psychocritical interpretation. Hewitt resumes her argument in the formula: "Sarraute's writing turns into a transgressive activity when it breaks with the modes of formal knowledge that the paternal order had instilled in her as a girl" (89). In my own reading of *Enfance*, I shall argue that the dramatic unraveling of the "pact" with the mother, with its consequent establishing of a strong bond between daughter and father, is at the source of the "ethical" style in Sarraute—which I do not view as a sign of the writer-daughter's subservience to paternal norms, but rather as her own conscious contribution to the creation of a *prepositional rhetoric*, as I define it in my discussions of Duras and Sarraute in this chapter.

Sarraute's writings as a whole are a challenge to psychocritical and feminist perspectives on literature, in that they pose the thorny question of gender in an embarrassingly acute and direct way. What do we make of Sarraute's conscious authorly decision, in a number of her fictions, to create a "neutral voice" that can be called neither masculine nor feminine in its abstract generality? Hewitt terms such a technical innovation a "stunning denial of gender" (63). But to say this is to presuppose that gender *defines* and that Sarraute's conscious decision not to write about sex is, of itself, a "denial" of sexuality (the added presupposition being that all genuine works of literature always write, consiously or unconsciously, about sex; that sex, as literary theme, is *always there* because it is all-determining). Another way of looking at this issue would be to say that sex, although present in filigree form in Sarraute, is simply not her principal concern and that her essential preoccupation is with the possibilities and limits of language— language as lawfulness *and* as transgression.

31. The meaning of the "ich werde es zerreissen" episode has been interpreted allegorically by both John Sturrock and Frank Kermode. For Sturrock, Sarraute has had "a splendid career of just such vandalism, as a novelist supremely gifted in the slicing open of our human upholstery and the laying bare of the shabby springs within" ("The Way of Disobedience," 596). Kermode writes: "We may reflect that this is what the writer later wishes to do to 'conversation'—to slash it so that its interior spills out" (50–51). See also Leah Hewitt for a psychocritical interpretation of the "escaping" or oozing of the gray substance from the split (*fente*) of the upholstery (77–78).

32. It is the narrator herself who uses the term *folie* (98) to describe the extreme limit toward which her private "ideas" (such as a failed comparison between her mother and a doll; see my analysis below) have taken her. There is potential for humor here, given the discrepancy in perspective between the experienced adult and the limited view of the child, who conceives of her difference from other, "normal" children in absolute, tragic terms. But the humor is muted and does not negate the pathos of the event in its lived intensity.

CHAPTER FIVE
BLANCHOT AND NARRATIVE

1. In the first group are (1) critics who discern an evolution in the writing style of Blanchot, who do not hesitate to divide his fictional and critical production into clearly

delineated "periods" (see Walter A. Strauss and Evelyne Londyn), and (2) critics who subordinate the disruptive force of Blanchot's essays to abstract aesthetic categories (see especially Tzvetan Todorov). In the second group one can mention Jean Starobinski, Emmanuel Levinas, Michel Foucault, Paul de Man, Françoise Collin, and Roger Laporte, whose pioneering analyses are included in the June 1966 issue of *Critique*, as well as Collin (*Maurice Blanchot et la question de l'écriture*), Levinas (*Sur Maurice Blanchot*), Gerald Prince, Jeffrey Mehlman, and Jacques Derrida.

2. For a development on this inward-spiraling movement, see Jacques Derrida, "La Loi du genre" (*Parages*, 251–87), an analysis of Blanchot's *La Folie du jour* (*The Madness of the Day*). The English translation of Derrida's essay ("The Law of Genre") can be found in *On Narrative*.

3. "Le Pont de bois" can be found toward the conclusion (568–82) of *L'Entretien infini*, one of Blanchot's most challenging and most exhaustive meditations on literary language, in which the key theoretical notions of *le désoeuvrement*, *l'absence*, and especially *le neutre* are developed and repeated in seemingly endless variations. Juxtaposed to "Le Pont de bois" is the crucial essay "La Voix narrative" (556–67) ("Narrative Voice"), some of whose implications I shall address later in this chapter.

4. On the question of whether Blanchot's critical essays ever reach the level of exegetical unveiling or uncovering, see the chapter on Camus's *La Chute* in this book and my discussion, within it, of Paul de Man's claim: "The clarity of his [Blanchot's] critical writings is not due to exegetical power; they seem clear, not because they penetrate into a dark and inaccessible domain but because they suspend the very act of comprehension" ("Impersonality in Blanchot," 62–63).

5. The one notable exception to this rule is Jacques Derrida who, in *Parages*, only occasionally refers to the critical writings of Blanchot as he seeks to encounter the dissimulated inaccessibility of the prose fictions on their own terms. For a statement on the difficulty of both Blanchot's critical and creative works and on the impossibility of classifying them in neat categories, see Derrida's introduction to *Parages*, 11–12.

6. Blanchot's critical works cover a vast period of time, from the 1930s until the present—a half-century of meditation on the act of writing and the essence of literature. It was not until *L'Espace littéraire* and *Le Livre à venir*, however, that Blanchot's essays began to crystallize around those nodal points—the reiterated problematic of *l'origine*, le neutre, le désoeuvrement—that interest us here and provide a point of departure for his later, more fragmented reflections in *Le Pas au-delà* and *L'Ecriture du désastre*.

7. On this question, see the aforementioned essay by Todorov, "Reflections on Literature in Contemporary France"—a curious comparison of two quite disparate figures: Roland Barthes and Maurice Blanchot.

8. Another—after the focal use of the Orpheus myth in *L'Espace littéraire* and of the Ulysses legend in the opening pages of *Le Livre à venir*.

9. Blanchot examines the question of *bavardage* as such and its link to narrative organization in his article on Louis René des Forêts's novel entitled *Le Bavard* (see "La Parole vaine," pp. 137–49 of *L'Amitié*) and in his study of Camus's *La Chute* ("La Chute: La Fuite," also in *L'Amitié*, 228–35).

10. Of the authors mentioned above, the poets most often examined in Blanchot's critical articles are Mallarmé and Rilke; the novelist who appears with the most obsessive regularity is Kafka. Blanchot's writings on the latter have been collected in the volume *De Kafka à Kafka* (1981).

11. On the Proust-Ruskin relation, and on the question of Ruskin's "idolatrous" betrayal of his own hermeneutical achievements, see Richard Macksey's excellent synthetic account in his introduction to *Marcel Proust: On Reading Ruskin*. See Paul de Man, *Blindness and Insight*, for a rigorous theoretical exposition of the "inevitably" erroneous and self-deluding process of reading.

12. "L'Expérience de Proust" is in Blanchot's *Faux Pas*. On the proximity of Blanchot to Heidegger and on the essential differences that separate the French writer from the German philosopher, see Françoise Collin's, "La littérature et le langage," pp. 55–79 of *Maurice Blanchot et la question de l'écriture*.

13. Indirectly and unexplicitly in this essay, but far more openly and unambiguously in the programmatic introductory chapter of *Faux Pas* entitled "De l'Angoisse au langage" (9–23).

14. The second version of "L'Experience de Proust" is part 2 of Blanchot's "Le Chant des Sirènes" (in *Le Livre à venir*).

15. Here, Blanchot anticipates Georges Poulet's masterful analysis of the Proustian metamorphosis of temporality into spatial relations, as described in *L'Espace proustien* (1963) (*Proustian Space*).

16. "Musil" is part 4 of Blanchot's "D'Un Art sans avenir" (in *Le Livre à venir*).

17. This essay can be found in both *L'Espace littéraire* and *De Kafka à Kafka*.

18. On the transformations from the first to the second version of *Thomas l'obscur*, see Evelyne Londyn, "L'Univers imaginaire de *Thomas l'obscur*," in *Maurice Blanchot romancier*; and Jean Starobinski.

19. For a provocative early assessment of *Aminadab*, see Jean-Paul Sartre, "Aminadab, ou du fantastique considéré comme un langage." On the mixture of Heideggerian allegory and the fantastic in *Le Très-Haut*, see Evelyne Londyn, pp. 177–89 of *Maurice Blanchot romancier*.

20. A number of the story's scenes have a surrealistic, hallucinatory quality. Thomas's *combat avec l'ange*—his wrestling with the word *rat* (which transmutes itself into a monstrous apparition with a concrete physical extensiveness)—is far from Giralducian: one thinks, rather, of Michel Leiris's *Aurora* for a work (and for wordplay) of similar oneiric power.

21. The proclamation "Je pense, donc je ne suis pas" is more than a parody or specular inversion of the Cartesian formula. The linkage of negation and absence to Being as it evolves through the passage contains within it unmistakable references to both Hegel and the Mallarmé of *Igitur*.

22. On the theme of vocal proximity in Blanchot (song and cry [*le chant, le cri*]), see Françoise Collin's, "Le Sujet et L'Autre" in her *Maurice Blanchot et la question de l'écriture*.

23. I refer to the now well known association of these three intellectuals with the currents of Nazism and anti-Semitism. For a cogent and imaginative reading of the traces of Fascist ideology in the rarified philosophical language of Heidegger, see Pierre Bourdieu. The ground-breaking study that relates Blanchot's early right-wing writings in *Combat* (1936–1938) to his later "pure" prose is that of Jeffrey Mehlman, "Blanchot at *Combat*: Of Literature and Terror."

In North America and in Europe, the controversy surrounding the belated discovery of Paul de Man's contributions to the (collaborationist) Belgian newspaper *Le Soir* from 1940 to 1942 has generated a steady and unabated stream of commentary. The collected articles of the young de Man can be found in the volume *Wartime Journalism*; reactions by European and American intellectuals to these articles appeared in *Re-*

sponses: On Paul de Man's Wartime Journalism (both books edited by the University of Nebraska Press). Other significant individual contributions by scholars close to de Man include those of Geoffrey Hartman ("Blindness and Insight"); Jacques Derrida ("Like the Sound of the Sea Deep within a Shell: Paul de Man's War"); and Barbara Johnson ("The Surprise of Otherness: A Note on the Wartime Writings of Paul de Man").

For those of us who worked closely with de Man (he was my dissertation adviser at Yale University), the revelation of his wartime writings was an unmitigated shock: nothing could have prepared us for the self-assured formulas and dubious ideology of "Jews in Contemporary Literature"—an article that, despite the tortuous unraveling to which Derrida submitted it in "Paul de Man's War," is irredeemable, *not to be rescued*. And it does not help that this article is the only one of de Man's 179 articles that is explicitly devoted to the "Jewish question." For the student of deconstruction, the revelation of the wartime writings poses the difficult question of the precise nature of the relation between the aesthetic and the ethical—or, in the terms of my own study, of the *inside* of the literary text conceived of as "self-referential" or "self-generated" "pure" narration, and the *outside* of the world to which this text *always points*, despite whatever assertions it might make to the contrary. Barbara Johnson formulated it well when she concluded, in "The Surprise of Otherness," that de Man's writings "remain indispensable in their insistence that the too-easy leap from linguistic to aesthetic, ethical, or political structures has been made before, with catastrophic results" (21). One thinks, naturally, of the "aestheticization of the political" performed systematically by the Nazis. I would add, however, that the failure of deconstruction (of a certain textually immanent subclass of this hard-to-define "movement") has been to retreat *into the text, back from the world and from history*, to *refuse the "leap" from text to world*. I have no quarrel with the assertion that this leap is not an easy one; indeed, it may be the most difficult, the most challenging leap possible. My point in the present study of Blanchot is that even the writer who has theorized most cogently the question of the "inaudible" and "relationless" *voix narrative* cannot avoid the inescapable fall into history that occurs when his narrative "betrays" itself by opening itself to the outside, when his words refer to the world—that extended space in which we live and in which our writings leave their traces.

CHAPTER SIX
BECKETT AND THE ETHICS OF FABULATION

1. In the present chapter I shall be quoting from both the French and the English versions of Beckett's works. *Fin de partie* was initially composed in French, then translated into English by the author. In the act of translation Beckett altered some passages in significant ways, and the traces of certain words that recurred in crucial contexts in the French original necessarily disappeared in English. In the second half of my analysis I shall deal with these microtextual linguistic peculiarities. Beckett composed *Company* in English, next wrote the French version, *Compagnie*, then came back to the English original and made some final changes (see Brian Finney, 69): in this case, the linguistic "crossover" is complete and the two texts are mutually dependent and mutually illuminating.

2. *Mal vu mal dit* was initially written in French, then translated by the author into English. *Worstward Ho* appeared first in English. As Beckett evolved in his writing style, he tended to alternate increasingly between English and French from work to work, whereas in the early stages of his career, the phases of writing exclusively in one lan-

178 NOTES TO CHAPTER SIX

guage were longer in duration. On the question of the original passage from English to French in Beckett, and on his linguistic ambivalence in general, see Erika Ostrovsky and John Fletcher. For a discussion of the place of translation within the creative and compositional processes unique to Beckett, see Brian T. Fitch.

3. On the temporary eclipse of the real referent in Beckett's prose, and on the central importance of "Imagination morte imaginez" (1965) ("Imagination Dead Imagine") and *Le Dépeupleur* (1970) (*The Lost Ones*) for an understanding of the "residual" phase of his fiction, see John Pilling.

4. *Compagnie* appeared two years after Deirdre Bair's useful, voluminous, but largely anecdotal biography of Beckett. As Brian Finney has observed, several of the fifteen autobiographical vignettes contained in *Compagnie* appeared in Ms. Bair's book (Finney, 69). It is possible that Beckett, having read his biography, decided to weave the now-public details of his life into a work of creative prose—the result being a hybrid text that shares elements of classical autobiography with hermetic fiction. On the mixture of these two modes, see Enoch Brater.

5. On this issue, see Ronald R. Thomas and Kateryna Arthur. Arthur derives her use of the term from the *schizo-analyses* of Gilles Deleuze and Félix Guattari in their provocative theory of writing as liberated (antifamilial) desire, as delineated in *L'Anti-Oedipe: Capitalisme et Schizophrénie* (1972) (*Anti-Oedipus: Capitalism and Schizophrenia*). Deleuze and Guattari apply their theory to the fictional universe of Franz Kafka in a subtle analysis entitled *Kafka: Pour une littérature mineure* (1975) (*Toward a Minor Literature*).

6. I borrow this term from M. M. Bakhtin, whose conception of novelistic discourse as an "orchestration" of diverse voices is illuminating for an understanding of Beckett's prose works. For the most concise development of this conception, see Bakhtin's essay "Discourse in the Novel."

7. Following are two examples of the first-person form:
"Et s'il parlait après tout. Si faiblement que ce soit. Quelle contribution à la compagnie ce serait. Tu es sur le dos dans le noir et un jour tu parleras à nouveau. Un jour! Enfin. Enfin tu parleras à nouveau. Oui je me rappelle. Ce fut moi. Ce fut moi alors" (27).

"If he were to utter after all? However feebly. What an addition to company that would be! You are on your back in the dark and one day you will utter again. One day! In the end. In the end you will utter again. Yes I remember. That was I. That was I then" 27.

"Tu naquis un vendredi saint au terme d'un long travail. Oui je me rappelle. Le soleil venait de se coucher derrière les mélèzes. Oui je me rappelle" (47).

"You were born on an Easter Sunday after long labour. Yes I remember. The sun had not long sunk behind the larches. Yes I remember" 46–47.

8. In engineering and surveying terminology, *point de repère* means *benchmark*, the already established point from which one measures new distances and levels.

9. Further along in the story, the third-person narrator reiterates this same idea: "Rares lueurs de raisonnement aussitôt éteintes. Espoir et désespoir pour ne nommer que ce vieux tandem à peine ressenti. Sur les origines de sa situation actuelle aucun éclaircissement. Point de là à rapprocher d'ici ni d'alors de maintenant" (61) ("Rare flashes of reasoning of no avail. Hope and despair and suchlike barely felt. How current situation arrived at unclear. No that then to compare to this now"[62].)

10. There are numerous passages in the text that evoke reminiscences from Beck-

ett's childhood, some of which (as previously noted) correspond directly to the anecdotal material contained in Deirdre Bair's biographical study. *Compagnie* is, on one level, a compendium of autobiographical fragments and can be read as a complex series of highly personal revelations from an author who is not usually prone to divulging such private information. The interpreter of *Compagnie* may be tempted to find in some of these primal familial scenes the representation of traumatic moments that the author himself considers pivotal, but the playfulness with which the narrator describes a number of these supposedly real occurrences in his life cannot be overlooked. See, for example, the passage in which the narrator conflates two episodes in the rustic summerhouse of his youth: the first, of his father reading *Punch* on a Sunday afternoon, the other of a rendezvous Beckett keeps with a young woman (*Compagnie*, 52–57; *Company*, 53–59). At the end of the episode, he brings together the image of his father's stomach protruding from unbuttoned trousers with that of the opulent girth of the young woman Beckett desires—a generic confusion of considerable interest to the earnest Freudian critic.

11. On the general question of genre transformation in Beckett, and on the specific matter of the adaptation of *Compagnie* to the theater, see S. E. Gontarski, "*Company* for Company: Androgyny and Theatricality in Samuel Beckett's Prose." In his essay, Gontarski describes his own adaptation of the prose text to the theater as well as that of Pierre Chabert and includes in his presentation pertinent remarks on the crucial role of voice as such in Beckett's evolving literary production.

12. On the symbolic potential of the stage setting as representation of life after the cataclysmic destruction of nature and of shared human values, see Theodor W. Adorno, 86–87. On the resemblance of the setting to the reduced universe of the skull and the interior realm of thought, see Ruby Cohn, 48–49.

13. On the significance of the distinction between the "inner space" observable by the spectator of *Fin de partie* and the "outer space" beyond his vision, see Ross Chambers, "An Approach to *Endgame*."

14. *FP*, 31; *EG*, 100. In his book *The Intent of Undoing in Samuel Beckett's Dramatic Texts*, S. E. Gontarski has studied the various existing early drafts of *Fin de partie* and has demonstrated the progressive disappearance of allusions to World War II. The reference to Sedan is one of the few details remaining in the final version of the text that evokes the War explicitly.

15. Following are two examples of the many one-line allusions to the incomprehensibility of time:

HAMM: Quelle heure est-il?
CLOV: La même que d'habitude.

(*FP*, 18)

HAMM: What time is it?
Clov: The same as usual.

(*EG*, 94)

CLOV: Tu crois à la vie future?
HAMM: La mienne l'a toujours été.

(*FP*, 69)

CLOV: Do you believe in the life to come?
HAMM: Mine was always that.

(*EG*, 116)

16. On the crucial notion of context or "situation" in narrative theory, see Ross Chambers, *Story and Situation: Narrative Seduction and the Power of Fiction*. In his introductory review of structuralist criticism ("grammatical" and "rhetorical" approaches to story telling), Chambers indicates what is missing in these methodologies—and what will be the subject matter of his own subtle analyses: "But what is lacking [in the structuralist, 'context-free' study of narration] is recognition of the significance of situational phenomena—of the social fact that narrative mediates human relationships and derives its 'meaning' from them; that, consequently, it depends on social agreements, implicit pacts or contracts, in order to produce exchanges that themselves are a function of desires, purposes, and constraints" (4).

17. The theme of abandonment is counterbalanced throughout *Fin de partie* by its diametrical opposite, pity (or aid) for one's fellow humans. In the early stages of the play, Clov accuses Hamm: "Tu n'auras eu pitié de personne" (54) ("You won't have had pity on anyone"110]); and, toward its conclusion, Hamm admits wistfully but with some violence: "Tous ceux que j'aurais pu aider. (*Un temps.*) Aider! (*Un temps.*) Sauver. (*Un temps.*) Sauver! (*Un temps.*) Ils sortaient de tous les coins" (91) ("All those I might have helped. [*Pause.*] Helped! [*Pause.*] Saved. [*Pause.*] Saved! [*Pause.*] The place was crawling with them!" [125]).

18. Here, Beckett touches on a classical literary motif—that of the sick, poor, or disadvantaged person in need of resources or psychological support to whom a healthy, rich, or privileged interlocutor refuses all aid. This is the situation of the famous "souliers rouges de la duchesse" episode that concludes *Le Côté de Guermantes*, the third volume of Proust's *A la recherche du temps perdu*: Swann is very ill, but the duc de Guermantes is more concerned with the color of his wife's shoes and with being late to a social gathering than with the state of health of his friend, to whom he addresses the following "reassuring" words: "Et puis vous, ne vous laissez pas frapper par ces bêtises des médecins, que diable! Ce sont des ânes. Vous vous portez comme le Pont-Neuf. Vous nous enterrerez tous!" (597) ("Now don't you be overly impressed by the stupidity of those doctors, for heaven's sake! They are all asses. You are as solid as a rock. You will bury us all!"). One thinks as well of Tolstoy's *Death of Ivan Ilyich*, in which the protagonist's family, with the notable exception of the simple but always devoted servant Gerasim, views the sick Ivan as a hindrance to its own pursuit of pleasure, as an incomprehensible dark figure casting a shadow over each day's sunrise, blocking the forces of vital renewal.

19. On two occasions Hamm makes it clear that he considers Clov to be his "son." First, in addressing Clov directly, he says: "Sans moi (*geste vers soi*), pas de père. Sans Hamm (*geste circulaire*), pas de home" (56) ("But for me [*gesture towards himself*] no father. But for Hamm [*gesture towards surroundings*] no home"110–11]). And later in the play, when imagining his imminent death, he prophesies: "Je serai là, dans le vieux refuge, seul contre le silence. . . . J'aurai appelé mon père et j'aurai appelé mon . . . (*il hésite*) . . . mon fils" (92) ("There I'll be, in the old refuge, alone against the silence. . . . I'll have called my father and I'll have called my . . . [*he hesitates*] . . . my son"[126]).

20. The interpretation of Clov's relation to the outside world (the grayness beyond Hamm's walls) and, in particular, of his link to the small boy observed just before the play's conclusion is made difficult not only by the author's calculated indefiniteness on this question (is Hamm's story real or a fiction, is Clov an actor in Hamm's story or not, etc.) but also by the differences between the French and English versions of the play at

the precise point at which Clov sees the boy. The French version (*FP* 103–5) is longer and far richer in symbolism (the boy is compared, successively, to the dying Moses facing the Promised Land and to a Buddhalike figure contemplating his navel), whereas the English version (*EG*, 130–31), in its elliptical simplicity, comes close to eliminating the importance of the scene (and the boy) altogether. On the question of the discrepancy between the two versions, see Bell Gale Chevigny (13), Martin Esslin (29–31), and Hugh Kenner (55).

CONCLUSION

1. This striking statement occurs in paragraph 59 of the *Critique of Judgment*. Its most general sense is well articulated by Gilles Deleuze, as follows: "As Kant says, *the beautiful itself is symbol of the good* (he means that the feeling of the beautiful is not a dim perception of the good, that there is no analytical relationship between the good and the beautiful, but that there is a symbolic relationship according to which the interest of the beautiful disposes us to be good, destines us for morality)" (*Kant's Critical Philosophy*, 55). The contextual significance of paragraph 59 within the totality of the *Critique of Judgment* is discussed by Ernst Cassirer (who warns against the "peril" of confusing the aesthetic sense of the "sublime" with the "awe" that is characteristic of the moral domain). An excellent close reading of the not-so-evident argumentational articulations that subtend the analogical connection between beauty and morality in the *Critique of Judgment* can be found in Ted Cohen's article.

WORKS CITED

Abbou, André. "Les Structures superficielles du discours dans *La Chute.*" *Revue des Lettres Modernes* 238–44 (1970): 101–25.

Adorno, Theodor W. "Towards an Understanding of *Endgame.*" In *Twentieth-Century Interpretations of "Endgame,"* 82–114.

Albert Camus 1980: Second International Conference on Albert Camus. Ed. Raymond Gay-Crosier. Gainesville: University Presses of Florida, 1980.

Arthur, Kateryna. "Texts for *Company.*" In *Beckett's Later Fiction and Drama: Texts for Company,* ed. James Acheson and Kateryna Arthur, 136–44. New York: St. Martin's Press, 1987.

Austin, J. L. *How To Do Things With Words.* Cambridge, Mass.: Harvard University Press, 1962.

Avni, Ora. *The Resistance of Reference: Linguistics, Philosophy and the Literary Text.* Baltimore: Johns Hopkins University Press, 1990.

Bair, Deirdre. *Samuel Beckett: A Biography.* New York: Harcourt Brace Jovanovich, 1978.

Bakhtin, M. M. "Discourse in the Novel." In *The Dialogic Imagination,* ed. Michael Holquist, trans. Caryl Emerson and Michael Holquist. Austin: University of Texas Press, 1981.

Barthes, Roland. *Fragments d'un discours amoureux.* Collection "Tel Quel." Paris: Seuil, 1977. Trans. Richard Howard as *A Lover's Discourse: Fragments.* New York: Hill and Wang, 1978.

―――. *Mythologies.* Collection "Pierres Vives." Paris: Seuil, 1957. Trans. Annette Lavers as *Mythologies.* New York: Hill and Wang, 1972.

―――. *Le Plaisir du texte.* Collection "Tel Quel." Paris: Seuil, 1973. Trans. Richard Miller as *The Pleasure of the Text.* New York: Hill and Wang, 1975.

―――. *Roland Barthes par Roland Barthes.* Collection "Ecrivains de Toujours." Paris: Seuil, 1975. Trans. Richard Howard as *Roland Barthes by Roland Barthes.* New York: Hill and Wang, 1977.

Baudelaire, Charles. "Assommons les pauvres!" *Le Spleen de Paris.* In *Oeuvres complètes,* 304–6. Text establ. Y.-G. Le Dantec. Rev. ed. Cl. Pichois. Paris: Pléiade, 1961.

―――. "De L'Essence du rire et généralement du comique dans les arts plastiques." In *Curiosités esthétiques, L'Art romantique et autres oeuvres critiques de Baudelaire,* ed. H. Lemaître, 241–63. Paris: Garnier, 1962.

―――. "Meditation." In *Les Fleurs du Mal/The Flowers of Evil,* trans. Richard Howard, 173. Boston: David R. Godine, 1982.

―――. "Recueillement." In *Les Fleurs du Mal/The Flowers of Evil,* trans. Richard Howard, 173. Boston: David R. Godine, 1982.

Beckett, Samuel. *Comment c'est.* Paris: Minuit, 1961.

―――. *Compagnie.* Paris: Minuit, 1980.

―――. *Company.* London: John Calder, 1980.

―――. *Le dépeupleur.* Paris: Minuit, 1970.

―――. *En attendant Godot.* Paris: Minuit, 1952.

Beckett, Samuel. *Endgame*. In *Samuel Beckett: The Complete Dramatic Works*, 89–134. London: Faber and Faber, 1986.

————. *Fin de partie*. Paris: Minuit, 1957.

————. *Happy Days*. London: Faber and Faber, 1962.

————. *How It Is*. New York: Grove Press, 1970.

————. *Ill Seen Ill Said*. New York: Grove Press, 1981.

————. "Imagination Dead Imagine." In *'First Love' and Other Stories*, 61–6. New York: Grove Press, 1974.

————. *Imagination morte imaginez*. Paris: Minuit, 1965.

————. *L'Innommable*. Paris: Minuit, 1953.

————. *The Lost Ones*. New York: Grove Press, 1972.

————. *Malone Dies*. New York: Grove Press, 1970.

————. *Malone meurt*. Paris: Minuit, 1969.

————. *Mal vu mal dit*. Paris: Minuit, 1981.

————. *Mercier and Camier*. New York: Grove Press, 1975.

————. *Mercier et Camier*. Paris: Minuit, 1970.

————. *Molloy*. Paris: Minuit, 1951.

————. *Molloy*. Trans. Patrick Bowles in collaboration with the author. New York: Grove Press, 1970.

————. *Oh les beaux jours*. Paris: Minuit, 1963.

————. *Textes pour rien*. Paris: Minuit, 1950.

————. *The Unnamable*. In *Molloy, Malone Dies, The Unnamable*, 293–418. London: Calder and Boyars, 1966.

————. *Waiting for Godot*. New York: Grove Press, 1970.

————. *Worstword Ho*. New York: Grove Press, 1983.

Beckett's Later Fiction and Drama: Texts for Company. Ed. James Acheson and Kateryna Arthur. New York: St. Martin's Press, 1987.

Berets, Ralph. "Van Eyck's 'The Just Judges' in Camus' *The Fall*." *Research Studies* (Washington State University), 42 no. 2 (1974): 112–22.

Birn, Randi. "Postface." In *Orion Blinded: Essays on Claude Simon*, ed. Randi Birn and Karen Gould, 189–91. Lewisburg, Pa.: Bucknell University Press, 1981.

Blanchot, Maurice. *Aminadab*. Paris: Gallimard, 1942.

————. *L'Amitié*. Paris: Gallimard, 1971.

————. *L'Arrêt de mort*. Paris: Gallimard "L'Imaginaire," 1971. Trans. Lydia Davis as *Death Sentence*. Barrytown, N.Y.: Station Hill Press, 1978.

————. *L'Attente l'oubli*. Paris: Gallimard, 1962.

————. *Au Moment voulu*. Paris: Gallimard, 1951. Trans. Lydia Davis as *When the Time Comes*. Barrytown, N.Y.: Station Hill Press, 1985.

————. *Celui qui ne m'accompagnait pas*. Paris: Gallimard, 1953. Trans. Lydia Davis as *The One who was Standing Apart from Me*. Barrytown, N.Y.: Station Hill Press, 1989.

————. "*La Chute*: La Fuite." In *L'Amitié*, 228–35. Paris: Gallimard, 1971.

————. *De Kafka à Kafka*. Paris: Gallimard "Idées," 1981.

————. *Le Dernier Homme*. Paris: Gallimard, 1957. Trans. Lydia Davis as *The Last Man*. New York: Columbia University Press, 1987.

————. "Le Détour vers la simplicité." in *L'Amitié*, 214–27. Paris: Gallimard, 1971.

————. *L'Ecriture du désastre*. Paris: Gallimard, 1980. Trans. Ann Smock as *The Writing of the Disaster*. Lincoln: University of Nebraska Press, 1986.

————. *L'Entretien infini*. Paris: Gallimard, 1969.

————. *L'Espace littéraire*. Paris: Gallimard "Idées," 1968. Trans. and intro. Ann Smock as *The Space of Literature*. Lincoln: University of Nebraska Press, 1982.

————. *Faux Pas*. Paris: Gallimard, 1943.

————. *La Folie du jour*. Montpellier: Fata Morgana, 1973. Trans. Lydia Davis as *The Madness of the Day*. Barrytown, N.Y.: Station Hill Press, 1981.

————. *Le Livre à venir*. Paris: Gallimard "Folio-Essais," 1971.

————. *Le Pas au-delà*. Paris: Gallimard, 1973.

————. *Thomas l'obscur*. New edition. Paris: Gallimard, 1950. Trans. Robert Lamberton as *Thomas the Obscure*. New edition. Barrytown, N.Y.: Station Hill Press, 1988.

————. *Le Très-Haut*. Paris: Gallimard, 1948.

Bloom, Harold. *The Anxiety of Influence: A Theory of Poetry*. New York: Oxford University Press, 1973.

Bonnefoy, Yves. "Lifting One's Eyes from the Page." *Critical Inquiry* 16, no. 4 (Summer 1990): 794–806.

Borgomano, Madeleine. "Romans: La Fascination du vide." *L'Arc* 98 (1985): 40–48.

Bourdieu, Pierre. *L'Ontologie politique de Martin Heidegger*. Paris: Minuit "Le Sens Commun," 1988.

Brater, Enoch. "The *Company* Beckett Keeps: The Shape of Memory and One Fablist's Decay of Lying." In *Samuel Beckett: Humanistic Perspectives*, ed. Morris Beja, S. E. Gontarski, and Pierre Astier, 157–71. Columbus: Ohio State University Press, 1983.

Brée, Germaine. *Camus*. New Brunswick, N.J.: Rutgers University Press, 1959.

————. Review of *L'Amant*, by Marguerite Duras. *International Fiction Review* 12, no. 2 (Summer 1985): 118–19.

Britton, Celia. "Diversity of Discourse in Claude Simon's *Les Géorgiques*." *French Studies* 38 (October 1984): 423–42.

Brochier, Jean-Jacques. Interview with Robbe-Grillet. "Robbe-Grillet: La Vraisemblance et la vérité." *Magazine Littéraire* 103–4 (September 1975): 84–86.

Brooks, Peter. *Reading for the Plot: Design and Intention in Narrative*. New York: Random House, Vintage Books, 1984.

Butor, Michel. *La Modification*. Paris: Minuit "Double," 1987. Orig. publ. 1957. Trans. Jean Stewart as *A Change of Heart*. New York: Simon and Schuster, 1959.

Butor: Colloque de Cerisy. Ed. Georges Raillard. Paris: Union Générale d'Editions, 10/18, 1974.

Camus, Albert. *La Chute*. In *Théâtre, Récits, Nouvelles*, 1477–1551. Trans. Justin O'Brien as *The Fall*. New York: Knopf, 1957.

————. *Essais*. Ed. R. Quilliot and L. Faucon. Paris: Pléiade, 1965.

————. *L'Etranger*. In *Théâtre, Récits, Nouvelles*, 1127–1212. Trans. Stuart Gilbert as *The Stranger*. New York: Knopf, 1946.

————. *L'Homme révolté*. In *Essais*, 413–709. Trans. Justin O'Brien as *The Rebel*. New York: Knopf, 1954.

————. *Le Mythe de Sisyphe*. In *Essais*, 90–211. (Also included in *The Myth of Sisyphus and Other Essays*, trans. Justin O'Brien. New York: Knopf, 1955).

————. *La Peste*. In *Théâtre, Récits, Nouvelles*, 1213–474. Trans. Stuart Gilbert as *The Plague*. New York: Knopf, 1948.

Carroll, David. *The Subject in Question: The Languages of Theory and the Strategies of Fiction*. Chicago: University of Chicago Press, 1982.

Cassirer, Ernst. *Kant's Thought and Life.* Trans. James Haden, intro. Stephan Korner. New Haven, Conn.: Yale University Press, 1981.

Chambers, Ross. "An Approach to *Endgame.*" In *Twentieth-Century Interpretations of "Endgame,"* 71–81.

———. "Are Baudelaire's 'Tableaux Parisiens' About Paris?" In *On Referring in Literature,* ed. Anna Whiteside and Michael Issacharoff, 95–110. Bloomington: Indiana University Press, 1987.

———. *Story and Situation: Narrative Seduction and The Power of Fiction.* Minneapolis: University of Minnesota Press, 1984.

Chevigny, Bell Gale. Introduction to *Twentieth-Century Interpretations of "Endgame,"* 1–13.

Claude Simon: Colloque de Cerisy. Ed. Jean Ricardou. Paris: Union Générale d'Editions, 10/18, 1975.

Cohen, Ted. "Why Beauty is a Symbol of Morality." In *Essays in Kant's Aesthetics,* ed. and intro. Ted Cohen and Paul Guyer, 221–236. Chicago: University of Chicago Press, 1982.

Cohn, Ruby. "*Endgame.*" In *Twentieth-Century Interpretations of "Endgame,"* 40–52.

Collin, Françoise. "L'Un et L'Autre." *Critique* 229 (June 1966): 561–70.

———. *Maurice Blanchot et la question de l'écriture.* Paris: Gallimard, 1971.

Dällenbach, Lucien. *Claude Simon.* Paris: Seuil, 1988.

———. "*Les Géorgiques* ou la totalisation accomplie." *Critique* 414 (Special Issue entitled *La Terre et la Guerre dans l'oeuvre de Claude Simon*) (November 1981): 1226–42.

———. *Le Récit spéculaire. Essai sur la mise en abyme.* Paris: Seuil, 1977. Trans. Jeremy Whiteley and Emma Hughes as *The Mirror in the Text.* Chicago: University of Chicago Press, 1989.

De Boisdeffre, Pierre. "Le Retour du romanesque." Review of *Le Miroir qui revient,* by Alain Robbe-Grillet. *Revue des Deux Mondes* (April–June 1985): 428–32.

Deleuze, Gilles. *Kant's Critical Philosophy: The Doctrine of the Faculties.* Minneapolis: University of Minnesota Press, 1984.

Deleuze, Gilles, and Félix Guattari. *Capitalisme et Schizophrénie. L'Anti-Oedipe.* Paris: Minuit, 1972. Trans. Robert Hurley, Mark Seem, and Helen Lane as *Anti-Oedipus: Capitalism and Schizophrenia.* Minneapolis: University of Minnesota Press, 1983.

———. *Kafka: Pour une littérature mineure.* Paris: Minuit, 1975. Trans. Dana Polan as *Toward a Minor Literature.* Minneapolis: University of Minnesota Press, 1986.

De Man, Paul. *Allegories of Reading: Figural Language in Rousseau, Nietzsche, Rilke, and Proust.* New Haven, Conn.: Yale University Press, 1979.

———. *Blindness and Insight: Essays in the Rhetoric of Contemporary Criticism.* New York: Oxford University Press, 1971.

———. "La Circularité de l'interprétation dans l'oeuvre critique de Maurice Blanchot." *Critique* 229: 547–60.

———. "Impersonality in the Criticism of Maurice Blanchot." In De Man, *Blindness and Insight,* 60–78.

———. *Wartime Journalism, 1939–1943.* Ed. Werner Hamacher, Neil Hertz, and Thomas Keenan. Lincoln: University of Nebraska Press, 1988.

De Martinoir, Francine. Review of *L'Amant,* by Marguerite Duras. *La Nouvelle Revue Française* 383 (December 1984): 92–95.

Derrida, Jacques. "Les fins de l'homme." In *Marges de la philosophie*, 129–64. Paris: Minuit, 1972. Trans. Alan Bass as *Margins of Philosophy*. Chicago: University of Chicago Press, 1982.

———. "Forme et signification." In *L'Ecriture et la différence,* 9–49. Paris: Seuil, 1967. Trans. and intro. Alan Bass as *Writing and Difference*. Chicago: University of Chicago Press, 1982.

———. "The Law of Genre." In *On Narrative*. Ed. W.J.T. Mitchell, 51–77. Chicago: University of Chicago Press, 1981.

———. "Like the Sound of the Sea Deep within a Shell: Paul de Man's War." Trans. Peggy Kamuf. *Critical Inquiry* 14, no. 3 (Spring 1988): 590–652.

———. "Limited Inc abc . . ." *Glyph* 2 (1977): 162–254.

———. *Parages*. Paris: Galilée, 1986.

———. "Signature Event Context." *Glyph* 1 (1977): 172–97.

Dowd, Maureen. "Nobel Panel's Pick Keeps Cognoscenti Guessing." *New York Times* (18 October 1985): C23.

Ducrot, Oswald, and Tzvetan Todorov. *Dictionnaire encyclopédique des sciences du langage*. Paris: Seuil, 1972. Trans. Catherine Porter as *Encyclopedic Dictionary of the Sciences of Language*. Baltimore, Md.: Johns Hopkins University Press, 1979.

Dulac, Philippe. "Claude Simon: *Les Géorgiques*." *La Nouvelle Revue Française* 347 (December 1981): 111–14.

Duras, Marguerite. *L'Amant*. Paris: Minuit, 1984. Trans. Barbara Bray as *The Lover*. New York: Pantheon Books, 1985.

———. *Un Barrage contre le pacifique*. Paris: Gallimard, 1950. Trans. Herma Briffault as *The Sea Wall*. New York: Farrar, Strauss and Giroux, 1967.

———. *Moderato cantabile*. Paris: Minuit, 1958. (Also Included in *Four Novels: "The Square," "Moderato cantabile," "Ten-Thirty on a Summer Night," "The Afternoon of Mr. Andesmas,"* trans. Sonia Pitt-Rivers et al. New York: Grove Press, 1965.

———. *Le Ravissement de Lol V. Stein*. Paris: Gallimard, 1964. Trans. Richard Seaver as *The Ravishing of Lol Stein*. New York: Grove Press, 1967.

Dury, Jean H. "*Les Géorgiques* by Claude Simon: A Work of Synthesis and Renewal." *Australian Journal of French Studies* 21 (May–August 1984): 161–79.

Ellison, David R. *Understanding Albert Camus*. Columbia: University of South Carolina Press, 1990.

Esslin, Martin. "Samuel Beckett: The Search for the Self." In *Twentieth-Century Interpretations of "Endgame,"* 22–32.

Felman, Shoshana. *The Literary Speech Act: Don Juan with J.L. Austin or Seduction in Two Languages*. Trans. Catherine Porter. Ithaca, N.Y.: Cornell University Press, 1983.

Finney, Brian. "*Still* to *Worstword Ho*: Beckett's Prose Fiction since *The Lost Ones*." In *Beckett's Later Fiction and Drama*, 65–79.

Fitch, Brian T. *Beckett and Babel: An Investigation into the Bilingual Work*. Toronto: University of Toronto Press, 1988.

———. "*La Chute* et ses lecteurs. II. Depuis 1962." *Revue des Lettres Modernes* 238–44 (1970): 20–32.

———. "Clamence en chute libre." In *Albert Camus 1970*, 43–48. Sherbrooke: CELEF, 1970.

———. "Le paradigme herméneutique chez Camus." In *Albert Camus 1980*, 32–48.

Fitch, Brian T. "Une voix qui se parle, qui nous parle, que nous parlons ou l'espace théâtral de *La Chute*." *Revue des Lettres Modernes* 238–44 (1970): 59–79.

Fletcher, John. "Ecrivain bilingue." In *Samuel Beckett*, ed. Tom Bishop and Raymond Federman, 212–18. Paris: Cahiers de l'Herne, 1976.

Foucault, Michel. "La Pensée du dehors." *Critique* 229: 514–22.

Gadamer, Hans-Georg. *Wahrheit und Methode*. 4th ed. Tübingen: J.C.B. Mohr [Paul Siebeck], 1975. Trans. Joel Weinsheimer and Donald G. Marshall. 2d rev. ed. New York: Crossroad, 1990.

Gassin, Jean. "*La Chute* et le retable de 'L'Agneau mystique': Etude de structure." In *Albert Camus 1980*, 132–41.

Gelfand, Elissa. "Suspicion and Scepticism." Review of *Enfance*, by Nathalie Sarraute. *The Women's Review of Books* 3, no. 6 (March 1986): 14–16.

George, François. "Robbe-Grillet dépose son armure blanche." Review of *Le Miroir qui revient*, by Alain Robbe-Grillet. *Critique* 41 (1985): 284–93.

Gontarski, S. E. "*Company* for Company: Androgyny and Theatricality in Samuel Beckett's Prose." In *Beckett's Later Fiction and Drama*, 193–202.

———. *The Intent of Undoing in Samuel Beckett's Dramatic Texts*. Bloomington: Indiana University Press, 1985.

Guérin, Jeanyves. Review of *Le Miroir qui revient*, by Alain Robbe-Grillet. *Esprit* 101 (May 1985): 119–20.

Habermas, Jürgen. "The French Path to Postmodernity." *New German Critique* 33 (Fall 1984): 79–102.

Hartman, Geoffrey. "Blindness and Insight." *New Republic* (7 March 1988): 26–31.

Heidegger, Martin. *Sein und Zeit*. 12th ed. Tübingen: Max Niemeyer, 1972. Trans. John Macquarrie and Edward Robinson as *Being and Time*. New York: Harper and Row, 1962.

Heuvel, Pierre van den. "L'Aide au lecteur en péril: Les 'Romanesques' d'Alain Robbe-Grillet." University of South Carolina *French Literature Series* (*FLS*) 17 (1990): 26–34.

Hewitt, Leah D. *Autobiographical Tightropes*. Lincoln: University of Nebraska Press, 1990.

Hutcheon, Linda. "Metafictional Implications for Novelistic Reference." In *On Referring in Literature*, 1–13.

Huyssen, Andreas. "Mapping the Postmodern." *New German Critique* 33 (Fall 1984): 5–52.

Jameson, Fredric. "The Politics of Theory." *New German Critique* 33 (Fall 1984): 53–65.

———. *Postmodernism, or the Cultural Logic of Late Capitalism*. Durham, N.C.: Duke University Press, 1991.

———. Janvier, Ludovic. "Lieu dire." In *Samuel Beckett*/ Cahiers de l'Herne: 193–205.

Johnson, Barbara. "The Surprise of Otherness: A Note on the Wartime Writings of Paul de Man." In *Literary Theory Today*, ed. Peter Collier and Helga Geyer-Ryan, 13–22. Ithaca, N.Y.: Cornell University Press, 1990.

Kant, Immanuel. *Kritik der praktischen Vernunft*. Ed. Karl Vorländer. Collection "Philosophische Bibliothek." Hamburg: Felix Meiner, 1967. Trans. and intro. Lewis White Beck as *Critique of Practical Reason*. New York: Macmillan, 1985.

―――. *Kritik der Urteilskraft*. Ed. Karl Vorländer. Collection "Philosophische Biblio-thek." Hamburg: Felix Meiner, 1968. Trans. and intro. Werner S. Pluhar as *Critique of Judgment*. Indianapolis: Hackett, 1987.

Kenner, Hugh. "Life in a Box." In *Twentieth-Century Interpretations of "Endgame,"* 53–60.

Kermode, Frank. "What Nathalie Knew." Review of *Enfance*, by Nathalie Sarraute. *New York Review of Books* 31, no. 16 (25 October 1984): 49–51.

Laporte, Roger. "Le Oui, Le Non, Le Neutre." *Critique* 229: 579–90.

Leiris, Michel. *Aurora*. Paris: Gallimard "L'Imaginaire," 1973.

Levinas, Emmanuel. "La Servante et son maître: A propos de *L'Attente l'oubli*." *Critique* 229: 514–22.

―――. *Sur Maurice Blanchot*. Montpellier: Fata Morgana, 1975

Lévi-Valensi, Jacqueline. Review of *Enfance*, by Nathalie Sarraute. *Esprit* 83 (November 1983): 166–67.

Locke, F. W. "The Metamorphoses of Jean-Baptiste Clamence." *Symposium* 21 (1967): 306–15.

Lohr, Steve. "Claude Simon of France Wins the Nobel Prize in Literature." *New York Times* (18 October 1985): A1 and C23.

Londyn, Evelyne. *Maurice Blanchot romancier*. Paris: Nizet, 1976.

Lottman, Herbert R. *Albert Camus: A Biography*. New York: Doubleday, 1979.

―――. Lyotard, Jean-François. "Answering the Question: What is Postmodernism." Trans. Régis Durand, in Lyotard, *The Postmodern Condition*, 71–82.

―――. *The Postmodern Condition: A Report on Knowledge*. Trans. Geoff Bennington and Brian Massumi. Minneapolis: University of Minnesota Press, 1984.

Macksey, Richard. Introduction to *Marcel Proust: On Reading Ruskin*. Trans. and ed. Jean Autret, William Burford, and Phillip J. Wolfe, xiii-liii. New Haven, Conn.: Yale University Press, 1987.

Mallarmé, Stéphane. "Crise de vers." In *Oeuvres complètes*, 360–68. Paris: Pléiade, 1945.

Marini, Marcelle. "Une Femme sans aveu." *L'Arc* 98 (1985): 6–15.

Mehlman, Jeffrey. "Blanchot at *Combat*: Of Literature and Terror." *MLN* 95, no. 4 (May 1980): 808–29.

―――. "Orphée scripteur: Blanchot, Rilke, Derrida." *Poétique* 20 (1974): 458–82.

Meltzer, Françoise. "Preliminary Excavations of Robbe-Grillet's Phantom City." *Chicago Review* 28, no. 1 (Summer 1976): 41–50.

Meyers, Jeffrey. "Camus' *The Fall* and Van Eyck's *The Adoration of the Lamb*." *Mosaic* 7, no. 3 (1974): 43–51.

Miller, J. Hillis. *The Ethics of Reading*. New York: Columbia University Press, 1987.

―――. "The Triumph of Theory, The Resistance to Reading, and the Question of the Material Base." *PMLA* 102, no. 3 (May 1987): 281–91.

Montalbetti, Jean. "Fantômes à revendre." Review of *Le Miroir qui revient*, by Alain Robbe-Grillet. *Magazine Littéraire* 214 (January 1985): 88–93.

Morot-Sir, Edouard. "Logique de la limite, esthétique de la pauvreté: Théorie et pratique de l'essai." In *Albert Camus 1980*, 189–209.

Morrissette, Bruce. *The Novels of Robbe-Grillet*. Ithaca, N.Y.: Cornell University Press, 1975.

―――. "Post-Modern Generative Fiction: Novel and Film." *Critical Inquiry* 2 (Winter 1975): 253–62.

Morrissette, Bruce. "Topology and the French *Nouveau Roman*." *Boundary 2* (Fall 1972): 42–57.

Murphy, Carol J. *Alienation and Absence in the Novels of Marguerite Duras*. Lexington, Ky.: French Forum, 1982.

Noël, Bernard. "D'une main obscure." In *Deux Lectures de Maurice Blanchot*, 14–52. Montpellier: Fata Morgana, 1973.

Nouveau roman: hier, aujourd'hui. 2 vols. Ed. Jean Ricardou and Françoise van Rossum-Guyon. Paris: Union Générale d'Editions, 10/18, 1972.

On Referring in Literature. Ed. Anna Whiteside and Michael Issacharoff. Bloomington: Indiana University Press, 1987.

Orion Blinded: Essays on Claude Simon. Ed. Randi Birn and Karen Gould. Lewisburg, Pa.: Bucknell University Press, 1981.

Ostrovsky, Erika. "Le Silence de Babel." In *Samuel Beckett*/Cahiers de l'Herne: 206–11.

Oxford Latin Dictionary. Oxford: Oxford University Press, 1968.

Pavel, Thomas. *Fictional Worlds*. Cambridge, Mass.: Harvard University Press, 1986.

Pilling, John. "Shards of Ends and Odds in Prose: From *Fizzles* to *The Lost Ones*." In *On Beckett: Essays and Cricitism*, ed. and intro. S. E. Gontarski, 169–90. New York: Grove Press, 1986.

Poulet, Georges. *L'Espace proustien*. Paris: Gallimard, 1963. Trans. Elliott Coleman as *Proustian Space*. Baltimore, Md.: Johns Hopkins University Press, 1977.

Prince, Gerald. "The Point of Narrative: Blanchot's *Au Moment voulu*." *Sub-stance* 14 (1976): 93–98.

Proust, Marcel. *A la recherche du temps perdu*. 3 vols. Paris: Pléiade, 1954.

Raillard, Georges. "Le grand verre de Robbe-Grillet." Review of *Le Miroir qui revient*, by Alain Robbe-Grillet. *La Quinzaine Littéraire* 432 (16 January 1985): 5–6.

Redfern, W. D. "Camus and Confusion." *Symposium* 20 (1966): 329–42.

Reitsma-La Brujeere, Cora. "Récit, métarécit, texte et intertexte dans *Les Géorgiques* de Claude Simon." *French Forum* 9 (May 1984): 225–35.

Responses: On Paul de Man's Wartime Journalism. Ed. Werner Hamacher, Neil Hertz, and Thomas Keenan. Lincoln: University of Nebraska Press, 1989.

Ricardou, Jean. *Pour une théorie du nouveau roman*. Paris: Seuil, 1971.

———. *La Prise de Constantinople*. Paris: Minuit, 1965.

Robbe-Grillet, Alain. *L'Année dernière à Marienbad*. Ciné-roman illustré de 48 photos extraites du film réalisé par Alain Resnais. Paris: Minuit, 1961. Trans. Richard Howard as *Last Year at Marienbad*. Text by Alain Robbe-Grillet for the film by Alain Resnais. Picture Editor Robert Hughes. New York: Grove Press, 1962.

———. *La Belle Captive*. Lausanne: La Bibliothèque des Arts, 1975.

———. *Djinn*. Paris: Minuit, 1981. Trans. Yvone Lenard and Walter Wells as *Djinn*. New York: Grove Press, 1982.

———. *Glissements progressifs du plaisir*. Paris: Minuit, 1974.

———. *Les Gommes*. Paris: Minuit, 1953. Trans. Richard Howard as *The Erasers*. New York: Grove Press, 1964.

———. *La Jalousie*. Paris: Minuit, 1957. Trans. Richard Howard as *Jealousy*. New York: Grove Press, 1978.

———. *La Maison de rendez-vous*. Paris: Minuit, 1965. Trans. Richard Howard as *La Maison de rendez-vous*. New York: Grove Press, 1966.

———. *Le Miroir qui revient*. Paris: Minuit, 1984. Trans. Jo Levy as *Ghosts in the Mirror*. New York: Grove Press, 1988.

———. *Pour un nouveau roman*. Paris: Minuit, 1963. Trans. Richard Howard as *For a New Novel: Essays on Fiction*. Freeport, N.Y.: Books for Librairies Press, 1970.

———. *Souvenirs du triangle d'or*. Paris: Minuit, 1978. Trans. J. A. Underwood as *Recollections of the Golden Triangle*. New York: Grove Press, 1986.

———. *Topologie d'une cité fantôme*. Paris: Minuit, 1976. Trans. J. A. Underwood as *Topology of a Phantom City*. New York: Grove Press, 1977.

———. *Le Voyeur*. Paris: Minuit, 1955. Trans. Richard Howard as *The Voyeur*. New York: Grove Press, 1989.

Robbe-Grillet: Colloque de Cerisy. 2 vols. Paris: Union Générale d'Editions, 10/18, 1976.

Robert, Marthe. *L'Ancien et le Nouveau: de Don Quichotte à Franz Kafka*. Paris: Grasset, 1963. Trans. Carol Cosman as *The Old and the New: From Don Quixote to Franz Kafka*. Berkeley and Los Angeles: University of California Press, 1977.

Roubichou, Gérard. "*Histoire* or the Serial Novel." In *Orion Blinded: Essays on Claude Simon*, 173–83.

Rousset, Jean. *Forme et signification*. Paris: Corti, 1962.

Salgas, Jean-Pierre. "Robbe-Grillet: 'Je n'ai jamais parlé d'autre chose que de moi'." Interview in *La Quinzaine Littéraire* 432 (16 January 1985): 6–7.

Sarkonak, Ralph. *Claude Simon: Les Carrefours du texte*. Toronto: Les Editions Paratexte, 1986.

Sarraute, Nathalie. *Enfance*. Paris: Gallimard, 1983. Trans. Barbara Wright in consultation with the author as *Childhood*. New York: G. Braziller, 1984.

———. *L'Ere du soupçon: Essais sur le roman*. Paris: Gallimard, 1956. Trans. Maria Jolas as *The Age of Suspicion: Essays on the Novel*. New York: G. Braziller, 1963.

———. *Les Fruits d'or*. Paris: Gallimard, 1963. Trans. Maria Jolas as *The Golden Fruits*. New York: G. Braziller, 1964.

———. *Martereau*. Paris: Gallimard, 1953. Trans. Maria Jolas as *Martereau: A Novel*. New York: G. Braziller, 1959.

———. *Portrait d'un inconnu*. Paris: Robert Marin, 1948. Trans. Maria Jolas as *Portrait of a Man Unknown*. New York: G. Braziller, 1958.

———. *Tropismes*. Paris: Denoël, 1939. Trans. Maria Jolas as *Tropisms*. New York: G. Braziller, 1967.

Sarte, Jean-Paul. "Albert Camus." In *Situations IV*, 126-29. Paris: Gallimard, 1964.

———. "*Aminadab*, ou du fantastique considéré comme un langage." In *Situations I*, 122–42. Paris: Gallimard, 1947.

Scutenaire, Louis. *Magritte*. Chicago: William and Norma Copley Foundation, 1962.

Searle, John R. "Reiterating the Differences: A Reply to Derrida." *Glyph* 1 (1977): 198–208.

Sherzer, Dina. *Representation in Contemporary French Fiction*. Lincoln: University of Nebraska Press, 1986.

Simon, Claude. *La Bataille de Pharsale*. Paris: Minuit, 1969. Trans. Richard Howard as *The Battle of Pharsalus*. New York: G. Braziller, 1971.

———. *Les Corps conducteurs*. Paris: Minuit, 1971. *Conducting Bodies*. New York: Grove Press, 1987.

Simon, Claude. *Les Géorgiques*. Paris: Minuit, 1981. Trans. John and Beryl S. Fletcher as *The Georgics*. New York: Riverrun Press, 1989.

——. *Histoire*. Paris: Minuit, 1967. Trans. Richard Howard as *Histoire*. New York: G. Braziller, 1968.

——. *Leçon de choses*. Minuit, 1975. Trans. Daniel Weissbrot as *The World About Us*. New York: Persea Books, 1983.

——. *La Route des Flandres*. Paris: Minuit, 1960. Trans. Richard Howard as *The Flanders Road*. New York: Riverrun Press, 1985.

——. *Triptyque*. Paris: Minuit, 1973. Trans. Helen R. Lane as *Triptych*. New York: Riverrun Press, 1986.

——. *Le Vent: tentative de restitution d'un retable baroque*. Paris: Minuit, 1957. Trans. Richard Howard as *The Wind*. New York: G. Braziller, 1986.

Starobinski, Jean. "*Thomas l'obscur* Chapitre premier." *Critique* 229: 498–513.

Steiner, George. "Real Presences." In *Le Sens du sens*, 69–91. Paris: Vrin, 1988.

Stourzh, Gerald. "The Unforgiveable Sin: An Interpretation of *The Fall*." *Chicago Review* 15 (1961): 45–57.

Strauss, Walter A. "Siren-Language: Kafka and Blanchot." *Sub-stance* 14: 18–33.

Sturrock, John. "At a Steady Temperature." Review of *Le Miroir qui revient*, by Alain Robbe-Grillet. *TLS* 4280 (12 April 1985): 412.

——. "The Way of Disobedience." Review of *Enfance*, by Nathalie Sarraute. *TLS* 4184 (10 June 1983): 596.

Suleiman, Susan. "Reading Robbe-Grillet: Sadism and Text in *Projet pour une révolution à New York*." *Romanic Review* 68, no. 1 (January 1977): 43–62.

Théâtre, Récits, Nouvelles. Ed. R. Quilliot. Paris: Pléiade, 1962.

Thomas, Ronald R. "In the Company of Strangers: Absent Voices in Stevenson's *Dr. Jekyll and Mr. Hyde* and Beckett's *Company*." *Modern Fiction Studies* 32, no. 2 (Summer 1986): 157–73.

Todorov, Tzvetan. "Reflections on Literature in Contemporary France." *New Literary History* 10, no. 3 (Spring 1979): 511–31.

Tolstoy, Leo. *The Death of Ivan Ilyich*. Trans. Lynn Solotaroff. New York: Bantam, 1981.

Tucker, Warren. "*La Chute*: Voie du salut terrestre." *The French Review* 43, no. 5 (April 1970): 737–44.

Twentieth-Century Interpretations of "Endgame." Ed. Bell Gale Chevigny. Englewood Cliffs, N.J.: Prentice-Hall, 1969.

Ungar, Steven. *Roland Barthes: The Professor of Desire*. Lincoln: University of Nebraska Press, 1983.

——. "Rules of the Game: First-Person Singular in des Forets' *Le Bavard*." *L'Esprit Createur* 20, no. 3 (Fall 1980): 66–77.

Van Roey-Roux, François. "*Enfance* de Nathalie Sarraute, ou de la fiction à l'autobiographie." *Etudes Littéraires* 17 (1984): 273–82.

Viggiani, Carl. "Fall and Exile: Camus 1956–58." In *Albert Camus 1980*, 269–76.

Virgil. *The Georgics*. Trans. C. Day Lewis. New York: Oxford University Press, 1947.

Whiteside, Anna. "The Double Bind: Self-Referring Poetry." In *On Referring in Literature*, 14–32.

——. "Theories of Reference." In *On Referring in Literature*, 175–204.

INDEX

Abraham, 125
absence, 73, 119, 121
absurde, l', 28
aesthetics: and Beckett, 140; and Blanchot,
   131; and Camus, 38, 39; and contemporary
   literary practice, 10, 12, 13, 16, 18; and ethics, 156–58, 177n.23; and Sarraute, 111–13
affective relations, 90, 122, 123, 127, 129,
   136–38
age of suspicion, 13–16
analytic envelopment, 105–6
antithetical meaning of primal words, 20, 151–
   54
anxiety of influence, 6
aphonie. See textual voicelessness
arbitrariness of the sign, 49
authenticity, 86, 87, 92, 113, 173n.28
authorial intrusion, 13
autobiography, postmodern, 69–95, 99, 133,
   135

Balzac, Honoré de, 6
Bataille, Georges, 124
bavardage. See chatter
Bible, the, 29, 35, 67, 115, 125, 145, 148, 150,
   153
bliss, 74, 82, 171n.14
Bosch, Hieronymus, 120
Butor, Michel, 16, 135

categorical imperative, 156
Char, René, 112
chatter, 40, 111, 175n.9
Christianity, 36, 38
commentary, 5, 10, 28, 99, 102, 156; in Blanchot, 106, 107, 111
confessional discourse: and Beckett, 135; and
   Camus, 29–31, 35, 41, 43; and postmodern
   autobiography, 69, 71, 81, 82, 94
connotation, 7, 11, 48, 54, 118
creux générateur, 77, 79, 81, 89, 94

Dante Alighieri, 41, 102
De Chirico, Giorgio, 47, 52
deconstruction, 8, 10–13, 103, 108, 137, 156,
   177n.23

Delvaux, Paul, 47, 50, 51, 52
démesure. See textual excess
denotation, 7, 155
dérive textuelle. See textual drifting
dérobade. See semantic elusiveness
desire, 19, 70; in Duras, 81–85, 155
dialogue: and Beckett, 20, 141, 147, 152, 158;
   and Blanchot, 127–31; and Camus, 31–32;
   and Sarraute, 70, 88
Dostoevsky, Fyodor, 77
duplicity, in *La Chute*, 27, 36, 38

écriture, 27
Eden, 30, 38
enfouissements. See textual buryings
eroticism: and Blanchot, 122, 124–27; and
   Camus, 30, 34; and postmodern autobiography, 70, 76, 81–87; and Simon, 50, 52
espaces textuels. See textual spaces
ethical, the: and aesthetics, 155–58; and Beckett, 140, 150, 154; and contemporary literary practice, 9, 10, 12, 15, 16, 20; and contemporary theory, 99–103; and Sarraute,
   90–95
Eurydice, 109, 119
existential humanism, 19, 25, 27, 155
experimental fiction, 9, 10, 16–18, 99, 155

Faulkner, William, 58, 83
figuration, poetic, 9; and Beckett, 139, 153;
   and Blanchot, 118, 121, 121–31; and Sarraute, 93–94
Flaubert, Gustave, 6, 15, 45, 77, 116, 120
formalism, 15, 45, 51, 54, 155, 158
Freud, Sigmund, 19
fuite textuelle. See textual escape

game theory, 32–35, 38, 42–43, 47, 49
generativity: in postmodern autobiography,
   77, 80; in Robbe-Grillet's *Topologie*, 19, 45,
   48, 49, 51-54, 99; in Simon, 63–64
Gide, André, 16, 17, 72, 73, 88, 135
God, 11, 150
Goethe, Johann Wolfgang von, 30, 172n.21
grotesque, the, 38–39
guilt, in *La Chute*, 31, 34, 36, 40–43, 99